*The Bibl* ... *oor*

**Liberation and Theology Series**

*Editorial Committee*
Leonardo Boff, Sergio Torres, Gustavo Gutiérrez,
José Comblin, Ronaldo Muñoz, Enrique Dussel,
José Oscar Beozzo, Pedro Trigo, Ivone Gebara,
Jon Sobrino, Virgil Elizondo, Juan Luis Segundo

*Ecumenical Consultant*
Julio de Santa Ana

*Titles in the series*
(latter volumes in preparation)

. . . "this is going to be a series which both illuminates Latin
American realities and provokes thought about the relevance
to the rest of the world of a theology which springs very
powerfully out of these realities – out of the people's suffering
and out of a still vibrant faith."—David L. Edwards, *The
Church Times*

*Jorge Pixley*
*Clodovis Boff*

# THE BIBLE,
# THE CHURCH
# AND THE POOR

## BIBLICAL, THEOLOGICAL AND PASTORAL
## ASPECTS OF THE OPTION FOR THE POOR

*Translated from the Spanish and Portuguese by*
*Paul Burns*

**BURNS & OATES**

First published in Great Britain in 1989
Burns & Oates Ltd., Wellwood, North Farm Road,
Tunbridge Wells, Kent TN2 3DR
and in the United States of America by Orbis Books,
Maryknoll, NY 10545

Originally published in Brazil under the title
*Opção pelos pobres* by Editora Vozes Ltda,
Petrópolis

Original edition © CESEP – São Paulo 1987

English translation © 1989 Burns & Oates Ltd

ISBN 0 86012 165 8

20029629    261·8

Typeset by Scribe Design, Gillingham, Kent
Printed and bound in Great Britain by
Biddles Ltd, Guildford and King's Lynn

# Liberation and Theology Series

In the years since its emergence in Latin America, liberation theology has challenged the church to a renewal of faith lived in solidarity with the poor and oppressed. The effects of this theology have spread throughout the world, inspiring in many Christians a deeper life of faith and commitment, but for others arousing fears and concerns.

Its proponents have insisted that liberation theology is not a sub-topic of theology but really a new way of doing theology. The Liberation and Theology Series is an effort to test that claim by addressing the full spectrum of Christian faith from the perspective of the poor.

Thus, volumes in the Series are devoted to such topics as God, Christ, the Church, Revelation, Mary, the Sacraments, and so forth. But the Series will also explore topics seldom addressed by traditional theology, though vital to Christian life – aspects of politics, culture, the role of women, the status of ethnic minorities. All these are examined in the light of faith lived in a context of oppression and liberation.

The work of over a hundred theologians, pastoral agents, and social scientists from Latin America, and supported by some one hundred and forty bishops, the Liberation and Theology Series is the most ambitious and creative theological project in the history of the Americas.

Addressed to the universal church, these volumes will be essential reading for all those interested in the challenge of faith in the modern world. They will be especially welcomed by all who are committed to the cause of the poor, by those engaged in the struggle for a new society, by all those seeking to establish a more solid link between faith and politics, prayer and action.

"This is a most enterprising series which should enable those of us who live in the West to listen to what the liberation theologians themselves have to say. It may well open the eyes of Western Christians to the need for liberation in the First World as well." – *The Expository Times*

# Contents

vii

# Contents

viii

# Contents

# Contents

x

# Foreword

by RT REV. MOACYR GRECHI, *Bishop of Acre and Purus*

## THE POOR WILL SAVE THE WORLD

The question of the poor and poverty is beyond doubt the major problem facing the world today. The nuclear threat is obviously a very serious matter, since it affects the very survival of the human race and of all life on the planet. But, effectively, the bomb has already been exploded, and still is exploding, as far as millions are concerned. It was first exploded at the time of European colonial expansion, and goes on being exploded through the process of continuing the arms race. What is spent on arms is in effect taken out of the mouths of the poor, as Pope John Paul II has said.

Poverty is an issue of special gravity for international ethics. As that great Christian Emmanuel Mounier wrote in 1933: "People are divided by the stand they take on the poverty of today." Two days before his sudden death, confiding his desire to be associated with the poor to a priest friend, he said: "My gospel is the gospel of the poor. I could never feel happy if there was any misunderstanding between me and those who have the trust of the poor. I can never rejoice at anything that divides the world and threatens the hopes of the poor." Another great layman, Jacques Maritain, said of the bloody Spanish Civil War: "Those who kill the poor are at least as guilty as those who kill priests."

The question of the poor affects all men and women today, but Christians above all. There would be something central missing from Christianity if it were to lose sight of the poor and the justice due to them. Without them, how can we understand the God of the exodus and the carpenter's son? This is why Paul VI, in his usual lapidary style, declared: "The church is tied by *inborn vocation* to indigent and suffering humanity" (17 May

xi

1971). And the best of Christians, in the midst of and despite all infidelities, have clearly understood this, from St Francis of Assisi to Charles de Foucauld.

Unfortunately, the evangelical banner of redemption of the oppressed has been picked up off the ground only by historical forces outside the faith, because it was Christians who let it fall to the ground. This is why the church has suffered under the blows of atheist regimes, just as Israel suffered under the hammer of Babylon, wielded by Yahweh (Jer. 51:20ff).

Now, thanks to the Holy Spirit, the church has reawakened to the problem of poverty and the poor. The option for the poor has to be seen as one of the greatest blessings that God has granted the church in recent times. The discovery of the poor has, for the church, been the same as rediscovering the true face of the Lord. Through knowing the poor better, the church knows its divine founder and Lord better.

## THE POPES IN DEFENCE OF THE POOR

Thanks to the Father of all gifts, recent popes have spoken out clearly to proclaim the good news of freedom for the poor, "the Lord's year of favour." Opening Vatican Council II, on 11 September 1962, John XXIII stated what was to become the definitive expression of an overall vision of the church: "The church is and desires to be the church of all, but principally the church of the poor."

Paul VI, to whom we owe so many enduring expressive gestures, made a prophetic contribution (which was censored in Brazil) to his public audience for the Brazilian authorities in January 1970, when the incidence of torture in the country was already known: "The church will know how to make the anger of the poor and the non-violent, and their rebellion against injustice, its own." He also coined the lapidary phrase, so often repeated, including by Cardinal J. Landázuri Ricketts in his closing address to the Medellín Conference: "The poor are the sacrament of Christ."

John Paul I, always poor himself, showed the same sensibility to the poor. On one occasion, he recalled St Laurence's famous words: "The poor and humble are the real treasure of the church." And on another, when he was greeted as "prince of the church," he retorted: "Prince? In what way and of what, if our church is the church of the humble?"

And finally, John Paul II has tirelessly proclaimed the good news of human dignity for the downtrodden throughout the world: "The option for the poor is my daily concern," he once said.

So the Spirit is with the church to a high degree. Prophecy of justice for the oppressed is alive again. The blood of martyrs for the sake of the Kingdom of God and its justice calls out once more. Archbishop Romero, assassinated for his preaching in defence of his downtrodden people, stands out as the supreme symbol of this "cloud of witnesses" of love for the "little ones" that was Jesus' love.

There is a great growth in the number of base Christian communities, which "embody the church's preferential love for the common people," as the Puebla Conference said (643). In them, the poor learn the liberating faith of the gospel, come together as church and as people and struggle for a better and fuller life. And outside the communities, there are the innumerable men and women, young people and not so young, who have placed their cultural and social advantages at the service of the poor in so many different ways.

## THE OPTION FOR THE POOR AS FRUIT OF VATICAN II

All this, surely, is a true fruit of the Council? There was the famous intervention by Cardinal Lercaro, Archbishop of Bologna, at the end of the first session, on 7 December 1962: "The central theme of the Council should be the church of the poor." There was the "Belgian College Study Group," which brought together some eighty bishops and advisers, with the aim of forwarding this theme within the Council. This led to the proposal in the third session that the bishops should abandon their sumptuous mode of dress, and that a basket should be passed round in which the Council Fathers should

place their precious crosses, chains and rings, which could then
be sold and the money devoted to the poor.

When a hundred bishops made a proposal in favour of
simplifying the ways of the church for the sake of evangelizing
the poor and the workplace, Pope Paul VI responded magnifi-
cently with an unforgettable symbolic gesture: during the mass
concelebrated in St Peter's on 14 November 1964, before the
assembled bishops and faithful, he laid the triple tiara solemnly
on the altar as a gift from the church to the poor of the world.

Finally, there was the famous "Schema XIV," produced by
the Belgian College Study Group and sent to all the Council
Fathers, a real commitment to evangelical poverty and the
poor. This specifically said: "We shall devote all the time
necessary to the apostolic and pastoral service of individuals
and groups of workers whose economic situation is one of
weakness or underdevelopment. We shall support those lay
people, religious, deacons and priests whom the Lord has called
to evangelize the poor and workers and to share their working
lives." This text came into the open at the end of the Council,
when some forty Council Fathers were concelebrating in the
catacombs of St Domitila, at the invitation of Bishop Himmer,
a member of the Belgian College Study Group, to ask the
apostles and martyrs for the grace to remain faithful to the
gospel of the poor.

Schema XIV could be described as one of the strongest
spiritual links between Vatican II and the Medellín and Puebla
Conferences, which, on a continental level, developed the
potential of the theme of the evangelical perspective of the
poor, springing from its concentrated expression—like the grain
of mustard seed—in *Lumen Gentium* 8.

These extracts from our historical memory of those times
serve to illustrate the strength and evangelical zeal with which
the church rediscovered the immense area of poverty as its
proper mission field. This was no innovation, nor was it a
modish or politically motivated invention. It was rather a
discovery, or rediscovery, since the poor are, by evangelical
right, the patrimony of the church, its "basic material," so to
speak.

## WHAT THE CHURCH LOSES WITHOUT THE POOR—AND VICE-VERSA

If we ask what the church loses without the poor, the only answer is: without the poor, the church loses practically everything:

—It loses its universality, becoming an elite church, a minority church;

—It loses the meaning of history and its function as leaven in the world, thereby removing itself to the margins of the march of men and women of our day, confining itself to a ghetto or "eschatological reserve";

—It loses its strength of incarnation in the world, of being rooted in the concrete, painful reality of the suffering majorities, since they alone experience and live the drama of the world, and is reduced to a church lost in the rarified atmosphere of a spirituality without flesh and bones;

—It loses the force of its oneness (what is a church without the poor as one of the epicentres of its unity, grouped round the permanent centre, Christ?), of its holiness (how can we enter the Kingdom passing by the masses fallen by the wayside of the world?), of its catholicity (how can it be the church of all if the poor, who are greatest in number and aspirations, find no welcome in it?), and of its apostolicity (how can it be the church of the apostles if it does not follow their way of life, as described in Acts, where "they held everything in common" and "there were no poor among them"?);

—Finally, without the poor, the church loses its Lord, who identified with them and elevated them into the final judges of this world. Without the poor, the church is simply lost. "I hold that the poor will save the world, and that they will save it without wishing to do so, will save it despite themselves, that they will ask it nothing in return, simply because they will not know the value of the service they have rendered it." The words are those of that great Christian Georges Bernanos, in his book *Les enfants humiliés*.

On the other hand, what do the poor lose without the church?

—They lose the basic and ultimate sense of their dignity, which the gospel alone can reveal fully;

—They lose the prospect of integral liberation, to which they aspire more than anyone else;

—They lose the "supreme advantage of knowing Jesus Christ" (Phil. 3:8), the full and final Liberator;

—Without the church, the poor lose an important historical ally and an unequalled well of inspiration.

The option for the poor constitutes the church's challenge to "honour the gospel." Because "if the hungry do not find faith, the fault lies with those who refuse them bread," as Bonhoeffer said. Today, in fact, the credibility of the gospel stands or falls by this, by solidarity with the lost.

"Those who help the lost are lost," said Bertolt Brecht. This is why the church has paid and is paying for its option for the poor with the blood and tears of so many of its sons and daughters. But *sub specie aeternitatis*, those who unite themselves to the lost of this world are saved for eternal life.

## FOR THE POOR, AGAINST ALL DIVISION

By siding with the poor, will the church contribute to an increase in the divisions in the world? On the contrary: it is only from the standpoint of the poor that the church can contribute to the reconciliation of humanity today. The First World looks, in Jean Guitton's words, "like a golden island battered on all sides by the waves of the deprivation of the rest." How can we prevent the ever-increasing fury of these waves of deprivation engulfing and swallowing these golden islands? Marcel Proust wrote: "A major social question consists in knowing whether the glass wall will everlastingly protect the celebrations of the wonderful animals and whether the dark men who look on avidly in the night will not seize them from their aquarium and devour them." Terrible words, with the ring of fateful prophecy.

The church, which is "a kind of sacrament or sign of intimate union with God, and of the unity of all mankind" (LG 1b), is called to effect the great task of reconciliation of which the world stands so much in need. This is a time of grace and a time for mission. The Spirit is keeping the church faithful to its one Lord and to the first after the one Lord: the poor.

# Abbrevations

Documents of Vatican II

AG    *Ad Gentes.* Decree on the Church's Missionary
Activity

GS    *Gaudium et Spes.* Pastoral Constitution on the Church
in the Modern World

LG    *Lumen Gentium.* Dogmatic Constitution on the
Church

PC    *Perfectae Caritatis.* Decree on the Appropriate
Renewal of the Religious Life

EN    *Evangelii Nuntiandi.* Apostolic Exhortation of Pope
Paul VI

LE    *Laborem Exercens.* Encyclical Letter of Pope John
Paul II

MM    *Mater et Magistra.* Encyclical Letter of Pope John
XXIII

PT    *Pacem in Terris.* Encyclical Letter of Pope John
XXIII

Puebla *Evangelization in Latin America's Present and Future.*
Final Document of the Third General Conference of
the Latin American Episcopate, held at Puebla,
Mexico, 1979. For a copy of the document see John
Eagleson and Philip Scharper, eds.,*Puebla and
Beyond* (Maryknoll, N.Y.: Orbis Books, 1979).

# Introduction

# Who Are the Poor Today, and Why?

The subject of this book is the "option for the poor." But who are these poor? This has to be determined before we can proceed further.

The "poor" here are understood in a real, not a metaphorical, sense. They are those who suffer from basic economic need, those who are deprived of the material goods necessary to live with any dignity.

The poor of today can be defined by three adjectives: collective, conflictive and alternative. The poor are a collective phenomenon, they are the product of a conflictive process and they demand an alternative historical process. Let us explain each of these three features.

## 1. THE POOR ARE A COLLECTIVE PHENOMENON

Poverty today is a social, structural, massive problem. The poor make up whole classes, masses and peoples. They are found above all in the urban areas of the Third World, in their shanty towns and sprawling slums, but also in the now largely depopulated rural areas.

These poor make up the majority—some 80 percent—of the total population of Latin America. Of the rest, some 15 percent might be called "middle class," leaving 5 percent who are rich, or upper-middle and upper class.

The difference between the societies of Latin America and those of the advanced capitalist nations is not one of kind (since

1

both are capitalist societies and therefore divided into classes), but one of degree. In "industrialized" societies, there is a wider range of levels within the middle class, and a much higher percentage of people in that class—they can account for over half the population. Both forms of society are pyramidal in structure, but there are pyramids and pyramids: some rise to a sharp point from a broad base, squeezed in the middle, as in Latin America; others tend to bulge outwards in the middle, as in the developed nations.

Taking the poor as a collective phenomenon in this way, the first view to discount is the empirical or common perception of the poor as individuals, as particular cases. This is an old view and not now generally held. It saw the poor as the Lazaruses of this world. It abstracted or separated the poor from their social conditions or from the structures that place and define them. It saw the trees, but not the wood.

In this vision, the poor existed because of two main causes:

(a) *Moral causes*: poverty is the fruit of ignorance or prejudice. Or it can also be the fruit of the egoism and greed of others. But in neither case is there a perception of the structures or social mechanisms that embody these moral forces.

(b) *Natural causes*: the poor are poor because they were born poor. It has always been thus. "Since Adam and Eve," there have been rich and poor.

The logical outcome of this vision is *aid*, or *charity*. We must *give* to the poor, not awaken them. They must be given alms, schools, etc. So the natural messiahs or saviours of the poor are the rich, those who *have*.

It must be said that the greater part of religious initiatives taken in the last century and this, springing from a desire to help the poor (initiatives by religious congregations, institutes of charity, various types of "crusades"), were motivated by sincere compassion for the poor. But it was an ingenuous compassion; its heart was evangelical, but its vision lacked any critical focus. It saw individual cases, not collective conditions. It concentrated on individuals, not the structures that hemmed these individuals in. The evidence for this is that this whole huge and inspiring effort to help the poor ended in failure. Poverty has not diminished; it has increased.

## 2. THE POOR ARE THE PRODUCT OF A CONFLICTIVE PROCESS

The poor constitute a social phenomenon that has been produced; that phenomenon does not come about naturally. They have been reduced to poverty (im-poverished) or held in poverty by the forces of a system of domination. In this sense, the poor are the dominated classes.

The poor are poor because they are exploited or rejected by a perverse economic system: in the case of Latin America, capitalism. This is an exploitative and excluding system, which means the poor suffer and are oppressed, means the system keeps them under it or outside of it. This is the real explanation for the fact that the poor are poor.

Who, though, are these poor? Taken as the oppressed classes, they fall into two main groups:

(a) *The marginalized*, which means those who are (still) outside the prevailing economic system or are positively excluded from it, such as:

—The *unemployed* or *part-employed* (who in Latin America make up some 25 to 30 percent of the working population);

—A whole gamut of *the wretched*: beggars, abandoned children, outcasts, prostitutes, and so on.

All these live deprived of the basic necessities for life, below or just at subsistence level. Those whom economists prudishly refer to as "absolutely poor," "lumpen proletariat," or "sub-proletariat," are in reality wretched, starving, stunted, lost, dependent in a hundred ways, and in Latin America they run into millions, making up at least a third of the oppressed classes. They make up a socially heterogeneous and politically incoherent whole, for whom the church, through the base communities and other organizations, represents virtually the only force that can give them human dignity and social coherence.

(b) *The exploited*, who are those whom the socio-economic system treats unjustly. They are the "working poor," the whole mass who live in the city or the country, the proletariat and the rural workers.

This group of poor is relatively easy to define. Its main sectors are: (i) *Industrial workers*, who are the most coherent group. They make up some 15 percent of the oppressed classes throughout Latin America. Though relatively few in number, they are more organized and combative than the rest and so possess considerable reserves of power. They form the class most directly confronting the forces of capitalism. (ii) *Rural workers*, who form a less definite class, but are greater in number, accounting for over half the total population, even though their numbers are decreasing with the advance of capitalist methods into the countryside. This diversified rural population, many of whom belong to the indigenous peoples, can be divided into:

—Full-time and seasonal *wage-earners*, with the seasonal element increasing and in some countries now accounting for the majority;

—*Smallholders*, who are finding their livelihood threatened by the advance of "agribusiness" and more and more being forced to leave the land or work for wages;

—*Settlers*, who can work the land for themselves, but are not recognized as having any title to it. They too are being swallowed up by capitalist farming and generally forced to emigrate to the cities;

—*Tenant farmers*, who are mostly going the same way.

The exploited classes would also include those on the lower rungs of the "service sector," such as clerks, primary school teachers, small shopkeepers and the like.

So the poor of this continent have many faces. But they all, as Puebla says, show the "suffering features" of Christ (31 – 39). When these different types of oppressed (marginalized or exploited) are also *refugees* because of the vicissitudes of the endless civil wars of Central America (from where thousands have fled to Mexico or the United States), then their situation is still more desperate. The aggravation of oppression by the fact of being black, Amerindian or female is something we shall come to later.

The classical image of the poor as a ragged figure begging a crust from door to door is something we have to put behind us, to be replaced by a less romantic and more realistic image of the poor. They are those who are oppressed in all manner of ways, and who seek their liberation. This vision is critical and differentiates among types of poor. It is basic to putting the option for the poor into practice. Just as it is one thing to be a poor agricultural labourer and quite another to be a poor metal worker, so it is one thing to work with abandoned children and quite another to work with the rural poor. Each group of poor people requires its own specific methodology and strategy, even if the liberation of all is the common factor.

## 3. THE POOR NEED A DIFFERENT SOCIAL SYSTEM

Just as the situation of the poor has a structural cause, so their liberation has to go through the process of changing the social system, which prevents them from growing and playing a positive part in history. The poor judge society as it is at present, and see that if their situation is to change, this change has to come about in a new form of society. This means that the poor are indissolubly wedded to the idea of revolution, in the real sense of a *basic* change in a social system.

What in the past belonged to the sphere of utopia, in the sense of an unrealizable project, has now moved into the realm of historical possibility. What was just an ideal has become a definite plan. In effect, humanity's material (technical and scientific) and cultural (political understanding) development has now made it possible to create a society in which there need be no deprivation of basic necessities (food, shelter, clothing, elementary education and basic health care), nor any domination of some over others (antagonistic classes).

This is what is shown by the historical process that has been going on for the past twenty-five years in the Third World, particularly in Latin America. The poor are rising up and organizing themselves for their collective liberation. In the early 1960s, Pope John XXIII had seen the appearance of the working classes on the historical scene and characterized it, together with the independence of former colonies and the emancipation of women, as one of the "signs of the times" (PT 40–42).

We shall examine the struggles of the oppressed to achieve their liberation, and the progress they are making, in Chapter VI.

## (a) The Poor Yesterday and Today

It is clear that the phenomenon of poverty today is different in kind from that of the past. Poverty today is not simply backwardness in the sense of lack of material development. This is still a factor, but no longer the most important one. Poverty today is mainly the result of a contradictory development, in which the rich become steadily richer, at the expense of the poor who are made steadily poorer. Poverty today is endogenous: it is internal to the system and a natural product of it. This is why poverty today means oppression and dependence in social terms, and injustice and social sin in ethical terms.

To illustrate the difference between the traditional idea of poverty and the modern view, we can compare the picture of Lazarus as painted in the gospels with that of the modern Lazarus, as Pope John Paul II would describe him on various occasions (address to the UN, in Brazil, etc.). There is a parallel between the two, as is to be expected:

| LAZARUS THEN | LAZARUS TODAY |
|---|---|
| 1. An individual, the poor seen as persons, cases, etc. | 1. Classes and masses (collective bodies) |
| 2. Abandoned by the selfishness of the rich; left poor | 2. Exploited at the profit of the ruling classes: made poor (conflictive situation) |
| 3. Asking for charity: for bread in this world, while waiting for his reward in "Abraham's bosom" | 3. Demanding justice: a place at table with the rest now, while not denying "heaven" (alternative system) |

This is dealing with the "type" of poor persons, not with the poor in general. The Lazarus of then is clearly still with us today, but is no longer the historical model of the poor. Equally, almsgiving is still needed, but there is no way it can solve the problem of poverty today.

*(i) Erroneous Conception of the Poor Today.* We have seen who the poor are and why they are poor. They are poor because of the existence of systems that exploit and exclude them. We might call this explanation "dialectical," since it explains that the growth of poverty is dependent on the growth of wealth. There is a different explanation at large, which we consider erroneous, and which might be called the *functionalist* or *liberal* view of poverty.

This view claims a scientific basis, and is in fact widespread in the intellectual, technical and political circles of the Third World. It sees poverty as a collective, but not conflictive, reality; the poor are simply backward, underdeveloped, not enjoying the fruits of material progress. To escape from their situation, the poor need only wait a while, with help from the others, the rich. They will then reach the level of the classes and peoples called developed. It is all a matter of technique: investment, forward planning, and so on.

This view, however, has failed the gospel test of being known by one's "fruits." With all their "help" to the poor, those who propose this solution—all rich, needless to say—have only produced greater poverty for the others and greater riches for themselves. We do not need to trade theories, merely to look at the facts, which have been exceedingly painful for those who have had and still have to bear them: the poor above all. This is the failure of "developmentism," of which the "Alliance for Progress" of the 1960s was the most typical example. All this brought the peoples of Latin America was greater dependence, even though it did serve to awaken the masses (a positive benefit) to a sense of their need—not for "development," but for liberation.

So only the critical and dialectical view of poverty which we set out at the beginning can really explain the phenomenon of poverty and its growth. And it alone will enable us to resolve the problem. How? By transforming the present social system from the standpoint of those most concerned, the oppressed.

This is a process of historical liberation, not of economic development. This conviction is growing among ever wider sectors of the oppressed themselves, and of the church, as the Puebla document shows.

*(ii) Other "Poverties": Blacks, Indians, Women.* Till now, we have looked at the poor as a socio-economic category, as a class or classes. They are the collective Lazaruses who live in a conflictive situation and seek an alternative humanity. They are poor not only because they are deficient in consumption, but also because they are exploited workers. They are poor because they are removed from the means to life (production), dependent on those who own these means, alienated and therefore powerless.

This understanding of the poor as a class is the most inclusive, or the only comprehensive view. There is no type of poor person in actuality who cannot be included in this view. It includes industrial workers (producers), rural labourers, and those on the fringes (under-employed, unemployed or marginalized). There are no poor outside this class, except those who are said to be poor in the *symbolic* sense (the "poor in spirit," "poor sinners" and the like).

Yet within the overall category of the actual poor there are other types of "poverty" besides the socio-economic. Strictly speaking, we should speak of separate types of "oppression," which are above all socio-cultural, producing socio-cultural "poverties." The first group of these is formed by three types of discrimination: *racial, ethnic* and *sexual.* There are others: against national or religious minorities, homosexuals, the physically and mentally handicapped, old people, and so on. But the major forms of discrimination are undoubtedly racism, ethnocentrism and sexism (*machismo*), and their objects are blacks, Indian peoples and women. It needs saying that these socio-cultural "poverties" do not generally exist alongside, but *inside* the generic socio-economic poverty, which is the basic determinant, to which others are added. These other "poverties" are variants, aggravating actual poverty and making the poverty of their poor victims a *concentrated* poverty. Each has its relative autonomy, its own consistency, which is separate from the economic aspect. But as a matter of actual fact, they are all tied in with economic poverty.

Take the case of blacks, for example. They are certainly set apart, but they are also generally, and especially at the bottom of the economic scale, exploited or marginalized. The same can be said of women: besides suffering sexual discrimination, they are generally more exploited economically.

Of course, racial discrimination against the black president of an African republic is one thing, and racial discrimination against a black mine worker in South Africa another. Equally, *machismo* affects the wife of a mine owner in one way and the wife of an unemployed miner in another. This shows that socio-*cultural* "poverty" is deeply conditioned by socio-*economic* or class poverty. So it cannot be dealt with outside a class context, which is its basic determinant, the setting for the main contradiction and the primary struggle. The struggle against socio-cultural oppressions cannot be waged except by combining and articulating it with the struggle against socio-economic poverty. Socio-cultural "poverties" must not be taken as a veil to be drawn over the real, brute fact of socio-economic poverty. There is no cloud to cover this massive mountain rising on the horizon of the world today, as an out-dated form of pietism still seeks to do. Socio-cultural "poverties" can be specific and, in a minority of cases, exist outside socio-economic poverty, but they are normally associated with it and cannot be attacked outside the context of an attack on it.

### (b) The "New Poor" of Industrial Societies

The advanced industrial nations above all, but also the more developed centres of Latin America, have seen the rise of a new type of poor. These "new poor" are: the physically and mentally handicapped who have been abandoned to the streets of huge cities, immigrant workers, the homeless, the unemployed, the suicidally depressed, old people dependent on a state pension and young drug addicts. These categories do not make up new classes besides the marginalized and exploited classes, but form part of them. Their class provenance may be different (the handicapped, pensioners and drug addicts come from all classes), but their actual class situation places these new poor among the socio-economic poor, and within this category, among those we have described as *marginalized*.

They are in any case both a typical product of, and a contestatory force in, societies living in general abundance, with materialist values that satisfy the body and leave the spirit hungry.

The nature and significance of this new type of poverty, which sometimes amounts to a social pathology, needs further examination. But it should be clear that these "new poor" cannot be considered apart from the social whole, but have to be seen within the social, and above all economic, conditions of their society. This is the only way to organize action effectively to free them from their alienation, thereby liberating the system that alienates them.

So we have come to identify three definite groups that make up the poor today:

—The *socio-economic* poor, consisting of the marginalized and the exploited;
—The *socio-cultural* poor, including blacks, indigenous peoples and women;
—The *new* poor of the most developed countries and areas.

As we have seen, these groups do not exist side-by-side, as though they formed three distinct social groupings. They are rather superimposed on each other and involve the same people. More specifically, they are three oppressed groups and therefore three groups with their own interests and struggles to pursue.

There is no doubt that their other interests will tend to be pursued within the context of their overall class cause. But "class" in this sense cannot be confined just to their economic situation. This is why, in Latin America, we tend to indicate this wider basis by talking of "oppressed peoples" rather than "classes," and of "integral liberation" rather than "economic advancement."

### (c) The Poor as an International Issue

The poor seek not only a new society in their own countries, but also a new world, a "new international order." In effect, the issue of poverty is worldwide: the poor are made poor and kept poor by structures of domination operating on an international basis. One could say that the present state of the world is a gigantic re-creation of the parable of Dives and Lazarus, as recent popes have often stated.

How can one explain the poverty of the Third World? Just as with the basic question of poverty, there are two sets of explanations of poverty on the international level—the phenomenon, that is, of underdevelopment. These opposing theories can be represented schematically:

| Liberal or Functionalist Explanation | Dialectical or Historical-structural Explanation |
|---|---|
| Underdevelopment | |
| = Economic backwardness. It is a situation. | = Dependence. It is a historical process. |
| = *Per capita* income under $800 annually. Low level of economic development. | = Absolute poverty and increasing gap between rich and poor. |
| Solutions | |
| = Increase *per capita* income by external "aid": technological, capital, commercial. | = Eradicate absolute poverty and liberate from external domination through popular participation. |

Note that the poverty of one country has its roots in other countries. It is an issue of dependence or oppression on the international level. What are the relationships that produce the riches of some at the expense of the poverty of others?

The relationship between North and South, between the First World and the Third, should not be seen primarily in terms of relations between nations or states, but between the classes of different nations. These complex relationships can be shown by the following diagram:

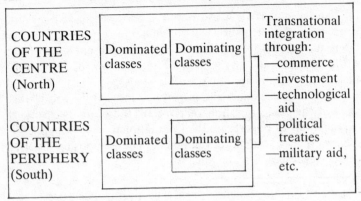

| COUNTRIES OF THE CENTRE (North) | Dominated classes | Dominating classes | Transnational integration through: —commerce —investment —technological aid —political treaties —military aid, etc. |
| COUNTRIES OF THE PERIPHERY (South) | Dominated classes | Dominating classes | |

Some comments on this diagram:

1. It shows the capitalist system as a transnational system. Both the centre (North) and the periphery (South) have dominated and dominating classes, because all capitalist countries develop unevenly and so produce class divisions. So there are poor in the rich countries too: 35 million of them in the US and 30 million in the EEC. And, conversely, there are small, but highly dynamic, pockets of development in the poor countries, with advanced industries, exporting agribusiness and the like, controlled by a small but very rich elite—in Brazil there is a group of 1 percent of the population with a total income higher than that of 50 percent of the total population.

2. There are dominated classes in the North as well as in the South. Nevertheless, those in the South have to be seen as *doubly dominated*. There is a process of transfer of wealth from South to North, resulting in workers in the North earning on average eight to ten times as much as their counterparts in the South. This happens because the laws of the capitalist system take from the latter and give to the former. This in turn means that societies in the North can afford to redistribute wealth and have liberal-democratic governments, while those in the South tend to concentrate wealth in a few hands and have authoritarian regimes.

3. Of course some nations of the South are relatively rich and some of the North relatively poor, but these are secondary variations that do not affect the system of exploitation itself. Equally, the "East-West" conflict is not really the major one of

our time. It takes place within the context of the greater conflict, which is that between the oppressed and the oppressor classes, as much in the North as in the South. This is the great contradiction, irreconcilable in nature, which affects both North and South in themselves, while at the same time being repeated between them. The dominant classes are internationally organized: they have their confederations, trusts and other organizations through which they defend their global interests. They can equally count on the protection and support of their liberal governments, as can be seen in the "Trilateral Agreement." For their part, the dominated classes in the system have only feeble defence organizations on the international level. Difficulty of making contacts, internal ideological and political splits (aggrevated by external intervention), lack of support and even opposition from their own governments, explain why the necessary alliance among the oppressed on a world scale is still so precarious.

4. The diagram also shows how many forces the oppressed have to overcome and replace if they are to liberate themselves. There are the ruling classes of their own countries, then the dictatorships that keep them in power; after this, the vested interests of the international community, which derives much of its hegemony from the Third World; and finally, the reactionary forces of the big landowners, who ally themselves with the bourgeoisie on vital matters affecting their own survival.

5. The reason for taking a world view of poverty is to show that any effective struggle to overcome it has to be equally worldwide. This is of vital concern to a worldwide institution like the Christian church and many of its internal organizations (religious orders, etc.). Such institutions are the only places where the universal dimension of poverty can be clearly appreciated and where there is a possibility of devising valid, equally universal, means of overcoming it.

# PART ONE

# THE BIBLICAL ASPECT

The next four chapters set out the biblical aspect of the issue of the option for the poor. The first two deal with the God of the Bible as the God who opts for the poor, in the Old and New Testaments respectively. Chapter III deals with the option for the poor from the human standpoint: it discusses solidarity as the biblical basis of the ethic concerning the poor. Finally, chapter IV examines the poor as first recipients of the word of God.

# Chapter I

# The Option for the Poor in the Old Testament

## 1. INTRODUCTION

This chapter seeks to establish just who the God of the Bible is. This might not seem necessary, as the question of who God is could seem to have been settled by the common understanding of our Western culture. God is the one perfect being, all-powerful and all-wise, creator of heaven and earth, whose goodness and justice never fail. But common understanding, in this as in so many other things, is deceptive. The long history of conflicts between Christians in Latin America has taught us that the common confession of one God hides different, and even opposing, ways of envisaging this all-powerful and all-wise creator God. The Bible takes great care to identify the God it speaks of, and does so using categories other than our common understanding. To simplify somewhat, but without distorting the matter in essentials, we can say that the God of the Bible is the God who led Israel out of Egypt and who raised Jesus Christ from the dead. This is the God who created heaven and earth, and this is the God whose perfection we have to postulate.

There is no reason to dispute the Western philosophical affirmation that for God's love to be perfect, it has to be universal. But this does need some qualification. The biblical narratives tell us that the concrete expression of this love favoured the slaves in Egypt and Palestine, and the poor of Galilee. God's love for Pharaoh was mediated through God's preferential love for the Israelite slaves. In the same way, God's love for the scribes and Pharisees was mediated through God's love for and solidarity with the fishermen and women of Galilee. And so the God whom the Bible calls creator of heaven and earth takes on specific characteristics.

So, having, we hope, established the importance of asking who the God of the Bible is, let us approach the question through the introduction to that admirable synthesis of law that we know as the Decalogue:

> I am Yahweh your God who brought you out of the land
> of Egypt, out of the house of slavery. You shall have no
> gods except me (Exod. 20:2–3).[1]

The words are so familiar to us that we hardly pay attention to them, yet they contain affirmations that are far from obvious at first sight. In the first place, the God Yahweh displays a polemical tone with regard to other possible gods. The text neither denies nor affirms that there are other gods. Their existence or non-existence is not the case at issue. What is at issue is that *you*, Israelite, to whom the law is addressed, must base your justice on the prohibition to worship them or ask them for favours. In other words, any god who has not brought you out of the house of slavery cannot be your God.

All the commandments dealing with just conduct among people—"honour your father and mother . . . you shall not kill . . . you shall not steal," etc.— are presented as the direct and personal commands of *this* God, who "brought you out of the land of Egypt, out of the house of slavery." There is nothing to show that it had to be this way; at least, there is nothing in the common understanding of Western culture that would indicate this. But let us look at the text a little more closely:

(a) "I am *Yahweh* your God." The proper name Yahweh serves to ensure that those gods who cannot or will not save Israel from the house of slavery in Egypt cannot hide under the generic term *god*. It is not possible to make definite assertions about the origin of the name Yahweh.[2] Nevertheless, the Elohist and priestly traditions, two of the three great narrative traditions in the Pentateuch, agree in placing the revelation of this divine name within the context of the exodus. In the Elohist tradition, Yahweh revealed his proper name to Moses in the desert at the time he was persuading him to undertake the liberation of his enslaved people (Exod. 3:14–15). In the priestly tradition, he revealed his name to Moses still in Egypt as a confirmation of his will to set the slaves free (Exod. 6:2–6). Both traditions coincide in having God already known to the patriarchs Abraham, Isaac and Jacob, though they did not know God's *name*. This was revealed only to the prophet who was to lead Israel in its liberation. So the name Yahweh asserts the singularity of God as liberator.

(b) "I am Yahweh *your* God." Because he brought Israel out of the land of Egypt, out of the house of slavery, Yahweh is the God of Israel. This liberation establishes a relationship of exclusive dependence on Yahweh. Yahweh cannot be adored except by those who confess themselves slaves liberated from the slavery in Egypt. To understand this, we have to be careful not to be confused by the patriarchal traditions. This *your* does not indicate a previous relationship independent of the liberation. The exodus formed the people of Yahweh. According to Exodus 12:38 (from the Yahwist tradition), "people of various sorts" (*erev rav*) joined the Israelites on the march, showing that the unity of Israel had to be constituted on the basis of the exodus. What was ordained for the Passover shows how the nation was defined:

> No alien may take part in it. . . . Should a stranger be staying with you and wish to celebrate the Passover in honour of Yahweh, all the males of his household must be circumcised: he may then be admitted to the celebration, for he becomes as it were a native-born. But no uncircumcised person may take part (Exod. 12:43, 48).

In other words, for Yahweh to be *your* God, you have to unite yourself to those who are celebrating their liberation from slavery. And no one who shows solidarity with the liberated people, demonstrating it through the circumcision of his foreskin, will be excluded from the community that celebrates its liberation from Egypt. In Israel's later practice, things were not that simple, but this expresses an intention: Yahweh is *your* God.

(c) "I am Yahweh your *God.*" Theology in the Old Testament is not organized round dogmatic themes. Strictly speaking, the Old Testament includes no Creed defining the nature of God. Its theology is narrative, and the great majority of the books that make up this collection of writings recognize the foundational character of the story of the exodus. Efforts at generalizing about the nature of God are based on this story:

> Yahweh your God is God of gods and Lord of lords, the great God, triumphant and terrible, never partial, never to be bribed. It is he who sees justice done for the orphan and the widow, who loves the stranger and gives him food and clothing (Deut. 10:16–18).

The God of the exodus account is a God who heard the cries wrung from the slaves by the slave-drivers of Pharaoh and so came down to set them free and lead them to a land flowing with milk and honey. Moses, the man chosen to lead this project, had gained his credentials by risking his high social position by killing an Egyptian who was maltreating a Hebrew (Exod. 2:11–15). So the exodus account clearly shows that justice means taking sides with the oppressed. The Yahweh of the exodus takes the part of the oppressed. From this our text draws the theological principle that God's impartiality makes God love the orphan and the widow with preference. Curiously, but nevertheless logically, not making exception of persons means making a preferential option for the oppressed in a situation of oppression.

These initial observations show that Yahweh, the God of the Bible, is characterized by his preferential option for the oppressed. The remaining sections of this chapter will examine some of the principal witnesses of the Bible concerning the way in which they appropiated this Yahweh God of the exodus. We need to remind ourselves here that the Bible is not one continuous work, but a collection of writings originating at different periods. This diversity of origin is also shown in the different ways it takes up the basic themes of Israel's tradition. Yahweh's option for the oppressed, as an integral element in the exodus narrative, which has a foundational character for

Israel, exercised a basic influence over virtually all the books of the Bible (the notable exception being Proverbs, which we shall examine in due course as an expression of the teaching of "wise men"). Our examination will seek to bring out the different shades with which God's preferential option for the impoverished and oppressed is presented.

## 2. THE EXODUS REVEALS YAHWEH AS LIBERATOR GOD: THE TEXT AND THE SOCIAL CONTEXT IN WHICH IT WAS PRODUCED

In the account of the exodus from Eygptian slavery under the inspiration of Yahweh and the leadership of Moses, Israel narrates its origins as a people and confesses that it owes these to Yahweh and is, in consequence, the people of Yahweh. Although the events narrated are earlier than the formation of Israel as a nation with its own language and identity, the account presupposes the existence of this nation. It is an "official" account; and, like the official accounts of any nation explaining its origins, it hides some elements while revealing others. We therefore need to have some idea of the social history of Israel, the context in which the account was produced. So in this section we begin by reconstructing the probable origins of Israel, and go on to examine the exodus narrative and what it tells us about Yahweh and his choice of a nation for himself, showing how the social changes that came about in Israel altered the way in which the foundational events were understood.

Israel first appeared on the historical scene around the end of the thirteenth century BC. The name features on the stele of Merneptah, king of Egypt, in the context of his campaign in Palestine in 1208 BC. Although this text tells us no more than the existence of Israel in Palestine at this date, later texts tell us that it originated in the central mountains of Palestine, which, till the thirteenth century, had been the least populated area of Palestine. There is an extensive correspondence between the Egyptian court and the kings of Canaan, dating from the fourteenth and thirteenth centuries. Letters from Tel-el-Amarna indicate that the centres of population were the coastal plain and the valley of Yezreel, which crosses the mountain range by Mount Carmel. These were precisely the areas Israel did not control at the time of its origins, which is significant. Another important fact derived from these letters is that Egypt was unable to maintain stable control in Palestine, owing to continuous wars among the kings of the cities.

According to its own traditions of the early period, as recounted in the Book of Judges, Israel consisted of various peasant groups scattered around the mountain areas. The valleys and plains were controlled by hostile tribes, whose material culture was superior to that of the Israelites (they possessed horses and carts).

Around 1200 BC, archaeology shows a vital transitional point in the material culture of Palestine, the introduction of iron tools. This must be the major factor leading at just this period to the clearing of mountain areas previously unserviceable for agriculture, producing the population shift that brought together groups who were to make up the nation of Israel.

All these facts are explained by the thesis that Israel arose in the thirteenth century BC from a process of internal migration in Palestine. Families and clans that had previously lived on the plain and in the valleys fled from the endless wars to seek a new life in country that had become cultivatable through the introduction of iron tools. This movement is illustrated in the biblical tradition of the migration of the tribe of Dan from the cities of Zorah and Eshtaol to the extreme Northeast of Galilee (Judg. 17–18). These migrations also had a social effect. Those who migrated were peasants; not only did they escape the political conflicts; they also escaped the tributes they had previously paid to the lords of the cities. In their new hill areas they did not build cities because they were not city people. Archaeological excavations have produced cases of cities destroyed at this period and rebuilt on a smaller scale, with humbler materials. This diminution of urban life can be explained by the incursion of peasant groups coming up from the plain. If this is the demographic origin of the clans that were to make up the nation of Israel, then one can talk of a movement of migration/uprising.[3]

These peasant groups were joined around 1200 BC by a group that came from Egypt, where it had carried out an uprising and an exodus into the desert under the leadership of Moses, a prophet of the God Yahweh. Their rebellion had been provoked by King Rameses II (1290–24), whose construction projects had placed an intolerable burden on the peasant population of Egypt. The social system obtaining in Egypt is described in Genesis 47:13–26: the people lived in their own villages and with their own families, but all the land belonged to the state and its produce was subject to a tax imposed by the Pharaoh. This was the same "Asiatic" system as in Palestine, aggravated by the fact that the Egyptian state was far more powerful. The Hebrews who came out of Egypt understood that their success had been due to Yahweh, their God, being with them. The coincidence of this experience with that of the clans of Israel was noteworthy, and the clans gradually came to accept Yahweh as their God. The exodus of the Hebrews came to be the founding history of Israel.[4]

So the material basis of confession of faith in Yahweh was the diffuse peasant movement arising from the particular conditions in Palestine in the fourteenth and thirteenth centuries BC. Israelite society was made up of small villages organized by ties of blood relationship into families, clans and tribes. At the beginning, they had neither cities nor kings. The arrival of the Hebrew group gave the movement a political and social consciousness, the axis of which was confession of Yahweh as their only king.[5] The laws given on Sinai lent coherence to the movement and a consciousness of the group's difference from the "Canaanites" who dwelt in the cities, subject to human kings and worshipping Baal. The Israelites spoke the language of Canaan (see Isa. 19:18), from where they had come. The telling of the exodus and their confession of faith in Yahweh gave weight to their consciousness of being different from the inhabitants of the valleys and the cities. They were the people of Yahweh and had no kings "like the other nations" (1 Sam. 8:5).

Reflecting on the importance of their movement, the tribes of Israel gradually came to see its universal significance, and to recognize Yahweh as God *tout court*, not simply as the God of Israel. One tradition held that Yahweh had promised Abraham: "All the tribes of the earth shall bless themselves by you" (Gen. 12:3). Deutero-Isaiah (sixth century) proclaimed that

Israel, the servant of Yahweh, would be a "light to the nations" (Isa. 49:6). So some biblical texts give universal value to the Israelite experience that God is a saviour of the oppressed. Logically, Israel also came to confess Yahweh as creator of heaven and earth. It also saw in Yahweh a companion to those who wander the face of earth without a home, a God who gave them land in which to settle.[6] And so the people of Israel came to understand that the Yahweh of the exodus was the one God who governs all nations. This is the historical thesis we follow here.

After this brief reconstruction of the origin of Israel, let us turn to its founding text, the account of the exodus. The book of Exodus, like the whole of the Pentateuch of which it forms part, was not finally completed till the fifth century BC, eight hundred years after the events it recounts. During these eight centuries, several major changes took place in the life of Israel:

(i) For two hundred years, Israel existed as a loose grouping of clans and tribes of peasants, surrounded by cities under monarchical regimes, generally hostile to Israel (with some exceptions, such as Gibeon and Schechem).

(ii) Around the year 1000 BC, the attacks from the cities forced Israel to create its own monarchical state, which lasted some four hundred years.

(iii) After the destruction of the capital (587 BC), the Jewish people organized themselves as a religious nation led by a priestly caste, under the tolerant suzereignty of the Persian empire.

As the account of the exodus is the founding document of Israel, it was naturally revised in each of these three epochs. The final text of the book of Exodus contains elements from each of these revisions. So it is a text made up of superimposed layers, with differing interpretations of those events in Egypt in the thirteenth century BC.

The earliest stage of the account, probably exclusively oral, calls the people of the exodus "Hebrews." This term did not originally denote a race, but was a designation given to various groups in several localities from Egypt to Mesopotamia. Such people were mercenaries, nomads, rebels; the name denoted the fact that they were not integrated into the broader framework of society, were outside the general rule of law.[7]

When the exodus narrative was the foundational text of the Israelite tribes, the experience in Egypt was read as that of a group of peasants who had rebelled and placed themselves outside Egyptian law. Those who heeded the call of Yahweh and Moses to undertake a struggle that would set them free from slavery in Egypt were, therefore, "Hebrews," "people of various sorts" who decided to break with the Egyptian legal system, under which they had to hold their flocks, lands and bodies at the king's disposition.

The central feature of the account for the tribes of Israel was the part played by Yahweh in their liberation. They did not read the exodus as a secular revolutionary movement. Yahweh was on their side and guided the movement through his prophet Moses. The fact that they succeeded in escaping from their enforced serfdom despite the powerful Egyptian army showed that God, who took the side of the poor in Egypt, was the true God.

With the establishment of the monarchical state in Israel, the exodus narrative was taken up by the official scribes and converted into a national epic, together with the ancient traditions concerning the patriarchs Abraham, Isaac and Jacob. This process of adapting the Israelite traditions for the ends of the new monarchy probably took place at the court of Solomon. This produced the written version of the traditions that exegetes call the Yahwist version (known as J), the earliest writings that survive as part of the Pentateuch.

At this period, when the state was seeking to create a consciousness of national identity built up round the Davidic dynasty, it had to re-read the exodus as a national liberation struggle. The children of Israel, according to this re-reading, had been enslaved in Egypt after settling there to escape the famine in their own land of Canaan. A perverse king took advantage of their presence as guests, and the struggle that followed was between Egyptians and Israelites. The Israelites conceived the plan of "returning" to the land of Canaan. In this way the account ceased to describe a social movement within Egyptian society and replaced it with a struggle between peoples, in which Yahweh took the side of Israel. Israel was an exploited people, but more importantly, it was the people of Yahweh, and this from before the time of its exploitation in

Egypt. This is the emphasis in the Yahwist version:

> Go and gather the elders of Israel together and tell them,
> "Yahweh, the God of your fathers, has appeared to me—
> the God of Abraham, of Isaac, and of Jacob; and he has
> said to me: I have visited you and seen all that the
> Egyptians are doing to you" (Exod. 3:16).

The children of Israel are shown as having a relationship with
Yahweh going back to the time of their ancestors who lived in
Canaan. They are his people and this is the reason Yahweh
intervened to rescue them from their slavery. In this way the
exodus lost a large part of its challenging content and could
become useful for the monarchical aim of creating a national
consciousness.

On the basis of this re-reading of the exodus, a theological
reflection on the election of Israel as the special people of God
was developed in the late monarchical period (seventh century
BC):

> If Yahweh set his heart on you and chose you, it was not
> because you outnumbered other peoples: you were the
> least of all peoples. It was for love of you and to keep the
> oath that he swore to your fathers that Yahweh brought
> you out with his mighty hand and redeemed you from the
> house of slavery, from the power of Pharaoh king of
> Egypt (Deut. 7:7–8).

The exodus changes from Yahweh's option for the oppressed
to being an inscrutable favour conferred by Yahweh in
fulfilment of his promises to the patriarchs. This does not mean
that the memory of the favour enjoyed by the poor in Yahweh's
eyes was lost, but it was carried on as part of a thought-process
that enhanced Yahweh's special relationship with his people
dating from commitments entered into with the patriarchs.

The final re-reading of the exodus further overlaid the
revelation of Yahweh as the liberator God who showed his
preference for the oppressed. This is the reading made by the
priests in the sixth century BC, when Judah existed as a national
group within the Persian empire, internally led by the priestly

caste. This re-reading could not quite efface the privilege of the poor, but it changed the emphasis so as to exalt the greatness of Yahweh. The following is an example:

> Yahweh said to Moses, "See, I make you as a god for Pharaoh, and Aaron your brother is to be your prophet. You yourself must tell him all I command you, and Aaron your brother will tell Pharaoh to let the sons of Israel leave his land. I myself will make Pharaoh's heart stubborn, and perform many a sign and wonder in the land of Egypt. Pharaoh will not listen to you, and so I will lay my hand on Egypt and with strokes of power lead out my armies, my people, the sons of Israel, from the land of Egypt. And all the Egyptians shall come to know that I am Yahweh when I stretch out my hand against Egypt and bring out the sons of Israel from their midst" (Exod. 7:1–5).

In the earlier layers of the account, the blows delivered against Pharaoh were to force him to let the Hebrews go. Every time Pharaoh hardened his heart, Yahweh visited a fresh plague on him so as to soften it. In the priestly re-reading, the marvels have another purpose: to demonstrate the greatness of Yahweh. This is why Yahweh himself hardens Pharaoh's heart so as to give himself new opportunities of showing his greatness.

In this priestly re-reading of the exodus, the desire to show the greatness of Yahweh has grown to such an extent that it obscures—though it cannot completely erase—Yahweh's predilection for the poor and oppressed. So Yahweh's option for the slaves and their liberation, the inspiration of pre-monarchical Israel, was gradually weakened in later re-readings. The original vision was kept in prophetic circles, which is something we shall examine in section 6 of this chapter.

## 3.   COULD ISRAEL HAVE KNOWN CLASS CONSCIOUSNESS?

Discussion of the origins of Israel as coming about through an uprising/migration and repudiation of the structures of domination personalized in the kings of the surrounding peoples raises a doubt: are we not imposing on these early years a level of social consciousness that could not have existed two thousand years before Christ? This is a legitimate concern, and needs examination.

Obviously, there were no "social sciences" either in Canaan or in Egypt in the thirteenth century BC. So there was no possibility of making a "scientific" analysis of the structure of society and the dynamics of its reproduction. Hence if we raise the above question with reference to a kind of social conscious-ness grounded in social–scientific analysis, the reply has to be affirmative.

So let us put the question differently. Was it possible for groups of peasants in Canaan to arrive at a realization that their interests as peasant groups were being threatened by their subjection to the king of their cities—Dor, Megiddo, Beth-shean? In a stable society, even though the king sequestered a large portion of agricultural produce and required significant labour quotas for state works, it is highly unlikely that a peasant class which had never known any other way of life would have hankered after alternative lifestyles. Furthermore, the king was not regarded as a man, but as a god, on whom they were dependent for such essentials as sun and rain.

Nevertheless, Canaan in the fourteenth and thirteenth centuries BC was going through a critical phase in the Egyptian domination, reflected in the continual wars among the kings of its cities. Such a situation would lead to each village undergoing changes of overlord, besides interruptions to its crop produc-tion. One god/king would take the place of another as "benefactor" responsible for giving life to the people of one place, without any internal change taking place within the people themselves. These changes would create the possibility of thinking of alternatives to the system of domination by kings. The peasants, well organized in large families on the local level, could come to realize that their interests were not identical with those of the city which demanded a quota of their produce. The presence of nearby virgin land, even if not as fertile as that of the plain, would have completed the process of "conscientiza-tion" concerning the possibility of an alternative to their traditional subjection.

In Egypt, conditions that could have led to an alternative consciousness among the peasants were different. Here there was only one state, and it was a very strong state, with a very convincing religious underpinning. Conditions for a consciousness of oppression were created by the excessive exploitation of the peasant base of society for funerary constructions. It was natural to attribute these excesses of exploitation to abuses by the king's henchmen, which the king would correct if he knew the wrong being done his servants. That is, exploitation in itself would not have produced an alternative consciousness. As long as everyone continued to believe in the supreme god, whose goodness was shown in the richness of the country, irrigated every year by the flood waters of the great river Nile, the social structure was very secure. There was no alternative cultivatable land in the region. No one suggested the possibility of an alternative, and the wrongs suffered by a particular group of workers were a very localized incident compared to the overall riches of a land blessed by heaven.

Here, consciousness of an alternative must have come principally from an outside element introduced, undoubtedly, from the East, in the form of the God Yahweh, who appeared on the holy mountain. Yahweh had presented himself as a God of the poor, promising their liberation. It seems certain that very few peasants in the land of Egypt were prepared to receive such a message, though the conditions of exceptional oppression produced by the construction works of Rameses II would have led some to this extreme. So a small group of "Hebrews" gathered round Moses, determined to understand their withdrawal from society as a repudiation of the oppression they now associated with Pharaoh, demystified for them by their acceptance of the God who had appeared to Moses with the promise of another land flowing with milk and honey.

## 4. THE DAVIDIC MONARCHY PROCLAIMS ITSELF YAHWEH'S INSTRUMENT FOR THE DEFENCE OF THE POOR

Toward the end of the eleventh century, a leader of the peasant militias called Saul of Benjamin obtained the support of large

sectors of Israel in forming a professional army to defend the
tribes against the predations of the militarized peoples surrounding them, the Moabites, Ammonites, Edonites and,
above all, the Philistines (1 Sam. 11; 14:47–52). Saul was given
the title *Melek*, king, though he continued to live in Geba of
Benjamin without fortifying it or converting it into a capital
city. In the ranks of Saul's army an exceptional fighter and
politician appeared, called David of Judah, who after Saul's
death succeeded in unifying the tribes for the sake of better
defence against the Philistines and, later, in order to wage wars
of conquest. In order to establish his power, this David
conquered a fortified city in the mountains of Canaan and
established his capital there. Jerusalem soon became the
luxurious centre of the small empire, controlling the whole of
Palestine and parts of Syria.

This section seeks to examine how the monarchy affected
faith in Yahweh, the God of the poor. Here we confine
ourselves to the outlook of the capital, the official religion of
Jerusalem, since sections 6 and 7 deal with other social entities
of the period, the prophets and the wise men. The most
important documents for understanding the "true ideology" of
Jerusalem are the Psalms, which were collected in the capital's
temple. Before examining them, it is worth taking a look at the
process that led to a peasant and anti-monarchic movement
accepting a king and a capital.

We have said that at the outset Israel was a people of
peasants, small landholders, a coalition of clans which had
withdrawn from the proximity of the cities on the coastal plain
and emigrated to the mountainous zones of the country. It was
an egalitarian society, in a particular sense we shall examine
later when looking at its legal tradition. The people occupied
relatively infertile lands, with uncertain rainfall, and they were
poor. Yet from a very early period they formed alliances with
cities already established in the mountain regions. We know of
two such cases, Gibeon and Shechem, both relatively large
cities, fortified and used to monarchical rule. Both came to be
important centres of the Israelite movement, and also religious
centres for the cult of Yahweh. So from the outset the
movement was not totally closed to urban life.

This situation conditioned Israel to consider the possibility of having a king when military pressures from both inside and outside became intolerable. There were armed conflicts within Israel itself; some of these were on a fairly large scale, such as the destruction of Succoth by a force from Manasseh headed by Gideon (Judg. 8:4–21), and the concerted attack by various tribes on Benjamin (Judg. 19–21). From outside the tribes there were pressures from the Moabites, the Ammonites, the Midianites and, above all, the Philistines. Israel lacked the political tools to impose peace among its clans or to defend itself from the Philistine threat. It was this situation that led to the formation of a professional army under Saul of Benjamin. Once this army was in existence, conditions existed for a clever and charismatic warrior such as David of Judah to take the next step of capturing a city and converting it into a capital.

An absolute monarchy of the "Asiatic" type needed religious legitimation. Furthermore, the actual social conditions of a tributary society lend verisimilitude to the teaching that the king was more than a man. In Israel there was the problem (for David and his successors) that Yahweh was the God of the peasants who had fled from the domination of kings. The narrative texts dealing with the birth of the monarchy (1 Sam. 8–12) tell of the prophet Samuel's opposition to this novelty. The text shows his opposition based on two points: that choosing a king meant rejecting Yahweh as king (1 Sam. 8:7); and that kings end by enslaving their people (1 Sam. 8:17). Later, the prophet Nathan followed the same lines of resistance in opposing David's plan to build a temple to Yahweh in his new capital (2 Sam. 7:7–17). Nevertheless, by the middle of the tenth century, Solomon was able to build the temple, and in time this became the principal sanctuary of Yahweh. It is the theology that was developed in this temple that concerns us in the remainder of this section.

The Psalms were used in the liturgy of the temple of Jerusalem, and are, therefore, direct testimony to how official-dom interpreted the function of the king in religious terms. The Psalms tell of the great richness of religious life at court, and also show how religious propaganda was effected.[8] The prophets and the Deuteronomist history generally distance themselves from the kings, denouncing them at times and at others questioning the whole institution of the monarchy. The Psalms, on the other hand, always depict the king in positive tones. One of the things they say of the kings is they are defenders of the poor, placed in their position by Yahweh for this purpose. As an example, we can take Psalm 72, a prayer for Yahweh's blessing on the king:

God, give your own justice to the king,
    your own righteousness to the royal son,
so that he may rule your people rightly
    and your poor with justice.

Let the mountains and hills
    bring a message of peace for the people.
Uprightly he will defend the poorest,
he will save the children of those in need,
    and crush their oppressors.

Like sun and moon he will endure,
    age after age,
welcome as rain that falls on the pasture,
    and showers to thirsty soil.

In his days virtue will flourish,
    a universal peace till the moon is no more;
his empire shall stretch from sea to sea,
    from the river to the ends of the earth.

The Beast will cower before him
    and his enemies grovel in the dust;
the kings of Tarshish and of the islands
    will pay him tribute.

The kings of Sheba and Seba
    will offer gifts;
all kings will do him homage,
    all nations become his servants.

He will free the poor man who calls to him,
  and those who need help,
he will have pity on the poor and feeble,
  and save the lives of those in need;

he will redeem their lives from exploitation and outrage,
  their lives will be precious in his sight.
(Long may he live, may gold from Sheba be given him!)
Prayer will be offered for him constantly,
  blessings invoked on him all day long.

Grain everywhere in the country,
  even on the mountain tops,
abundant as Lebanon its harvest,
  luxuriant as common grass!

Blessed be his name for ever,
  enduring as long as the sun!
May every race in the world be blessed in him,
  and all the nations call him blessed!

Abundant harvests are asked for the king, and victory over
his enemies; but the main thrust is the prediction that he will
defend the poor and needy against those who oppress them.
This is of course language with an ulterior motive: it is not
describing what is, but what ought to be, and also what it wants
people to believe is. The king of flesh and blood might be a
protector of the weak, or he might be a crony and accomplice
of the rich; whichever he is, the stability of his social control
requires the people to see him as their benefactor and defender.
  According to official teaching, Yahweh chose David and his
offspring in perpetuity to govern his people Israel (2 Sam. 7:16;
Pss. 89:4–5; 132:11). This flatly contradicts the conviction that
Yahweh was king of Israel, and that therefore Israel could have
no human kings (Judg. 8:22–3; 1 Sam. 8:4–15). It would take
too long to explain here how David managed to overcome
opposition to his reign. In fact, he never succeeded in
overcoming it entirely and till the end of his reign had to deal
with a series of uprisings. One fact, however, concerns the

subject we are examining here: the way the court developed the thesis that Yahweh had chosen David to protect the poor. Though such an idea was common in Eastern monarchies, it carried special force in Israel's case, since Yahweh was a God of the poor. It was also very necessary to proclaim the king's function in this way in order to overcome religious opposition to the monarchy. Nathan's parable and David's reaction show the king carrying out this function:

> Yahweh sent Nathan the prophet to David. He came to him and said:
> "In the same town were two men,
> one rich, the other poor.
> The rich man had flocks and herds
> in great abundance;
> the poor man had nothing but a ewe lamb,
> one only, a small one he had bought.
> This he fed, and it grew up with him and his children,
> eating his bread, drinking from his cup,
> sleeping on his breast; it was like a daughter to him.
> When there came a traveller to stay, the rich man
> refused to take one of his own flock or herd
> to provide for the wayfarer who had come to him.
> Instead he took the poor man's lamb
> and prepared it for his guest."
> David's anger flared up against the man. "As Yahweh lives," he said to Nathan, "the man who did this deserves to die! He must make fourfold restitution for the lamb, for doing such a thing and showing no compassion" (2 Sam. 12:1–6).

Absalom, David's son, managed to win the hearts of the people of Israel and so gain popular support for his uprising against his father by promising all who had a lawsuit or plea that he could provide justice for them better than the king (2 Sam. 15:1–6). And Solomon, at the beginning of his reign, prayed to Yahweh in his sanctuary at Gibeon for the wisdom to discern between good and evil in governing the people (1 Kings 3:9).

The complexities of this doctrine can be seen in the case of Isaiah. Isaiah subscribed to the official religion and believed that the king was Yahweh's designated benefactor of the poor. This is why he addressed strong condemnations to the kings of his time for failing to carry out what Yahweh expected of them. He attacked the kings and their officials for robbing orphans and preying on widows (Isa. 10:1–4). He prophesied the purification of Jerusalem by fire, and the replacement of judges who failed to hear widows' causes (1:21–6). Thinking within the framework of official theology, Isaiah cannot conceive that the monarchy might be destroyed; only that it must be renewed through a new king whom Yahweh will raise up to deal justice:

> A shoot springs from the stock of Jesse,
> a scion thrusts from his roots;
> on him the spirit of Yahweh rests,
> a spirit of wisdom and insight,
> a spirit of counsel and power,
> a spirit of knowledge and of the fear of Yahweh. . . .[9]
> He does not judge by appearances,
> he gives no verdict on hearsay,
> but judges the wretched with integrity,
> and with equity gives a verdict for the poor of the land.
> His word is a rod that strikes the ruthless,[10]
> his sentences bring death to the wicked (11:1–4).

Despite the radical nature of his critiques, Isaiah fails to see beyond a society in which kings have the final word. Within these limits, the best a believer in the Yahweh of the Bible could hope for was a good king inspired by Yahweh to judge the cause of the poor with power and integrity.

The official theology of Jerusalem, as we know it from the Psalms, held that, when Yahweh chose David, he chose him and his descendants forever. On the other hand, the Deuteronomist history or tradition (contained in the books of Deuteronomy, Joshua, Judges, 1 and 2 Samuel and 1 and 2 Kings, and known as "D"), written under the shadow of the destruction of Samaria, re-evaluates these unconditional promises and makes the covenant conditional on the kings obeying

the commandments given to Moses on Sinai and proclaimed to
the people by Moses in the desert of Moab. These are found in
Moses' exposition of the law in the series of discourses we know
as Deuteronomy. Jeremiah, influenced by Deuteronomic theology, proclaimed the conditional nature of the famous promise
made by Yahweh to David; Jeremiah made this proclamation
from Jerusalem, the very centre of royal theology:

> Yahweh said this, "Go down to the palace of the king of
> Judah and there deliver this message: 'Listen to the word
> of Yahweh, king of Judah sitting on the throne of David,
> you, your servants too, and the people who go through
> these gates. Yahweh says this: Practise honesty and
> integrity; rescue the man who has been wronged from the
> hands of his oppressor; do not exploit the stranger, the
> orphan, the widow; do no violence; shed no innocent
> blood in this place. For if you are scrupulous in obeying
> this command, then kings occupying the throne of David
> will continue to make their entry through the gates of this
> palace mounted on chariots and horses, they, their
> servants and their people. But if you do not listen to these
> words, then I swear by myself—it is Yahweh who
> speaks—this palace shall become a ruin!'" (Jer. 22:1–5).

So the kings will be judged according to the justice they show
to the oppressed, and it is possible for the royal line to be wiped
out. This contradicts the official theology of texts such as Psalm
89:31–8, and makes Yahweh's predilection for the poor, as
revealed in the exodus, more emphatic.

To sum up: according to texts attributed to Samuel (1 Sam.
8; 1 Sam. 12), the proposal to have a king "like the other
nations" was a rebellion against Yahweh, the God of the
exodus. Yahweh consented, but unwillingly. Official theology
stressed that the king was the instrument chosen by Yahweh to
protect the interests of the poor. So the official theology of the
kings, which served to legitimize their power and succession,
recognized that Yahweh, the official God, was a defender of
the poor.

## 5. SOCIAL RELATIONSHIPS COMMANDED BY YAHWEH: THE PRIVILEGE OF THE POOR IN LEGAL TRADITION

Approximately half the Pentateuch is devoted to the transmission of laws. The central block of the work deals with the stay of the people on Mount Sinai, where Yahweh, the God who had rescued the people from slavery, revealed to Moses the norms by which they were to live in the future as the people of Yahweh (Exod. 19:1; Num. 10:11). Later, before the people entered the land of Canaan, in the desert of Moab, it is said that Moses gave them another series of laws that Yahweh had revealed to him on Sinai (Deut. 12–26, the Deuteronomic code). Overall, all Israel's laws derived from Yahweh. The state that was later created could issue edicts, but the laws of Sinai imposed the limits within which these could be framed. Even when Israel had kings, its legal tradition did not depend on them.

Modern scholars accept that a large part of this ample body of law, sociologically speaking, originated and was transmitted as popular law. The tradition was carried on by the ancients sitting by the gates of the towns and villages. There they heard disputes that had arisen in the villages and, on the basis of the law of Yahweh they had received from their fathers, pronounced their judgments (Ruth 4:1–8; Amos 5:10, 12). In this way it was understood that the social life of Israel was carried on in conformity with the will of Yahweh, the God of their liberation.

In the course of compiling this popular law emanating from Yahweh, three major legal codes were produced, now found in the Pentateuch. These are the code of the Covenant (Exod. 20: 22–23:19), the Deuteronomic code (Deut. 12–26) and the law of Holiness (Lev. 17–26), which were compiled in this order in time. A notable lack in all of them is any regulation governing the king and his court. The only law in the whole corpus that mentions the king is Deuteronomy 17:14–20, which seeks to curb the excessive power of kings. This lack is not fortuitous; it confirms the independence of the kings of Israel from their court and is also consistent with Israel's confession of Yahweh as their only king.

Some examples from the code of the Covenant will serve to illustrate the privilege accorded to the poor in these laws given by Yahweh:

> You must not molest the stranger or oppress him, for you lived as strangers in the land of Egypt (Exod. 22:20).

> You must not be harsh with the widow, or with the orphan; if you are harsh with them, they will surely cry out to me, and be sure I shall hear their cry; my anger will flare and I shall kill you with the sword, your own wives will be widows, your own children orphans (22:21–3).

> If you lend money to any of my people, to any poor man among you, you must not play the usurer with him; you must not demand interest from him (22:24).

The subject who gives out these laws is Yahweh, the God of the exodus; their recipients are the Israelites who have been freed from Egypt. Being written after several centuries, this convention had become somewhat artifical, but it did serve to keep the memory of Israel's origins alive, and did have practical effects on the conduct of Israelite society.

This is popular law. It was not till much later that king Jehoshaphat of Judah (870–48) first appointed judges from the court (2 Chron. 19:5), and even then legal tradition did not take much notice of them. The penalty for murder was death; executions were carried out not by official executioners, but by the people themselves, by stoning. The legislation had no place for imprisonment as a punishment, since this would involve prison administration. The penalty for theft was rather the duty to make restitution:

> If a man steals an ox or a sheep and then slaughters or sells it, he must pay five oxen for the ox, four sheep for the sheep (Exod. 21:37).

This law and the prohibition of usury quoted above show how the law set life above property. There is a duty to lend to the poor because they need it, not in order to profit from their poverty. Those who steal will be obliged to make restitution, but their lives will not be demanded in exchange for stolen property. Thieves' lives are also protected in another way:

> If a thief is caught breaking in and is struck a mortal blow, there is to be no blood-vengeance for him, but there shall be blood-vengeance for him if it was after dawn (Exod. 22:1–2).

This means that if someone kills a thief breaking into his house by night, it is not counted as homicide, but it is if the thief breaks in and is killed by day.

The Deuteronomic code is the product of a revision of the ancient legal tradition made after the destruction of Samaria, when Israel had already had three centuries of monarchical rule. It was seeking to recover the best of the old tradition before corruption and forgetfulness of Yahweh led to the downfall of the nation. It contains many laws designed to protect the basic economy of the poor:

> You must not allow a master to imprison a slave who has escaped from him and come to you. He shall live with you, among you, wherever he pleases in any one of your towns he chooses; you are not to molest him (Deut. 23:16–17).

> You are not to exploit the hired servant who is poor and destitute, whether he is one of your brothers or a stranger who lives in your towns. You must pay him his wage each day, not allowing the sun to set before you do, for he is poor and is anxious for it; otherwise he might appeal to Yahweh against you, and it would be a sin for you (24:14–15).

> When reaping the harvest in your field, if you have overlooked a sheaf in that field, do not go back for it. Leave it for the stranger, the orphan and the widow, so

that Yahweh your God may bless you in all your
undertakings (24:19).

The law of Holiness was given this title because it systematically links the holiness required of each Israelite with the
holiness of Yahweh. Its literary composition dates from after
the exile, and though it certainly incorporates very ancient legal
traditions, it is difficult to use with any certainty as a guide to
the social life of independent Israel. It keeps the preoccupation
with the poor, particularly in the laws on land tenure in
Leviticus 25. Arable land cannot be sold, since it is considered
a patrimony which Yahweh has given to the landholder and his
family. If through circumstances beyond his control, the
landholder is forced to hand over his plot in order to survive,
this is considered a conditional transaction, until such time as
the seller can find the wherewithal to "redeem" the land. Even
if he cannot find the money, the land has to be returned to him
in the next jubilee year, which comes round every fifty years
(Lev. 25:23–34).

This brief selection from the laws deriving from Sinai gives
some idea of how Israel organized its social patterns in
conformity with the privileged position held by the poor in
Yahweh's eyes.

## 6.   THE PROPHETS OF YAHWEH SPEAK OUT AGAINST EXISTING CONDITIONS

There must certainly have been a great number of prophets,
most of whose names we do not know, living and acting in Israel
with neither disgrace nor glory. From the first period, when
Israel organized its life without kings and on the simple lines of
a peasant society, we know nothing about any prophets in the
strict sense. But the old story of the seer Balaam (Num. 22–
24), and the mention of divine inspiration of warriors, leaders
and judges, plus the ancient testimonies to prophets in Mari,
Byblos and Babylonia lead us to suppose that there was
prophetic activity in Israel at that time, even though it has left
no trace.

When Saul and then David had established a monarchy among the peasant clans of Israel, on the other hand, we see the appearance of outspoken prophets who, in the name of Yahweh, denounced the injustices of the new ruling classes. Some of these were attached to the court and took up their critical stance from there, but the most outspoken of them kept their distance from the monarchical apparatus. There was also a host of lesser prophets, some of whose names are preserved in the two books of Chronicles. These are not our concern here.

In religious terms, a prophet is a person, who announces a message received through direct inspiration by a god and who speaks from the fringes of the religious institution.[11] Because of their direct link with the divinity, prophets can preserve a relative autonomy from the dominant religious and political structures of their society. When a society had an egalitarian and anti-monarchical tradition, as did Israel, prophets were bound to take on greater importance during the period when the people were subject to indigenous royal dynasties. The classical period of biblical prophecy corresponds to the time of the monarchy, from the tenth to the sixth centuries BC. From the fifth century onwards, there were "Deutero-Prophets," whose sayings were added to the collections of sayings of the great earlier prophets without attribution, and also minor prophets such as Haggai and Zechariah.[12] During the centuries of the monarchy, it was the prophets who kept alive the tradition of Yahweh as the God who took the part of the poor in a society dominated by a ruling class dependent on the court.

The first major prophet in Israel was Samuel, in the eleventh century, at the period when Saul and later David were building up the monarchical state. The texts are somewhat contradictory about Samuel. On the one hand, he is said to reject the overtures of sectors of society who sought his support to legitimize the monarchy (1 Sam. 8:12). On the other, there are texts which say he took the initiative in conferring Yahweh's legitimacy first on Saul (1 Sam. 9) and later on David (1 Sam. 16). The texts link him more closely to Saul than to David, and it is likely that he supported Saul's monarchy, even if his support was conditional and only for a limited time.

By contrast, the prophet Nathan had close links with the

court of David, and supported him in the name of Yahweh. To him is attributed the important oracle which for several centuries served as the main divine justification for the dynasty: "Your House and your sovereignty will always stand secure before me and your throne be established for ever" (2 Sam. 7:16). Through him all rebellions against the dynasty were shorn of legality. Nevertheless, his close contact with David did not prevent him from reproaching him for the death of Uriah the Hittite leader (2 Sam. 12:1–15).

Ahijah of Shiloh begins the line of prophets who stood up to domination by the kings in the name of Yahweh and the poor. Ahijah, in the name of Yahweh, supported Jeroboam in his unsuccessful revolt against Solomon (1 Kings 11:26–40). Once Solomon was dead, Jeroboam was able to carry out his plan. The kingdom Jeroboam established leads one to suppose that Ahijah supported a limited form of monarchy, without pomp and without a capital, in the name of Yahweh. But Ahijah later turned against Jeroboam and announced the fall of his house (1 Kings 14:1–18).

In a similar incident, Elisha had Jehu, an army captain, anointed as king of Israel, so that he would overthrow Jehoram and assassinate the royal family (2 Kings 9). In this, Elisha was continuing the opposition of his master, Elijah, to the Amorites of Samaria. Elijah had denounced Ahab for having Naboth of Jezreel killed so that he could take over his vineyard (1 Kings 21). The text presents the struggle between the prophets and the Amorites as one between Yahweh and Baal. Behind this religious rivalry lay a defence of the poor people of Israel, as the incident of Naboth's vineyard shows.

The great prophets of the eighth century, Amos, Micah, Hosea and Isaiah, lived at a time of prosperity for both Israel and Judah, which lasted till the start of the Syrian invasions in 734. Samaria was ruled by the dynasty of Jehu, the king who restored the cult of Yahweh after the deviations of the Amorites. But Amos showed how love of luxury was making a mockery of their devotion to Yahweh. For Amos, the great sinners were the swindling traders, who, "by lowering the bushel, raising the shekel, by swindling and tampering with the scales . . . can buy up the poor for money, and the needy for a pair of sandals" (Amos 8:5–6). The great people of Israel lay on ivory beds, over-ate, bawled songs, drank wine by the bowlful and used the finest oil for anointing themselves, caring not at all for the ruin of Joseph (i.e. the impending collapse of Israel: Amos 6:4–6). This is why the nation would come to an end and not a single person escape (9:1–4).

Micah too defended the poor in the name of Yahweh. This country prophet (rightly) saw the root of the problem in the ruling class of Jerusalem, with its corrupt princes, judges, priests and prophets (Mic. 3:9–12). Because of their evil doings, "Zion will become ploughland, Jersualem a heap of rubble and the mountain of the temple a wooded height" (3:12). The dispossessed peasants will take over the lands at present held by the landowners through force, and the rulers will lament that they are now the despoiled, with "no one to measure out a share in the community of Yahweh" (2:1–5). [13]

Hosea, more than Amos and Micah, denounces the way religion is being used as a deceitful cloak for the accumulation of riches. The so-called Yahwism of the ruling classes is at bottom nothing other than worship of Baal, the god who brings rain and material abundance. Religion had become prostitution; its rites carried out not for love but for gain. But there will come a day when Israel will again call Yahweh "My husband" and not "My Baal" (Hos. 2: 18). The lack of knowledge of God in the country is shown in its general corruption: perjury, lies, slaughter, theft, adultery and violence, murder... (4:1–3). The priests are as guilty as the kings for this state of affairs (5:1); Hosea concludes that the monarchy must fall if the people are to live well (13:9–11). Once the monarchy and luxury have been put aside, the people can once more live their good life with Yahweh (2:16–25).

The only one of the great prophets of Israel and Judah who came from the capital was Isaiah of Jersualem. This is perhaps why his analysis of the basic problem afflicting the country lacks the radical edge of the three previous prophets, who saw the reality of the nation from out in the country. He also denounces the rulers as murderers and chasers after bribes (1:21–6), who fail to take notice of widows and orphans (10:1–4). He also recognizes the problem denounced by Micah: that the landown-

ers are buying up all the land, for which Yahweh will make their
lands fail to produce, even though they work them (5:8–10).
Yahweh's judgment will, in effect, lay the towns waste and
leave the countryside desolate (6:11–13). And yet, Isaiah hopes
for a king who will defend the poor with integrity (11:1–9); that
is, he looks forward to a society in which one class will not
exploit another.

A century later, Jeremiah attacked king Jehoiakim for
building palaces by "making his fellow man work for nothing"
(Jer. 22:13–19). Though he did not criticize king Josiah
personally, he attacked his famous reform as false (3:6–13). The
temple too had become part of the system of exploitation of the
people: the devices of the ruling classes had made it a "den of
thieves," used as a religious cloak under which they could go
on committing crimes against strangers, widows and orphans
(7:1–15). Yahweh's anger against the wrongs done to the poor
reached such a pitch that when the Babylonians attacked the
city of Jerusalem, Yahweh supported Nebuchadnezzar the king
of Babylon in his attack on the city (21:1–10). Jeremiah looked
forward to the restoration of a more modest society, with a
strong peasant base. During the anxious days of the seige of
Jerusalem, he bought a field at Anathoth, as a demonastration
of faith in the future of the countryside (32). When the
Babylonians took the city and freed him from prison, he
preferred to remain in the country with the humble people,
whom the Babylonians allowed to stay, to dress the vines and
harvest the fruit, when they took the leaders of the country to
Babylonia (40:7–12). In order to defend his people, Yahweh
had had to destroy the monarchy and the temple!

This brief look at the great prophets of Israel shows how,
each in their different way, they kept alive the tradition of
Yahweh as God of the poor.

## 7. THE PETITION OF THE PSALMS: THE POOR TURN
##    TO YAHWEH AS THEIR DEFENDER

The book of Psalms is a collection of prayers and hymns used
in the temple of Jerusalem. This means that they represent only
one aspect of Israel's religious practice: the sector linked to the

state. And as we have seen, the state of Judah had an ambiguous relationship with the Yahweh of the exodus, defender of the poor. On one hand, the mere fact of having mounted a state apparatus was seen by those sectors of society most faithful to the foundational experience of Israel as a sin against the Yahweh of the exodus. On the other, the state proclaimed itself chosen by Yahweh to defend the poor in his name; prophets of the stature of Isaiah saw the king as the best hope of the poor. As one might expect, it is this second viewpoint that was expressed in the liturgy of Jerusalem.

Many of the Psalms are petitions of those in need who turn to the temple seeking deliverance from their troubles. Such petitions clearly show the general expectation that Yahweh will be the protector of the weak and unprotected, particularly the poor, strangers, widows and orphans. This is the aspect that concerns us here. To take one short Psalm as an example:

Yahweh, do not punish me in your rage,
or reprove me in the heat of anger.
Pity me, Yahweh, I have no strength left,
heal me, my bones are in torment,
my soul is in utter torment.
Yahweh, how long will you be?

Come back, Yahweh, rescue my soul,
save me, if you love me;
for in death there is no remembrance of you:
who can sing your praises in Sheol?

I am worn out with groaning,
every night I drench my pillow
and soak by bed with tears;
my eye is wasted with grief,
I have grown old with enemies all round me.

Away from me, all you evil men!
For Yahweh has heard the sound of my weeping;
Yahweh has heard my petition,
Yahweh will accept my prayer.

Let all my enemies, discredited, in utter torment,
fall back in sudden confusion (Ps. 6).

This Psalm, like most of those of petition, has three *dramatis
personae*: the supplicant struck down with woes, the enemy or
enemies who attack him, and Yahweh the king and judge,
whose intervention can save the supplicant from his torments.
To understand the dynamic of this religious poetry, we have to
note that God appears above all as judge (and not father), that
God's right judgment is what the supplicant petitions for. The
enemy appears as someone of ill will, whose tongue is
poisonous and whose sword bloody; who thinks he can oppress
the innocent with impurity because he does not believe that
God will see him or concern himself with the cause of the
needy. In the great majority of such Psalms, the supplicant
presents himself as a just man fallen into misfortune; he invites
the judge to examine him so as to confirm his innocence and
the evil of his enemy. By asking for vengeance on his enemy, he
is doing no more than seek the justice-dealing intervention of
the divine judge:

Peering and prying for the out-of-luck,
lurking unseen like a lion in his hide,
lurking to capture the poor man,
the poor man seized, he drags him away in his net.

Questing of eye, he stoops, he crouches,
and the luckless wretch falls into his power
as he thinks to himself, "God forgets,
he hides his face, he does not see at all."

Rise, Yahweh, God raise your hand,
do not forget the poor!
Why does the wicked man spurn God,
assuring himself, "He will not make me pay"?

You yourself have seen the distress and the grief,
you watch and then take them into your hands;

the luckless man commits himself to you,
you, the orphan's certain help (Ps. 10:8–14).

Logically, those who turn to a judge to right their wrongs will
be the weak and the poor, those who lack their own resources
to remedy the evils they suffer. It is not surprising, then, that
the supplicants in the Psalms often describe themselves as poor
and their enemies as insolent rich people.[14]

Yahweh, how much longer are the wicked,
how much longer are the wicked to triumph?
Are these evil men to remain unsilenced,
boasting and asserting themselves?

Yahweh, they crush your people,
they oppress your hereditary people,
murdering and massacring
widows, orphans and guests.
"Yahweh sees nothing," they say
"the God of Jacob takes no notice" (Ps. 94:3–7).

But Yahweh is a just judge, and his justice implies that he
will respond to the plaints of the poor who suffer the assaults
of the uncaring rich:

Though the wicked draw the sword,
and bend their bow, to kill the upright,
their swords will only pierce their own hearts
and their bows will be smashed.

The little the virtuous possesses
outweighs all the wealth of the wicked,
since the arms of the wicked are doomed to break,
and Yahweh will uphold the virtuous (Ps. 37:14–17).

The hope of the poor who make these petitions is Yahweh, he
who will defend them from their powerful enemies. This is why
it is so important that the poor whom Yahweh has rescued from
their misfortune should make this known in the assembly of the

poor, so that all in their misery will know always to place their
trust in Yahweh:

> Then I shall proclaim your name to my brothers,
> praise you in the full assembly:
> you who fear Yahweh, praise him!
> Entire race of Jacob, glorify him!
> Entire race of Israel, revere him!

> For he has not despised or disdained the poor man in his
>     poverty,
> has not hidden his face from him,
> but has answered him when he called.

> You are the theme of my praise in the Great Assembly,
> I perform my vows in the presence of those who fear him.
> The poor will receive as much as they want to eat.
> Those who seek Yahweh will praise him.
> Long life to their hearts! (Ps. 22:22–7).

Examples demonstrating the dynamic of petition in the
Psalms could be multiplied, but these will suffice. The supplicant as poor knows he is the object of Yahweh's special
attention and approaches God with a confidence astonishing to
the modern reader. Without reservation, he asks for the most
terrible calamities to befall his enemy, who is seen as an
apostate whose oppressive actions declare that he does not
believe there is a just God. Whatever he may say with his lips,
his acts of oppression against the chosen of Yahweh cry out that
he does not believe Yahweh will protect the weak.

## 8.  GOD AND THE POOR IN THE WISDOM LITERATURE
    OF ISRAEL

Two great collections, the Proverbs of Solomon and the
Wisdom of Jesus ben Sirach (Ecclesiasticus), provide us with a
broad spectrum of the proverbial wisdom of Israel. This is a
different world from the one we have been examining till now:
one in which the liberating gesture of the exodus does not play

much part. The wisdom culture had its roots in the popular culture of Israel; the form in which we have it, however, is a recompilation edited by professional teachers dedicated to intellectual pursuits in the court and temple. Despite this, it has its vision of reality, one that does not belong to the court or to the temple. God is seen as creator of the natural order and the Supreme Being underlying the moral order of social relationships. It is God who gives understanding to the wise to enable them to discern the affairs of the world. The saviour God who throws down the mighty from their seat falls outside the wise men's sphere of reflection.

The theological basis of the wisdom collections is not, then, the salvation worked by Yahweh when he led Israel out of slavery in Egypt. Wisdom theology stems from acute observation of life, in which God's work is seen in the setting of the stars, the seasons of the year, and order in social life. This is a markedly different world from that of the prophets. So what role do the poor play in it, and what is their relationship to God?

In the world as it appears to the wise, poverty is a great calamity. Poverty and foolishness are the worst fates that can befall a human being:

The poor man is detestable even to his neighbour,
> but the rich man has friends and to spare (Prov. 14:20).

Wealth multiplies friends,
> But the one friend the poor man has is taken from him!
> (Prov. 19:4).

The rich man lords it over the poor,
> the borrower is the lender's slave (Prov. 22:7).

The rich man wrongs a man and puts on airs,
> while the poor man is wronged and apologizes (Ecclus. 13:3).

What peace can there be between hyena and dog?
> And what peace between rich man and poor?

> Wild donkeys are the prey of desert lions;
>> so too, the poor are the quarry of the rich.
>
> The proud man thinks humility abhorrent;
>> so too, the rich abominate the poor (Ecclus. 13:18–20).

Yet riches are not the only good to be desired, nor is poverty the sum of the miseries that can befall in this life. There are values to be desired that surpass riches, and evils that surpass poverty. But whatever gloss can be put on the situation, poverty can never be considered something good:

> A poor man is honoured for his wits,
>> and a rich man for his wealth.
> Honoured in poverty, how much the more in wealth!
>> Dishonoured in wealth, how much the more in poverty!
>> (Ecclus. 10:30–31).
>
> Do not set your heart on ill-gotten gains,
>> they will be of no use to you on the day of disaster
>> (Ecclus. 5:8).
>
> Better to have little and with it the fear of Yahweh
>> than to have treasure and with it anxiety (Prov. 15:16).
>
> Better have little and with it virtue
>> than great revenues and no right to them (Prov. 16:8).
>
> Better a poor man living an honest life
>> than a man of devious ways, rich though he be (Prov. 28:6).

Clearly, this vision of God and the world is not going to produce the passion for justice that moved the prophets to proclaim the destruction of cities that lived on the exploitation of the poor. Nor will it lead to the proclamation of a new dawn of the new and better society that Yahweh will bring for the poor.

Nevertheless, one of the functions of the God of the wise in this world is to defend the interests of the poor who lack the means to defend themselves:

To oppress the poor is to insult his creator,
   to be kind to the needy is to honour him (Prov. 14:31).

Yahweh pulls down the house of the proud,
   but he keeps the widow's boundaries intact (Prov.
   15:25).

Because a man is poor, do not therefore cheat him,
   nor, at the city gate, oppress anybody in affliction;
for Yahweh takes up their cause,
   and extorts the life of their extortioners (Prov. 22:
   22–3).

The Most High takes no pleasure in offerings from the
   godless,
   multiplying sacrifices will not gain his pardon from sin.
Offering sacrifice from the property of the poor
   is as bad as slaughtering a son before his father's very
   eyes.
A meagre diet is the very life of the poor,
   he who withholds it is a man of blood.
A man murders his neighbour if he robs him of his
   livelihood,
   sheds blood if he withholds an employee's wages
   (Ecclus. 34: 19–22).

Offer him no bribe, he will not accept it,
   do not put your faith in an unvirtuous sacrifice;
since the Lord is a judge
   who is no respecter of personages.
He shows no respect of personages to the detriment of a
   poor man,
   he listens to the plea of the injured party.
He does not ignore the orphan's supplication,
   nor the widow's as she pours out her story (Ecclus.
   35:11–14).

In its own quiet way, the wisdom literature also recognizes
that God favours the poor. But here this favour poses no sort
of threat to the ruling classes in society. Only the unjust rich

(which supposes that there are also just ones!) need to worry. Yahweh upholds the cause of the weak to prevent the rich from trampling on them with impunity. But there is no hint of the idea that God supports the poor in a struggle to do away with the injustices of this world. This is the obvious limitation of this literature.

# Chapter II

# The Option for the Poor in the New Testament

## 1. PAUL: IN CHRIST, GOD SHOWS SOLIDARITY WITH AN INTRINSICALLY POOR HUMANITY

For Christians, the life, death and resurrection of Jesus introduce a new element into history. In Jesus Christ, we know who God is. In Jesus Christ, God establishes a relationship with humanity that breaks with the patterns of "natural" thinking. The incarnation is God taking on the human condition out of pure gratuitousness, without there being any inherent attraction in the condition taken on. There is a break between God and humanity, the radical nature of which can be seen only in the moment when it is healed by divine grace. But the newness of the incarnation is also the full manifestation of something we already knew; it does not deny the Yahweh of the exodus, nor does it pass over the witness of Yahweh given by the prophets of Israel. In Jesus Christ all this is confirmed, but condensed and manifested in a radical way which is new. The very God, the God of the exodus, became present in Jesus to set humanity free from all expressions of sin. The God of the prophets who loved everyone through his preferential love for the poor is revealed in a definitive form which from now on becomes the norm for recognizing God in all future manifestations. Despite their previous formation, this event shook and astonished the apostles.

The earliest witness we possess to the Messiah event is a collection of letters written by the Apostle Paul, dating from a

53

little more than twenty years after the Lord's crucifixion and resurrection. These missionary letters show a man of enormous intellectual and spiritual power and have rightly become the basis for theology.

In view of this, the lack of reference to Jesus' life in these is disconcerting. It is of course likely that Paul never knew Jesus in the flesh. This does not explain his lack of interest in passing on what he must have heard from other witnesses. It is rather that he saw the materiality of the historical Jesus as a possible cause of theological confusion: From now onwards, therefore, we do not judge anyone by the standards of the flesh. Even if we did once know Christ in the flesh, that is not how we know him now" (2 Cor. 5:16).

Paul believes that reflection on the historical Jesus can detract from what is really important: the cross. It would seem that the fact that God came to humanity and submitted to crucifixion made such an impression on Paul that everything else pales into insignificance beside the transcendental importance of this fact. Given the immensity of God's decision to take on human flesh and to suffer death in the flesh for and with humanity, the facts of Jesus' human life are not important, nor even interesting. So he writes to the Corinthians: "During my stay with you, the only knowledge I claimed to have was about Jesus, and only about him as the crucified Christ" (1 Cor. 2:2).

Paul's concentration on God's action in Jesus Christ meant that in his letters, and most likely in his ministry as well, he showed a certain blindness to poverty as a social fact. For him, true poverty was anthropological, inherent in the human condition. The solidarity that interested him theologically was God's solidarity with humanity as made manifest in Christ:

> In your minds you must be the same as Christ Jesus:
> His state was divine,
> yet he did not cling
> to his equality with God
> but emptied himself
> to assume the condition of a slave,
> and became as men are;
> and being as all men are,

he was humbler yet,
even to accepting death,
death on a cross.
But God raised him high
and gave him the name
which is above all other names
so that all beings
in the heavens, on earth and in the underworld,
should bend the knee at the name of Jesus
and that every tongue should acclaim
Jesus Christ as Lord,
to the glory of God the Father (Phil. 2:3–11).

So Paul's thought displays great richness in reflecting on the solidarity of the rich and powerful God with poor and weak humanity. But alongside this, it shows limitations in dealing with poverty as a social problem and solidarity as something enjoined on believers. But this limitation does not amount to a total lack: faced with the conflicts among the community in Corinth, which were in part economic, Paul takes his christological reflection as an interpretative key: "It was to shame the wise that God chose what is foolish by human reckoning, and to shame what is strong that he chose what is weak by human reckoning; those whom the world thinks common and contemptible are the ones that God has chosen—those who are nothing at all to show up those who are everything" (1 Cor. 1:27–8). That is, the predominance of the poor among believers is not accidental: it is God's nature to work with strength through human weakness.

Even more important in showing Paul's understanding of the implications of divine solidarity for solidarity among believers is his argument in favour of the collection for the poor in Jerusalem: "Remember how generous the Lord Jesus Christ was: he was rich, but he became poor for your sake, to make you rich out of his poverty" (2 Cor. 8:9). Here Paul is drawing out the implications of divine solidarity and applying them to behaviour among human beings. The authentic way of opting for the poor is to make oneself poor with them in order together to deny inhuman poverty and together emerge into human riches. Human riches turn out to be like strength or wisdom: they can neither be given nor won on one's own; only in community can truly human strength, wisdom or riches be won. Paul does not derive this from an analysis of human relationships, but from the way in which God made salvation known, by becoming strong in the weakness of the cross.[1]

To sum up, then: Paul saw in Jesus Christ God's solidarity with poor humanity. He was so impressed by the inherent poverty of humanity compared to the greatness of divine favour that the problem of human differences between rich and poor was relegated to a secondary level in his thought. He did not offer any theological outline of the option for the poor, though he did touch on it in some cases of intra-church conflicts.

## 2. JOHN: THE SON OF GOD IS ACCEPTED BY THE OUTCASTS AND MAKES THEM CHILDREN OF GOD

The writer of the fourth Gospel, like Paul, sees the incarnation as the central mystery revealed in Jesus. His emphasis, however, is different: God sends the Son into the world as if it were a distant land, in order to redeem from the world those who accept him. The attention of this writer, whom tradition identifies with the Apostle John, is focused on the mystery of the division (Greek *krisis*, John 3:18–19) between those who rejected and those who accepted the Son, who is indeed the author of the lives of all and should therefore have been accepted by all:

> He came to his own domain
> and his own people did not accept him.
> But to all who did accept him
> he gave power to become children of God,
> to all who believe in the name... (John 1:11–12).

There is nothing to indicate that the fourth Gospel derives from the Pauline Epistles, though both Paul and John share the common purpose of understanding the enormity of the events they focus upon. For Paul, the overriding impression is made by the fact that the greatness of God should have deigned to

take on the human condition so as thereby to free humanity
from its slavery to sin. The cross reveals both the immensity of
God's saving will and the depth of human degradation. There
is no point in asking who is responsible for this, since we have
all sinned. For John, what makes the greatest impression is that
the world should reject him who made it, but most particularly
that "his own" should reject him. It was "the Jews" who sought
to kill him and who handed him over to Pilate to be crucified.
Pilate, the Roman, showed himself cleverer at discerning events
than the Jews, since he called Jesus "king of the Jews," a title
that was rejected by "the high priests of the Jews" (John 19:17–
22).

A comparison of John's Gospel with the Synoptic Gospels
shows that geography has a different meaning in the two, and
examination of this shows it to have theological significance. It
is not possible to decide whether the Synoptics precede John
chronologically or vice-versa, and the relative accuracy of their
accounts of Jesus' ministry in Judaea need not concern us here.
What does concern us is the relative importance of John's
geography for the theme of the option for the poor.

John's geography is ordered by the contrast between Judaea,
on one hand, and Samaria and Galilee, on the other.[2]
Nathanael introduces the matter with his questions: "From
Nazareth? Can anything good come from that place?" (1:40).
Jesus begins to give his signs in Cana *in Galilee* (2:11). On his
first appearance in Judaea, he uses a whip to drive the traders
out of the temple, and the sign he proclaims is the destruction
of the temple (2:18–19). He receives one of the masters of law,
Nicodemus, by night, and Nicodemus cannot understand what
he says (3). Yet he is accepted without question by a woman in
Samaria (4). In view of this astonishing contrast, Jesus
"declared that there is no respect for a prophet in his own
country" (4:44—this saying has another meaning in the Synoptics, where it is understood as referring to Nazareth).

According to John, Jesus was able to move freely round
Samaria and Galilee, but could not stay in Judaea, because "the
Jews were out to kill him" (7:1). At one time, "the Jews"
accused him of being a Samaritan and of having a devil; Jesus
replied to the accusation of having a devil, but passed over the

other accusation in silence, tantamount to tacit acceptance of it
(8:48–59). In all this, Judaea is the centre; Samaria and Galilee
the periphery. The Pharisees knew that the Christ could not
come from Galilee, because the scriptures said that he would
come from Bethlehem of Judaea (7:41—it is significant that
John leaves his readers to think that Jesus was born in
Nazareth). The Pharisees declared that "this rabble knows
nothing about the Law—they are damned" (7:49—the context
showing that "this rabble" was supposed to make up most of
the population of Galilee). So, seen from Judaea, Samaritans
and Galileans are equally outcasts. And Jesus' rejection by the
Jews and acceptance by (some of) the Samaritans and Galileans
has for John the sense of a revelation about God. Jesus is the
Word, the only-begotten Son of the Father, so that who sees
Jesus sees the Father:

> The Word was made flesh,
> and lived among us,
> and we saw his glory,
> the glory that is his as the only Son of the Father,
> full of grace and truth (1:14).

> Philip said, "Lord, let us see the Father and then we shall
> be satisfied." "Have I been with you all this time, Philip,"
> said Jesus to him "and you still do not know me? To have
> seen me is to have seen the Father" (14:8–9).

For John, the Son of God came to the whole world equally;
but when his own people did not accept him, it was the outcasts
of the periphery of Palestine who did. And they, the outcasts,
were made children of God.

## 3.   LUKE RECOUNTS GOD'S OPTION FOR THE POOR IN JESUS' LIFE

While Paul and John deal with the meaning of the life, death
and resurrection of Jesus on the level of discourse, the three
Synoptic Gospels use a narrative approach. The result of this is
that in these texts attention is concentrated on the man Jesus,

though he is certainly seen as inspired by God. Through his actions and words, Jesus is presented here as one of the poor, and as a poor man who showed solidarity with other poor people. We propose here to look at Luke's Gospel alone, the one that places most emphasis on this aspect of Jesus.[3]

In his account of the birth of Jesus, Luke stresses the fulfilment of the hopes of pious Jews, represented by Zechariah and Elizabeth, Mary and Joseph, Simeon and Anna. He also stresses the fact of Jesus' poverty, and the meaning of his life as a sign of hope for the poor. Jesus was born in a stable because his parents could provide nothing better, and those who celebrate the event to the accompaniment of a heavenly chorus are humble shepherds looking after their flocks in the fields.

Also significant is the way, in Luke, in which Jesus proclaims his mission in the synagogue of Nazareth by reading a text from Isaiah:

> The spirit of the Lord has been given to me,
> for he has anointed me.
> He has sent me to bring the good news to the poor,
> to proclaim liberty to captives
> and to the blind new sight,
> to set the downtrodden free,
> to proclaim the Lord's year of favour! (Luke 4:18).

In effect, Jesus' public activity from that moment on consisted of intense progress from one town or village to another seeking contact with all the needy so as to proclaim in healing words and deeds the good news of the coming of the Kingdom to the poor.

The Kingdom of God, as proclaimed by Jesus (in Luke), produces a division in society, between the rich and the poor: "How happy are you who are poor: yours is the Kingdom of God" (6:20); "But alas for you who are rich: you are living your consolation now" (6:24). In the parable of the rich man and Lazarus, the beggar is taken up into Abraham's bosom when he dies; whereas the rich man is despatched to a place of torment, without any difference being established between them other than that one is rich and the other poor (16:19–31). Following the same line of dividing society in relation to the Kingdom that is to come, Jesus tells the young aristocrat who asks him what he must do to inherit eternal life to sell all his goods and distribute the money to the poor, and then follow him like any other poor person (18:18–23).

Luke's Jesus collects together a small group of followers who are warned that "foxes have holes and the birds of the air have nests, but the Son of Man has nowhere to lay his head" (9:58). So this is a movement of poor people, a movement that is to reveal an alternative lifestyle in which solidarity among equals will be the distinguishing mark. The privatization offered by the family is not allowed:

> Another to whom he said, "Follow me," replied, "Let me go and bury my father first." But he answered, "Leave the dead to bury their dead; your duty is to go and spread the news of the Kingdom of God" (9:59–60).

In the new society being formed around Jesus, most merit is accorded to those who are most disposed to serve:

> An argument started between them about which of them was the greatest. Jesus knew what thoughts were going through their minds, and he took a little child and set him by his side and then said to them, "Anyone who welcomes this little child in my name welcomes me; and anyone who welcomes me welcomes the one who sent me. For the least among you all, that is the one who is great" (9:46–8).

> "Among pagans it is the kings who lord it over them, and those who have authority over them are given the title Benefactor. This must not happen with you. No; the greatest among you must behave as if he were the youngest, the leader as if he were the one who serves" (22:25–6).

The reply Jesus sends to John the Baptist's question from prison demonstrates that Jesus believes that his actions toward the poor are sufficient evidence that he is the one all are waiting for (7:18–23). The Kingdom of God, the hope of the poor, is being made actual in the actions of Jesus and his followers: "If it is through the finger of God that I cast out devils, then know that the Kingdom of God has overtaken you" (11:20).

Besides the division between rich and poor established by the proclamation of the Kingdom, Jesus and his followers found another division: between themselves and the masters of the Law, the Pharisees and scribes. This is illustrated by the dispute over the healing of the man with a withered hand in the synagogue on the sabbath (6:6–11). Jesus counters the objections of the scribes and Pharisees with the question, "Is it against the law on the sabbath to do good, or to do evil; to save life, or to destroy it?" (6:9). The Jesus of the Synoptics seeks to establish the opposition between the custodians of the Law and the promises of life that constitute the Kingdom of God. It is an opposition he sometimes provokes. This would seem to be because the custodians of the Law were respected by the humble people, with the result that in Palestinian society of the time the biblical tradition had ceased to mean life and liberation, but a burden to be borne (11:46).

The divisions provoked by the proclamation of the Kingdom reached their most acute stage when Jesus went to Jerusalem for the feast of Passover. On one side were the authorities who sought ways to kill him, fearful of him because the people listened to his preaching with enthusiasm; on the other side, the people themselves:

> Then he went into the Temple and began driving out those who were selling. "According to scripture," he said, "my house will be a house of prayer. But you have turned it into a robbers' den." He taught in the Temple every day. The chief priests and the scribes, with the support of the leading citizens, tried to do away with him, but they did not see how they could carry this out because the people as a whole hung on his words (19:45–8).

Luke shows Jesus as fully conscious of the danger to his life. He had accused the Pharisees of being guilty of killing all the

prophets (11:49–51). He knew that Herod Antipas had assassinated John the Baptist, whom Luke presents as Jesus' cousin.
Despite this, he goes on with his prophetic denunciations:

> While all the people were listening he said to his disciples,
> "Beware of the scribes who like to walk about in long
> robes and love to be greeted obsequiously in the market
> squares, to take the front seats in synagogues and the
> places of honour at banquets, who swallow the property
> of widows, while making a show of lengthy prayers. The
> more severe will be the sentence they receive" (20:45–7).

He foretold his own death at the hands of the elders and the
chief priests as something natural falling within the sphere of
divine providence (9:22). He had already shown his followers
that they would be persecuted as a result of identifying
themselves with the cause of the Son of Man: "Happy are you
when people hate you, drive you out, abuse you, denounce
your name as criminal, on account of the Son of Man" (6:22).
Without being afraid of death, since he knew that the
authorities would not rest till they had done away with him,
Jesus took refuge in the crowds during the week of Passover.
By day he was surrounded by the people; by night he retired
to remote places: "In the daytime he would be in the temple
teaching, but would spend the night on the hill called the Mount
of Olives. And from early morning the people would gather
round him in the Temple to listen to him" (21:37–8). His option
for the poor, then, deserved the option the poor made for him.
And yet, through the betrayal by one of his closest circle, the
authorities managed to discover his night refuge, arrested him,
tried him hurriedly that same night and the next morning
handed him over to the Roman procurator.

There is nothing to indicate that Jesus sought any power or
position through all his intense activity. His purpose—always
as presented by Luke—was to open the eyes of the mulitude to
the hope of the Kingdom given to the poor, and to the fact that
with all their piety, the scribes and priests were not working for
the good of the people. Through his work—which today we
should call true conscientization—Jesus took the risks run by

all those who stand up to the great ones of this world, laying himself open to the fate of the prophets, killed by the ancestors of the Pharisees. Luke presents his death as serene, making him able to say from the cross: "Father, into your hands I commend my spirit" (23:46). And the context implies that it was not just his spirit that he was confidently commending to his Father, but also the cause of the Kingdom he had proclaimed.

In this way, Luke and the other Synoptics took up Paul's (and John's, if he wrote before they did) affirmations that in Christ the God of the Bible was taking on the human condition in all its crudity. Luke, through his account of the public actions of Jesus, provides a historical basis for Paul's statements. The result is a Jesus Christ who emerges as surprisingly "political" in his option for the life of the poor.

## 4. IN WHAT SENSE WERE JESUS' ACTIONS POLITICAL?

Modern readers may well find it surprising that the one we confess as God incarnate should be presented by the Synoptic Gospels as having a public career so full of political overtones. Nothing in the letters of Paul and little in church life today prepare us for this discovery. Some reflection on the political implications of Jesus' words and deeds is needed if we are not to jump to false conclusions.[4]

There is one fact of unquestionable historical veracity that brings us dramatically face-to-face with the matter: the notice that Pilate had fixed to Jesus' cross, reading "This is Jesus, the King of the Jews" (Matt. 27:37; cf John 19:20). The very fact that he was executed by being crucifed corroborates the notice: this form of death was reserved for politicial criminals and rebel slaves. There would seem to be no way of avoiding the fact that Jesus was executed as a political rebel. This is not, of course, to say he was in fact the sort of rebel for whom this manner of death was usually reserved. But the Roman procurator took him for such; this much cannot be denied.

In fact, the witness given by the Synoptic Gospels is that since his public ministry in Nazareth, Jesus had come into conflict with the Pharisees. It would seem that, while he was still in

Galilee, it was the religious authorities who sent a commission of investigation (Mark 3:22). And it was these conflicts with the religious authorities that led to his arrest, sentence and execution. The unanimous witness of the Gospels is that the Roman governor was drawn into this judicial crime by the Jewish religious authorities, who were the instigators of the whole process.

This leads to a first and important clarification. Even though Jesus was sentenced by Pilate as a subversive, the arguments adduced to show that he was a rebel against the Romans are not conclusive. He was not a Zealot. His struggle was not against Rome; furthermore, the witnesses declare, he avoided coming into conflict with the imperial power. And again, he explicitly rejected armed struggle as a way of advancing the Kingdom of God. It should be clear enough that his condemnation by the Roman authorities as a subversive did not correspond to the reality of what he said and did. Neither was he a political figure in the sense we generally use the term: he did not aspire to power either for himself or for the movement he led.

It is clear that Jesus conceived the whole of his public activity in terms that today we would call religious. Fundamentally, all he did was to proclaim the coming of the Kingdom of God and show the way into this Kingdom. It was precisely from within the religious sphere that Jesus came into conflict with the religious authorities of his country. Since the authority of the Sanhedrim rested solely on the legal tradition, which formed the basis of the religion of the Jews, to question the religious legitimacy of the scribes and priests who made up the Sanhedrim was to question its entire legitimacy. And the way Jesus did this was not through academic discussion about true religion. It was through a play of forces, in which Jesus met with the support of the ordinary people, who heard him with joy. The most dramatic illustration of the way he worked was his confrontation with the temple authorities shortly before the Passover. Buoyed up by the demonstration of a crowd that was acclaiming him as king, Jesus went into the temple and gave a show of force, of which the least result was the expulsion of the traders.

To sum up: Jesus' public actions concentrated on the proclamation of the Kingdom. His practice revolved around seeking the way to God. But because he understood that the Kingdom was preferentially for the poor, his religious practice brought him objectively into conflict with the authorities of his nation, authorities whose power rested on a religious Law. Jesus appreciated the political realities affected by his prophetic practice. It was not his intention to seize power, but to use the strength of the weak to unmask the falsity of the religious legitimation of the power of the temple and the Pharisees. By accepting the imminence of his death at the hands of these authorities, Jesus was recognizing that God's strength alone gave meaning to a political practice based on the poor and the weak.

## 5. LIFE IN THE FIRST CHURCHES: SEEKING COHERENCE WITH THE GOD OF JESUS

We have seen that Jesus, at least the Jesus described in the Synoptic Gospels, organized a small movement of poor followers as part of his proclamation of the Kingdom of God. These disciples formed the nucleus of what in time was to become the Christian church. The immediate problem facing the disciples after Jesus' death and resurrection was how to organize the life in community in his absence. The results of this organizational process were mixed.

According to Luke (now as author of the Acts of the Apostles), one group of disciples remained in Jerusalem. There they formed a community in which those who had possessions sold them and shared out the proceeds (Acts 2:42–7; 4:32–7). There were no needs left unsatisfied among them, at least at first, since the resources of the community were sufficient to look after the poorest of them. But they were soon being persecuted by the city authorities, the same who had been responsible for executing Jesus. The community of disciples began to go hungry, possibly on account of this persecution, or possibly because of defects in their primitive system of distribution. Whatever the reason, those who had fled to

Antioch responded by sending food to relieve the situation in
Judaea (Acts 11:27–30).

Some year later, Paul was actively engaged in organizing a
collection among the churches of Asia and Greece for "the poor
among the saints at Jerusalem" (Rom. 15:26; 2 Cor. 8–9). In
this way the churches expressed their special concern for the
poor, even if they did not follow the example of the Jerusalem
community of meeting all needs out of a common purse.

Paul tells us that on his first visit to the community in
Jerusalem he had explained his mission to James, Cephas and
John, who recognized that he had been commissioned to preach
to the pagans, and agreed that he should continue to do so,
laying down the sole condition that he and his followers should
remember to help the poor, "as indeed I was anxious to do"
(Gal. 2:9–10).

In 1 Corinthians 1:26–31 Paul embarks on a theological
reflection on the fact that most of the Christians come from
humble backgrounds. God, he says, uses "those who are
nothing at all to show up those who are everything." This is the
logic of the power of the poor, which is that of the God of the
Bible. Despite the fact that this is also the God of the
Corinthians, Paul has to reproach them for their faulty
eucharistic practice, with each bringing his or her own food and
not sharing it with the poorer among them (1 Cor. 11:17–22).
This scandalous deviation shows the general rule that the
practice of the early churches was to favour the poor.

The general letter attributed to James denounces the spread
of worldly values in the churches. The example he gives is the
respect shown to rank in the congregations as in the world:

> Listen, my dear brothers; it was those who are poor
> according to the world that God chose, to be rich in faith
> and to be heirs to the kingdom which he promised to those
> who love him. In spite of this, have you respect for
> anybody who is poor? Isn't it always the rich who are
> against you? ... Aren't they the ones who insult the
> honourable name to which you have been dedicated?
> (James 2:5–7).

So both Paul in his correspondence with the Corinthians and James in his general letter are trying to make the preference for the poor effective in practice, while indicating the natural resistance to this shown by the communities in continuing to grant privileges to the rich.

The letter from Paul to Philemon shows the same tension between recognizing the privileged position of the poor in principle and the difficulty of institutionalizing it in practice. Philemon was rich enough to have a church in his house and to keep at least one slave, Onesimus. Onesimus was not a believer in Christ when he fled from Philemon's house, but Paul has been able to awaken the faith in him. With diplomatic arguments, Paul urges Philemon to take him back and treat him as a brother and no longer as a slave. But he does not go so far as to present him with a stark choice between going on being a slave owner and being a Christian. He would not take it well if Philemon continued to regard Onesimus as a slave, but he does not tell him that his faith in Jesus Christ makes this impossible.

So, in general, the picture of the early Christian communities that emerges from the letters of their pastors is similar to that presented by many Christian groups today. They recognised the privileged place due to the poor in their theology, but were not always successful in according them this privileged place in day-to-day reality.

# Chapter III

# Solidarity with the Poor: Basis of the Bible Ethic

## 1. FOLLOWING JESUS

This chapter and the next begin with a christological introductory section to situate the theme of each: ethic and mission.

The Gospels tell us that Jesus is the way to God. Those who seek to come to the Father must identify with the Son and follow him on their journey: "I am the Way, the Truth and the Life. No one can come to the Father except through me" (John 14:6).

Being a disciple means learning from Jesus' teaching, as the voice from the cloud said: "This is my Son, the Beloved. Listen to him" (Mark 9:7); but it also implies following what Jesus did in his life. The early church recognized the importance of combining doctrine with life by producing four accounts of Jesus which place his sayings in the context of his actions. This recognition was formalized when these four "Gospels" were taken into the canon to make up the greater part of the New Testament. To be a Christian it is not sufficient to confess the exceptional nature of Jesus—Messiah, Son of God, incarnate Word, and so on. We do not need the Gospels to be able to do this; we need only some professions of faith. Nor is it sufficient to know and believe what Jesus taught, for which all we would need would be a collection of parables and sayings like the (non-canonical) Gospel of Thomas. For the apostles, who are our privileged witnesses, what mattered was Jesus' life, because God's call is to follow him.

Even when we understand that we have to follow Jesus, it is not always easy to see what this might imply in the various late twentieth-century societies we live in: the dominant capitalism of the First World, the Party-led bureaucracy of the Second, the dependent capitalism of the Third, ... all very different from the society of first-century Palestine in which Jesus lived. So we have to seek out those elements in Jesus' life that are valid as guides to Christian life in situations that are not the same as those in which Jesus lived.

As a start, we would do well to look at what Paul took from Jesus' life in order to explain the message to believers who also lived in very different circumstances from Jesus'. Paul took part in the formation of Christian communities in various cities of the Roman Empire. These cities were places where people of many different races, languages and cultures mixed, in marked contrast to the culturally homogeneous people among whom Jesus moved. The cities lived off the work of slaves, a situation which, though not unknown in Palestine, was not the dominant factor there. So Paul can be a useful guide in learning how to follow Jesus in social situations different from those of first-century Palestine.

A key text for understanding how Paul saw the way marked out by Jesus is 2 Corinthians 8:9: "Remember how generous the Lord Jesus was: he was rich, but he became poor for your sake, to make you rich out of his poverty." From Jesus' life, Paul picks the quality we would call solidarity. By making himself poor, Jesus opted to enrich those who were sunk in poverty. The riches he brought to them in this way would not be the sort of riches that distinguish the rich from the poor, but simply equality for all. The commentary Paul himself makes on his observation proves that point; he is not proposing that the Corinthians should suffer want by collecting for the poor in Jerusalem, nor that the recipients of the collection should live in luxury: "it is a question of balancing" (2 Cor. 8:14); if there is a surplus in one place it can supply the needs of another, and one day perhaps that place will have a surplus to supply the needs of others in its turn.

If we examine the results of Paul's application of Jesus' practice to the situation of urban communities and then examine what these communities have to tell us about Jesus, one thing that stands out is that Jesus abandoned his own town and the security of his family in order to be in solidarity with a community of equals; in doing that he was questioning the way the religion held by the Pharisees served to bolster a differentiated society. He placed himself at the side of the "least" in society: the possessed, prostitutes, lepers, the homeless; from their side he questioned not so much the power structures directly, but rather the religious tradition which made the poor accept social differences as something inevitable. It was only after a time spent quietly in this work in the Galilean villages that he went to the centre of domination in Palestinian society, the temple of Jerusalem. From there, now with the support of the "multitude," he prophetically denounced the temple. He suffered the penalty reserved by that society for those who questioned it. In this way, through active solidarity, but not seeking confrontation till he had to, Jesus sought to liberate the poor who were kept in their place by a religious tradition.

The "salvation" that Jesus set before his followers when he proclaimed the Kingdom of God was not the paternalist gift of that religion which imagines God sitting in his heaven above the bustle of the world. The God of Jesus, as we saw in the preceding chapter, is with the poor, showing solidarity with their needs and struggles. Jesus shows us the way to the Father by showing solidarity with the poor—with the spiritually and materially poor. The road to the Kingdom of God, which passes through the strength of the weak, has to be followed by understanding the need to live in a common struggle. This emphasis on abolishing privileges and seeking a spiritual and material "balance" or equality is what Paul seems principally to have learned from Jesus' way to the Father. It is an element in Jesus' life that can be applied universally.

That emphasis in Jesus' life is related to the importance Jesus attached to service of the humblest (cf Matt. 25:31–46). Jesus' life of service was something he proposed as a model:

> You call me Master and Lord, and rightly; so I am. If I then, the Lord and Master, have washed your feet, you should wash each other's feet. I have given you an example so that you may copy what I have done to you.

I tell you most solemnly, no servant is greater than his master, no messenger is greater than the man who sent him (John 13:13–16).

In his actions, Jesus showed a complete lack of attention to the demands of the protocol that served to uphold social differences. He required his followers to ignore social protocol in the same way, something they did not always grasp, as shown by John and James arguing over who should be greater in the Kingdom of God (Mark 10:41–5).

As a result of his way of life, Jesus was persecuted. He knew and said that this persecution was not accidental, but for the sake of justice; and that those who followed the same way would be subject to the same fate:

Blessed are you when men hate you, drive you out, abuse you, denounce your name as criminal, on account of the Son of Man. Rejoice when that day comes and dance for joy, for then your reward will be great in heaven. This was the way their ancestors treated the prophets (Luke 6:22–3).

If anyone wants to be a follower of mine, let him renounce himself and take up his cross and follow me (Mark 8:34).

So following Jesus demands solidarity with the poor, service to the needs of the humblest, and readiness to suffer the persecution that will follow from these actions. It was not out of masochism, nor because poverty is a virtue, that Jesus required his followers to lead a life of poverty and be ready to serve and to suffer. His message was rather that the coming of the Kingdom would make the poor have their fill and those who mourn rejoice (Luke 6:20–24). The way to this happiness, Jesus tells us, is fully to take on the cause of the poor and the needy. This is the way to the Father that Jesus demonstrated with his life. This is the way to the Kingdom of God. It is valid not only in the particular circumstances of the Palestinian society in which he lived. With the modifications imposed by the circumstances of other societies, it is applicable to any social situation in which there are rich and poor, rulers and ruled.

The last section of this chapter applies these principles of following Jesus to the situation in Latin America today. Before doing so, we need to look at other major figures in the Bible, to see that the way to God put forward by Jesus was not basically new. If the true God is the God of the exodus, then the way of solidarity, of service and persecution, is the only way to that God. In Jesus, the apostles first and we later have been able to see the Son of God because he showed, in the clearest, most perfect form, the true way toward the God of the exodus.

## 2. MOSES IDENTIFIES WITH THE PEOPLE OF ISRAEL

The Pentateuch endows Moses with characteristics that place him well out of the ordinary. He devoted his life to the mission of being a servant of Yahweh and to solidarity with the enslaved people he led, a solidarity that he maintained till his death:[1]

> Yahweh would speak with Moses face to face, as a man speaks with his friend (Exod. 33:11).

> "Speak to us yourself," they said to Moses, "and we will listen; but do not let God speak to us, or we shall die" (Exod. 20:19).

> "Yahweh was angry with me too, on your account. 'You shall not go in either,' he said" (Deut. 1:37).

As is to be expected with someone from such a remote past, we do not possess the sort of sources that would enable us to reconstruct anything like a biography of Moses. So our examination of him here has to rely on the Pentateuch, which gives us a model of this servant of the Lord.

Moses moved into the public eye as the adopted son of the daughter of the king of Egypt. One day, going out from the palace, he killed an Egyptian overseer in a fit of anger for maltreating a Hebrew (Exod. 2:11–15). As a consequence, he had to flee from Egypt and take refuge in the land of Midian, looking after sheep for a group of Midianites. This first incident says a lot about Moses: his exile and loss of the luxuries of palace life were due to an act in defence of the poor.

The next incident recorded in his life, while he is settled as a shepherd in the land of Midian, is that Yahweh, the God of the Hebrews, entrusts him with the mission of returning to Egypt and leading his people out of their slavery there (Exod. 3). By accepting this mission, albeit with misgivings, Moses progressed a step further in his passion for justice, his desire to act in solidarity with the oppressed, running the same risks as they did in their quest for liberation.

The relationship between Moses and the Hebrews/Israelites was to prove a difficult one, as they were a "headstrong" people. More than once, he was forced to renew his solidarity with them in difficult circumstances brought about by their ingratitude. The most dramatic case is the incident of the golden calf (Exod. 32; Deut. 9). Moses had been summoned by Yahweh to the summit of Mount Sinai, there to receive the laws that were to create the structures for the new life of this people who had received their freedom. When the people saw that Moses had been a long time on the mountain ("This Moses, the man who brought us up from Egypt, we do not know what has become of him" [Exod. 32:1]), they made an image of Yahweh so that God himself, without human intermediary, would lead them to their destiny.[2] Yahweh took this action very much amiss, as a rejection of the agreements that he and Israel had made for Moses, his prophet, to be the leader who would guide them. He suggested to Moses that the project be abandoned: "Yahweh said to Moses, 'I can see how headstrong these people are! Leave me, now, my wrath shall blaze out against them and devour them; of you, however, I will make a great nation'" (Exod. 32:9–10). This was a magnificent opportunity for Moses to free himself from a people who shortly before had threatened to kill him when there was a shortage of water (Exod. 17:4). But Moses, as a model of solidarity, replied by interceding for the people, finishing with these dramatic words: "This people has committed a grave sin, making themselves a god of gold. And yet, if it pleased you to forgive this sin of theirs. . .! But, if not, then blot me out from the book that you have written" (Exod. 32:31–2). Moses identified with this people moulded by their sufferings to the extent that he preferred to give his life rather than allow Yahweh to abandon them in the desert.

There are various views on why Moses never entered the land of Canaan. The most interesting is that of Deuteronomy, that Moses had to die in solidarity with his people in their rebellion. He was allowed to see the promised land, but not to set foot in it. According to Deuteronomy, the major rebellion was at Kadesh-barnea, when Israel refused to take possession of the land of Canaan out of fear of its inhabitants—"a people, they say, bigger and stronger than we are" (Deut. 1:28). Faced with this rebellious attitude,

> "Yahweh heard this talk of yours and, in his anger, took this oath, 'Not one of these men, this perverse generation, shall see the rich land that I swore to give to your fathers, except Caleb son of Jephunneh. He shall see it. To him and to his sons I will give the land he has set foot on, for he has followed Yahweh in all things.' Yahweh was angry with me (Moses) too, on your account, 'You shall not go in either,' he said. 'Your servant Joshua son of Nun, he shall be the one to enter'" (Deut. 1:34–8).

Deuteronomy does not say, as the Yahwist does (Num. 14:1–4), that the people sought to replace Moses (and kill him?) and appoint another leader who would be prepared to take them back to Egypt. In the form we have the Pentateuch, combining Yahwist and Deuteronomic accounts, the solidarity Moses chose proved doubly tragic, since it meant he was unable to enter the promised land as part of Yahweh's punishment on his people for a rebellion of which Moses was nearly a victim.

To underline this implication of solidarity with the people implied by Moses' prophetic calling, the account is repeated:

> "And I pleaded then with Yahweh. My Lord Yahweh, I said, you that have begun to reveal your greatness and your power to your servant, you whose works and mighty deeds no one in heaven or on earth can rival, may I not go across and see this prosperous land beyond the Jordan,

this prosperous country of hills, and Lebanon? But because of you, Yahweh was angry with me. 'Enough!' he said, 'Speak to me no more of this. Climb to the top of Pisgah; let your eyes turn towards the west, the north, the south, the east. Look well, for across this Jordan you shall not go'" (Deut. 3:23–7).

So Moses left the people and climbed Mount Pisgah, or Nebo, and there died in the presence of Yahweh alone, after seeing from afar the land that Yahweh had promised to Abraham, Isaac and Jacob. And Yahweh buried him on the mountain (Deut. 34:1–6). And the next generation, which had not taken part in the rebellion at Kadesh-barnea, was able to enter the land that Moses had struggled so long to reach.

Moses was such a prophet as "since then, never has there been" in Israel, the man to whom Yahweh spoke face to face as though to a friend. The texts present him as a true man of God. In him, then, we find a model for those who seek the God of the Bible.

To sum up: Moses was a man whose mission from God led him to solidarity with the oppressed. As spokesman for the oppressed Hebrews in Egypt, he came into conflict with the authorities. Even more significant is the fact that his solidarity with the people led him into conflict with Yahweh, when, without justifying the people's rebelliousness, he identified himself with their fate, for good or ill. As a result of his intercession, Yahweh forgave the people for the golden calf episode, but Moses had to share in their punishment for the Kadesh-barnea rebellion. And finally, he died by Yahweh's hand without entering the promised land.

## 3. ELIJAH PERSECUTED FOR DEFENDING THE FAITH OF YAHWEH

What we know of the ninth-century prophet Elijah comes through a group of prophetic legends, which show him enjoying extraordinary powers—raising the dead, bringing rain and performing other marvels. In this aspect, he is a difficult model for those of us who lack these powers. Nevertheless, there is one constant element underlying all the legends: Elijah was persecuted for defending the traditions and worship of Yahweh.

Elijah lived and carried out his prophetic ministry during the brief but significant period of the Omri dynasty (885–841). His persecution cannot be understood without some knowledge of the situation of Israel during this dynasty. When Omri seized power in 885, Israel had existed as a kingdom independent of the Davidic dynasty of Judah for forty-six years. It had no fixed capital city, probably as a reaction against the excesses and preponderance of Jerusalem during the years when it had been united with Judah. Omri and his descendants wanted to change this and make Israel a strong nation. A basic step in this process was Omri's purchase of the hill from Shemer in order to build the city of Samaria on it as a new capital of Israel (1 Kings 16:24). He made his capital a Canaanite city, setting up a temple to the god Baal in it, and probably peopling it with sectors of the population who had not been integrated into the mainly peasant society of Israel.

Part of Omridic policy was to forge alliances with Phoenicia and Judah so as to establish a common front against their greatest enemy, Aram. As was the custom, these alliances were sealed by marriages, of which the most important was that of Ahab, Omri's son and heir, to Jezebel, princess of Sidon (1 Kings 16:31). Jezebel came to be the patroness of the temple of Baal in Samaria, presiding over a large number of prophets of Baal. Now Baal had long been known to the Israelites as a god who brought rain, vital to a peasant economy. Joash, father of Gideon, of the clan of Abiezer and the tribe of Manasseh, had an altar to Baal on his land, although he knew of Yahweh (Judg. 6). Baal was nothing new; what was new was the cult of Baal Mercart (Baal, god of the city) in the towns, raised to the status of official state religion. Jerusalem had had an official religion, that of Yahweh, for over a hundred years, and now Omri and his son Ahab were trying to establish an official religion of Israel. This may have been complicated somewhat because official policy may have sanctioned a two-part state, united under the person of the king but with some different political and religious emphases. One part would be the city of Samaria, a city-state of the Canaanite type, with an absolute monarchy; the other the Israelite nation, with its capital in Jezreel, observing the traditional law of Sinai and acting as a brake on the king's power.[3] The conflict between Elijah and the kings should be seen in this context.

Elijah was a champion of Yahweh, and this made him a special enemy of Queen Jezebel, patroness of Baal. She had been slaughtering the prophets of Yahweh, possibly just in Samaria (1 Kings 18:4). Elijah and his followers opposed the prophets of Baal, going so far on one occasion as to slaughter them (1 Kings 18:40) in turn. At one point Elijah had to flee to the desert to escape the queen's wrath (1 Kings 19:1–8). Why so much bloodshed? What was at stake in the struggle between Yahweh and Baal?

In the first place, undoubtedly, Elijah and the prophets of Yahweh were fighting for national identity. Yahweh had been the exclusive God of the tribes of Israel; Baal and his city of Samaria were an insult to national traditions, threatening to turn Israel into just another Canaanite state.

But more than this was at stake, because Yahweh was a completely different sort of God from Baal. Yahweh had liberated the slaves from Egypt and given laws for the protection of his people on Mount Sinai. At issue now was this protection of the people from the arbitrary rule of capricious kings. The story of Naboth of Jezreel illustrates this. Naboth had a vineyard "close by the palace of Ahab, King of Samaria," and Ahab wanted it. He offered Ahab a better vineyard somewhere else, or money, in exchange for it. But Naboth's answer was: "Yahweh forbid that I should give you the inheritance of my ancestors!" (1 Kings 21:1–3).

Sinaitic law forbade the sale of cultivatable lands for profit; they were family inheritances, which could be made over to others only in cases of need, for a certain period (Lev. 25:23–4). The original owner always retained the right to redeem lands made over in this way, never losing the title to them. While in Egypt the titular lord of all land was the king, in Israel this was Yahweh. In the Egyptian (and Canaanite) system, the monarchy could demand a percentage of the products of the land; in the Israelite system, Yahweh's title served to protect peasants who fell on hard times against losing their land. In the account in 1 Kings 21, Ahab took Naboth's refusal as putting an end to his ambitions. Jezebel, on the other hand, brought up in the traditions of Baal, held that there could be no authority above that of the king's wishes. So she ordered Naboth to be killed and his land given to King Ahab. In the Canaanite tradition, legitimated by Baal, such a procedure was not unusual. Elijah raised his voice against it: "You have committed murder; now you usurp as well" (1 Kings 21:19).

To sum up: Elijah, in defending the national religion of Yahweh, was defending the interests of the civil population against the despotism of the king. His championing of their cause meant he had to live in hiding, fleeing from official persecution. Of him it was said that Yahweh validated his ministry by taking him up into heaven without his undergoing death, the common fate of all human beings (2 Kings 2:1–18).

## 4. JEREMIAH OPTS FOR THE PEASANTS

Jeremiah lived out his prophetic ministry during a turbulent period in the history of Judah, a period which came to an end with the destruction of Jerusalem by the Babylonian army in 587 BC. He had to take a stance in reponse to rapidly changing situations, to events of the highest importance in the nation's life. The stance he adopted made him the object of more than one assassination attempt, and resulted in his being put in prison on several occasions. Let us try to see how his actions showed a coherent commitment to the peasants, the country folk despised by the inhabitants of Jerusalem.

Jeremiah began his prophetic ministry in the thirteenth year of the reign of King Josiah (627 BC). Josiah was an important king, remembered for his efforts at reforming the life of Judah in accordance with the precepts of the newly-discovered Book of the Law (Deuteronomy). Because of the emphasis he gave to the reform process, the historians of Judah judged that "he did what is pleasing to Yahweh, and in every respect followed the example of his ancestor David, not deviating from it to right or left" (2 Kings 22:2). It was probably at the same time as this reform that Jeremiah launched his stinging attack on the inhabitants of Jerusalem, a city in which not one just man "who

does right" could be found, so that Yahweh would strike them
all down like a lion (Jer. 5:1–6). Yahweh would send an invader
from the North who would lay the city waste (4:5–31). So was
the reform worth nothing? Surprisingly (to us, used as we are
to seeing the reform through the accounts given in Kings and
Chronicles), Jeremiah did not believe it went to the heart of
the evil in the nation. On the contrary: it had an adverse effect
through disguising this evil under superficial changes:

> "Worse than all this [the 'shameless whoring' of Israel]:
> Judah, her faithless sister, has not come back to me in
> sincerity, but only in pretence—it is Yahweh who speaks."
> And Yahweh said to me, "Besides faithless Judah,
> disloyal Israel seems virtuous" (Jer. 3:10–11).

Probably as a result of his opposition to the reforms, Jeremiah
was the target of an assassination plot by men from his home
town of Anathoth (11:18–23). We do not know how this plot
was foiled. King Josiah was killed in combat at the age of thirty-
eight, in 609 BC, and his son Jehoiakim either would not or
could not pursue the reform plans of his father with the same
vigour.

Early in Jehoiakim's reign, Jeremiah was the target of
another assassination plot, this time an official one drawn up
by the authorities of the city of Jerusalem (Jer. 26:7–8). Their
motive was the fact that in his denunciations of the injustices
of the city, he had proclaimed the destruction of the temple,
which was being used to legitimize all sorts of crimes and
abuses; according to Jeremiah the temple had been turned into
a "robbers' den" (7:1–15). Jeremiah inveighed directly and
personally against King Jehoiakim for his injustices, particularly for building palaces without paying the builders' wages,
something his father Josiah would not have done (22:13–19).

In the year 598, when the young Jehioachin, son of
Jehoiakim, was king, the Babylonians took the city of Jerusalem and promptly deported an initial 3,023 people (Jer. 52:28).
There was a problem of legitimacy when Zedekiah, the king's
uncle, occupied the throne while Jehioachin was still living as
a prisoner of the Babylonians. Zedekiah, though he had been

appointed by the Babylonians, began to conspire with the kings of neighbouring nations. The situation was complex: injustices continued to be committed against the poor people of Judah. But those who held firm to their faith in Yahweh were convinced that Yahweh would come and save his people. Some thought their salvation would come through the alliances Zedekiah was forging. Others thought salvation would come through the behaviour of the colony in exile, which included the legitimate king and the priests who had directed the reform which had purified the religion of Judah. But Jeremiah was clear and outspoken in his opposition to Zedekiah's alliances and in preaching loyal submission to the king of Babylon (Jer. 27). This led to his being considered a traitor and being thrown into prison during the siege of the city (37:11-16). This was done probably because he asked the young men to lay down their arms and surrender to the Babylonians, since Yahweh was fighting against the city (2:1-10).

With regard to hopes centred on an early return from exile, Jeremiah was equally clear. He sent the exiles a letter urging them to marry, build houses and pray for the wellbeing of Babylon, since their exile would be a long one (29:1-23). In due course, after seventy years, Yahweh would bring them back home again. His position should be interpreted in the light of the vision of the two baskets of figs in Jeremiah 24. The good figs were the exiles, and Yahweh would have compassion on them in his own good time. The bad figs were Zedekiah and those who stayed with him, and they would be destroyed.

So Jeremiah recognized the legitimacy of the national leadership of the colony in exile, but announced a long recess in the life of the nation as punishment for all the injustices that had been committed in Jerusalem under cover of the temple of Yahweh. But this recess did not mean that life was not to go on. At the height of the Babylonian attacks, Jeremiah made a deal to buy a field from his cousin in Anathoth, as a sign that life should proceed normally (Jer. 32). The destruction of Jerusalem and the long period of vassalage to the Babylonians did not mean the end of the life of the nation. The peasants who worked the land, the country people from the provinces, did not need Jerusalem to carry on with their lives. Jeremiah sided with them; when Jerusalem was destroyed and its inhabitants deported, the commander of the guard released him from prison and offered him safe conduct to Babylon, or, if he preferred, to go back to "live with the people." Jeremiah chose the second course and went to Mizpan, "living with the people still left in the country" (40:1–6).

If we have understood the complexities of Jeremiah's position correctly, he, faced with the turbulent events of his time, was consistent in defending the interests of the poor. This led him to oppose Josiah's reforms, to see the Babylonian conquest of Jerusalem as a punishment sent by God, and to put his faith and personal fate in the hands of "those humbler people of the country who had not beeen deported to Babylon" (40:7), since the Babylonians regarded them as unimportant. Through always taking a position against the official line, Jeremiah was subjected to constant persecution throughout his life.

## 5.   THE SERVANT OF YAHWEH IS KILLED BY NATIONS THAT DESPISE HIM

Much has been written about the figure of the servant of Yahweh in the preaching of Deutero-Isaiah, most specifically in the four songs of the servant in Isaiah 44:1–1; 49:1–6; 50:4–9 and 52:13—53:12. And much of what has been written has obscured rather than clarified the subject. The texts themselves, if we discard modern inventions such as the "suffering servant," are not so difficult. They show us the figure of a minister of God (this is what "servant" means in this context, in the verse in which David was a "servant of Saul" in 1 Samuel 29:3), a figure who accords with what we have seen embodied in Moses, Elijah and Jeremiah.[4]

Deutero-Isaiah was a prophet, whose actual name we do not know, who lived among the exiles in Babylon for a few years before 538 BC, the year in which Cyrus of Persia conquered Babylon. His sayings were added to those of Isaiah and form chapters 40–55 of the book of Isaiah. Judah had spent a generation in exile, and Deutero-Isaiah took Cyrus's military victories as a sign of hope, a sign that Yahweh would soon restore his people. He assures them that they have already

received "double punishment" for all their sins (40:1–2). Now
it is time to take heart and wait for salvation at Yahweh's hand
(40:27–31).

In this situation of hope after so much suffering. Yahweh has
assigned a special role to Israel in the scenario of history:

> You, Israel my servant,
> Jacob whom I have chosen,
> descendant of Abraham my friend.
>
> You whom I brought from the confines of the earth
> and called from the ends of the world;
> you to whom I said, "You are my servant,
> I have chosen you, not rejected you,"
>
> do not be afraid, for I am with you;
> stop being anxious and watchful, for I am your God.
> I give you strength, I bring you help,
> I uphold you with my victorious right hand.
> Yes, all those who raged against you,
> shall be put to shame and confusion;
> they who fought against you
> shall be destroyed, and perish (41:8–11).

One of the most disputed points in the exegesis of the servant
has been whether the subject of the four songs is, like that of
this text and others in Deutero-Isaiah, the whole people of
Israel, or whether the prophet is speaking of an individual (a
prophet, perhaps himself, a king, a Messiah). It is probable that
the people of Israel as a whole are meant, but who their subject
is does not really matter for our examination of the songs.
Suffice to know that they present us with an image of the true
minister of Yahweh. The servant of Yahweh in these songs has
no political or military function. According to Deutero-Isaiah,
Yahweh has assigned this to one whom he has anointed for the
purpose: Cyrus of Persia (45:1–7; 41:1–5). The function of the
servant of Yahweh is one that might be called rather prophetic
and kerygmatic: that of spreading right and justice to the ends

of the earth, a process that will be carried out through
persuasion, not through imposition from above:

> Here is my servant whom I uphold,
> my chosen one in whom my soul delights.
> I have endowed him with my spirit
> that he might bring true justice to the nations.
>
> He does not cry out or shout aloud,
> or make his voice heard in the streets.
> He does not break the crushed reed,
> nor quench the wavering flame.
>
> Faithfully he brings true justice;
> he will neither waver nor be crushed
> until true justice is established on earth,
> for the islands are awaiting his law (42:1–4).

Despite the servant's lack of political power, his mission will
provoke the enmity of the powerful. He will have to bear the
opposition of "the nations." He has to suffer serenely the
blows, insults and spittle in the confidence that Yahweh will
come to his help (50:4–9). He knows that the evil ones will be
like a garment consumed by moths, whereas Yahweh will set
his face like flint.

In the last song (52:13—53:12), Deutero-Isaiah beautifully
brings out the final consequences of the logic of this mission.
The nations will visit death on the one who represents justice
without the use of force. They will see him as so contemptible
that he seems no longer human (52:14), or else they will justify
their actions by saying he has been struck by God (53:4). So it
will be simply the logic of his mission to represent Yahweh and
bring justice that leads the servant to his suffering and death.

The mystery of faith is that this is not the end. Yahweh will
exalt his servant, who will "divide the spoil with the mighty"
(53:12). The nations will look with astonishment at the
vindication of the one they despised and tortured. They will
come to see that it was their own sins the servant bore (53:4–5).

In words of extraordinary beauty, these songs give us the mystery of solidarity, which is the strength of the weak. The justice proclaimed from below, with no show of force, is the justice of God. The one called to be its bearer will suffer at the hands of those who believe they have the right to impose their will by force. The servant suffers because he bears their sins! And their conversion will come about through the strength of the weak.

The four evangelists saw here a key to understanding the mission of Jesus the Messiah, and their accounts of the passion are shot through with the language of these songs. In effect, Jesus Christ, to an unparalleled extent, lived out his commitment to justice and to the God of life through showing the strength of the weak. This is why it is difficult to read these songs now without thinking of him.

## 6.  THE POOR WOMAN MARY LIVES HER LIFE IN THE HOPE OF THE POOR

Of the four evangelists, it is Luke who takes most care in his presentation of the admirable figure of the woman Mary, mother of the saviour. From the first two chapters of Luke we learn that both John the Baptist and Jesus the Christ were born in the bosom of a group of poor and pious Jews who lived in anxious hope of the revelation of the salvation of Israel. With incredulity and great joy Zechariah and his wife Elizabeth received the news that God had chosen them, a poor priest and his barren wife, "both getting on in years," to be the parents of the one who was to go before the Lord in the spirit of Elijah. Mary, a young woman not yet married, was a relative of Elizabeth, though she lived at a distance, in a town in Galilee called Nazareth (this according to Luke; Matthew places her from the start in Bethlehem of Judaea, ending up in Nazareth only for safety after the birth of Jesus and the flight into Egypt). Joseph, to whom Mary is betrothed, also shares his fiancée's expectations about the salvation of Israel. To these people, Luke adds the old and pious Simeon and Anna, who in their old age were favoured with the knowledge that their hopes were fulfilled in the child Mary and Joseph brought to the temple.

Within this environment of confident waiting for the salvation God has reserved for his people, Mary, despite her evident youth, stands out as the best model. In the sixth month of Elizabeth's pregnancy, at a time of great expectations among those who knew of God's announcement to Zechariah, the angel Gabriel appears to Mary in Nazareth. He tells her that she has been chosen to bear a son who will be called Jesus and also the Son of the Most High. His conception will come about without the intervention of any man, not even Joseph. Mary's reaction, as presented by Luke, is not complicated by any consideration of the scandal this extra-matrimonial pregnancy will cause: "I am the handmaid of the Lord; let what you have said be done to me" (Luke 1:38).

The interpretation of Mary's reaction to this astounding event is given by the text of the Magnificat, in which Mary sets her own life in the historic context of the hopes of the poor of Israel:

My soul proclaims the greatness of the Lord
and my spirit exults in God my saviour;
because he has looked upon his lowly handmaid.
Yes, from this day forward all generations will call me
    blessed,
for the Almighty has done great things for me.
Holy is his name,
and his mercy reaches from age to age for those who fear
    him.
He has shown the power of his arm,
he has routed the proud of heart.
He has pulled down princes from their thrones and
    exalted the lowly.
The hungry he has filled with good things, the rich sent
    empty away.
He has come to the help of Israel his servant, mindful of
    his mercy
—according to the promise he made to our ancestors—
of his mercy to Abraham and to his descendants for ever
(Luke 1:46–55).

It is not often that anyone can interpret his or her personal life within a context of historical transformation in the way Mary does in this famous exclamation. One might be able to understand it of people in high positions coming to the end of distinguished careers. Here we need to remember that it applies to a *woman* (in a society in which men were the makers of history), to a *young* woman, and, finally, to a young, *poor* woman. This poor woman awaits the historical salvation of her people and commits her life to its cause.

Luke stresses the poverty of Mary in his account of the birth of the child Jesus in a stable. The only people who succeed in recognizing him are some shepherds looking after their flocks in the vicinity (Matthew adds recognition by wise men from the East).

In his treatment of the presentation of the child in the temple, and the family's pilgrimage to Jerusalem for Passover, Luke shows Jesus' family upbringing in Mary and Joseph's house as a Jewish upbringing, respectful of the temple as the centre of Israel's tradition of religious faith. This in itself accentuates the contrast with the later situation, in which Jesus approaches the traditional religion of the Pharisees and the temple as burdens laid on the people. Mark, in a brief reference which smacks of authenticity, says that Jesus, relatives set out to take charge of him, possibly convinced he was out of his mind (3:31); these relatives included his mother (3:31–5). Luke mentions the fact of his mother coming looking for him, but omits any suggestion that Mary wanted to take him away fearing he might be mad (8:19–21). It is of a piece with what Luke tells us of the religious tenor of Mary and Joseph's marriage that Mary should not immediately understand why her son had to offend the teachers of Israel.

The fourth Gospel tells us that Mary was present in Jerusalem at the time of Jesus' passion and death (John 19:25). This fits in with what Luke says about Mary and Joseph's custom of going to Jerusalem every year for the Passover (2:41), though Luke does not mention Mary's presence at the time of Jesus' death. But since he mentions the mother of Jesus among those followers who gathered by the temple after his death and resurrection (Acts 1:14), we can assume that he too believed she had been there. We are not told what Mary thought about such momentous events as the violence in the temple when Jesus attacked the authorities there, his arrest and subsequent execution, the way the disciples abandoned him in the hour of his anguish, his resurrection and the formation of a community of his followers in Jerusalem. What we are told is that she accompanied Jesus and later his followers. The eloquent young woman of the Magnificat, it would seem, had suffered through the hard succeeding years, and her later sharing in the hope of the poor was a silent one. She is a model of a poor person identifying with the cause of the poor, a woman who was poor and believing.

## 7.　PAUL THE TEACHER TAKES UP MANUAL WORK FOR THE SAKE OF THE GOSPEL

Paul tells us of his impeccable origins in Judaism: "I was born of the race of Israel and of the tribe of Benjamin, a Hebrew born of Hebrew parents, and I was circumcised when I was eight days old" (Phil. 3:5). And Luke tells us that Paul had studied under the famous rabbi Gamaliel (Acts 22:3). He was a citizen of Tarsus and also a Roman citizen (Acts 22:3; 16:37). He came, therefore, from the cream of the Jewish nation in the diaspora, with a privileged education.

Paul rejected all this in order to embrace Jesus as the way to God. In his first letter to the Corinthians he writes:

Take yourselves for instance, brothers, at the time when you were called: how many of you were wise in the ordinary sense of the word, how many were influential people, or came from noble families? No, it was to shame the wise that God chose what is foolish by human reckoning, and to shame what is strong that he chose what is weak by human reckoning; those whom the world thinks common and contemptible are the ones that God has chosen—those who are nothing at all to show up those who are everything (1 Cor. 26-8).

Following Jesus, for Paul, meant accepting the priorities of the God of Jesus, who chooses those who are nothing in the eyes of the world.

Having taken up Jesus' way to God, Paul devoted the best years of his life to travelling to the cities of the eastern part of the empire teaching rich and poor, especially the poor, Jesus' way to the Father. He paid for these journeys by working with his hands, making leather tents.[5] This is a very important fact. Manual workers had a very hard life at the time, since the value of their work was undercut by the presence of slave labour. Paul's manual work was a source of pride to him, since it gave him a missionary independence that others, such as Peter, did not have. There were times when he stayed in the houses of wealthy Christians (Acts 16:40; 17:6–7), but he preferred to live in his workshop (Acts 18:3). From there he could make known the God who is seen in what the world holds common and contemptible.

> If we have sown spiritual things for you, why should you be surprised if we harvest your material things? Others are allowed these rights over you and our right is surely greater? In fact we have never exercised this right. On the contrary we have put up with anything rather than obstruct the Good News of Christ in any way. Remember that the ministers serving in the temple get their food from the temple and those serving at the altar can claim their share from the altar itself. In the same sort of way the Lord directed that those who preach the gospel should get their living from the gospel. However, I have not exercised any of these rights, I am not writing all this to secure this treatment for myself, I would rather die than let anyone take away something that I can boast of (1 Cor. 9:11–15).

It was not usual in the Greco-Roman world for a teacher, philosopher or preacher to live like a labourer. Manual workers were held in contempt; a good teacher could usually find a benefactor to house and maintain him. If Paul did not do this, it was because he did not want to. It was a costly decision, both in terms of long hours of hard work, and because of the opposition this missionary policy provoked. "My answer to those who want to interrogate me is this: Have we not every right to eat and drink?" (1 Cor. 9:3–4). He does not deny the principle that those who preach the gospel have the right to live from the gospel. He takes pride in not exercising this right himself. In this way, he could keep a healthy distance from the wealthier Christian families in his churches. And by adopting this way of life, he gave a sign, without spelling it out, of his following of Jesus. In Corinth there were some rich people who brought abundant food and drink to the eucharist, while others went hungry (1 Cor. 11:17–22). It was probably these rich people who questioned the authenticity of the apostolate of someone who lived like a simple worker. And they would probably have liked to take Paul into their own homes.

It could not have been easy for Paul to keep up his missionary activity while earning his living by the work of his hands. As he himself says, exaggerating a little, he had to work "slaving day and night so as not to be a burden on any one of you" (1 Thess. 2:9). This probably meant that he worked abnormally long hours in order to have some days free to meet with the brethren and share the message of God with them. But he probably also used his working hours to discuss the gospel with those who came to visit him in his workshop.

## 8. FOLLOWING JESUS IN LATIN AMERICA TODAY

This look at some of the main personalities of the Bible has confirmed our initial understanding of the way to God that Jesus showed through his life. Moses, Jeremiah and Paul realized that the mission entrusted to them by God required solidarity with the poor. Elijah, the "servant of Yahweh," and Jesus provoked the opposition of the powerful through their strategy of salvation, which favoured the poor, and suffered persecution on account of it. Elijah and Mary showed a disposition to help the needy. The whole Bible shows that Jesus is the way to God and that we have read his life correctly when we have emphasized his solidarity with the poor, his service to those in need and his firmness in confronting the opposition of the powerful.

Throughout the Bible, widely differing situations show a coherence in the way to the God of the Bible. But there are also important differences among the biblical figures we have been looking at. Moses led a social and political movement that led to the establishment of a new social order, in which Yahweh was the only king and the whole people performed the military and judicial functions which in Canaan and Egypt were carried out by the king. Deutero-Isaiah's servant of Yahweh, on the other hand, left the administrative and military functions to a pagan king, Cyrus, and exerted his influence on behalf of the poor through the peaceful implantation of justice. And Paul, in a society torn apart by the forced migration of Germanic, African and Asian slaves, formed little cells—churches— through his life of solidarity with working people; in these it was shown to be possible, even within the Roman empire, to live as brothers and sisters, as God wills. Elijah, through his disciple Elisha, provoked the violent overthrow of the house of Omri (1 Kings 19:17; 2 Kings 9), while the servant of Yahweh never raised his voice in the street. Jeremiah sought out public places, such as the temple, to attack the powerful for their abuses, while Paul tried to avoid confrontation with those in power and devoted his efforts to building communities of faith. So different circumstances demanded different responses, all within the same way to God and salvation.

This is not the place for a detailed examination of Jesus' strategy.[6] But we need to indicate its general lines. Jesus lived in a society characterized, at first glance, by the domination of the Roman empire. But inside Palestine there was another domination, that of the priestly caste and its adherents over the poor and religious population. The enmity between Jesus and the Pharisees seems to stem from the emphasis he placed on this second domination exercised from the temple and based on the intellectual work of the Pharisees in the townships of Galilee and Judaea. His solidarity with the poor was expressed in his efforts to break the ideological hold of the Pharisees over the people. He took a distant stance toward the Zealots, who were engaged in armed rebellion against the Romans, seemingly recognizing a degree of justice in their cause while not sharing their analysis of the problem, or, consequently, their strategy for the struggle. Jesus' silence on the subject of the uprising in which Barabbas and others in Jerusalem took part should, it would seem, be interpreted in the same sense. This distant attitude is in strong contrast to the violent diatribes Jesus directed against the scribes and Pharisees. So Jesus chose his enemies, just as he chose his allies.

Today in Latin America there is a broad consensus among those who work in solidarity with the cause of the poor that the basic oppression in our societies is that of capital over the workers—not just, or even chiefly, industrial workers, but all sorts of workers, including those who, owing to the accumulation of capital in few hands, cannot find any work. Following Jesus, which we have characterized as solidarity, service and sacrifice, has to develop within the conflictive reality of this overriding opposition between capital and labour. But the particular forms it takes will be dictated by the circumstances in which different people live within specific societies.

The popular movement in Latin America is made up of many parts: trade unions, rural and urban guerrillas, student movements, base Christian communities, and so on. It would seem that there is a time and place for everything.[7] Given this complex panorama, it would be foolhardy to put forward actual examples of how to follow Jesus in Latin America today. A general principle, founded on healthy prudence, would be not to condemn outright any of the different forms of popular struggle which seek to establish the rights of the humblest to the means of life.

Within the overall situation characterized by the main contradiction between capital and labour, there are many other forms of oppression bearing on the lives of the poor, which cannot be ignored either. Women are still dominated in many ways in a patriarchal society and in a church also marked by male domination. Indians and blacks have their own just demands, and the cause of their oppression cannot be reduced solely to the relation between capital and labour. It is through actual solidarity with the poor that we shall go on learning how to discern what following Jesus means among those poor in whose midst God has placed us and in whose faces God hopes we shall see the Son of Man (Matt. 25:31–46).

# Chapter IV

# The Poor: First Recipients
# of the Bible Message

## 1. INTRODUCTION: JESUS PROCLAIMS THE GOOD NEWS TO THE POOR

We who have opted for following Jesus toward meeting the God of the Bible are bearers of a message of hope. This is because following Jesus on his way to the Father not only involves a practice of solidarity with the poor, but also means being, like Jesus, bearers of a message of hope, a message the Bible calls gospel, good news. Jesus was a messenger of this gospel, and we who follow him have to be so likewise. This is common knowledge, but we should still like to look briefly, in this chapter, at what it involves.

Let us begin with the charge laid on the Eleven by the risen Christ. Matthew closes his Gospel with it, thereby attaching great importance to it, making all that has been said about Jesus, what he did and what he said, and how he fulfilled what had previously been proclaimed by the prophets, culminate in this mandate to his followers:

> Meanwhile the eleven disciples set out for Galilee, to the mountain where Jesus had arranged to meet them. When they saw him they fell down before him, though some hesitated. Jesus came up and spoke to them. He said, "All authority in heaven and on earth has been given to me. Go, therefore, make disciples of all the nations; baptise them in the name of the Father and of the Son and of the Holy Spirit, and teach them to observe all the commands

92

I gave you. And know that I am with you always; yes, to
the end of time" (Matt. 28:16–20).

As is the case with many things in Matthew's Gospel, the
ecclesial context of the early communities has modified what
must undoubtedly have been an authentic saying of the Master,
the modifications being especially evident in the trinitarian
formula and the emphasis on baptism. There is no mention of
the content of the teachings of Jesus that are to be spread; the
saying refers back, to what has already been recorded in the
account which these words conclude. The recipients of the
message the disciples are to proclaim are "all the nations," in
contrast to Jesus' practice, which was limited to Israel (Matt.
15:24); these are the same people who will have to appear
before the Son of Man to give an account of how they have
taken care of the needs of the poor (Matt. 25:32).

We know that a large part of the Gospels are devoted to an
account of what Jesus preached, and that this can be summed
up in the announcement of the coming of the Kingdom of God.
Mark puts it like this: "After John had been arrested, Jesus
went into Galilee. There he proclaimed the Good News from
God. "The time has come," he said, "and the Kingdom of God
is close at hand. Repent, and believe the Good News" (Mark
1:14–15). All Jesus' preaching is here summed up in the
announcement of the Kingdom of God, which is presented as
good news, or gospel. All his parables are on the same theme:
the Kingdom is like a mustard seed, which, though small, grows
into a tree in whose shade the birds of the air can take shelter
(Mark 4:30–32); like a man who finds a hidden treasure (Matt.
13:44), or a merchant who finds a pearl of great price (Matt.
13:45–6). The news that the Kingdom is possible and close at
hand is like the joy felt by the bridegroom's friends at a wedding
(Mark 2:19). Yet the call to repentance shows that this joy is
not innocent. The hope evoked by Jesus' announcement brings
judgment with it, and so requires repentance and faith of those
who receive it. The wheat and the darnel have to be separated
on that day (Matt. 13:24–30), and it will be like a shepherd
separating the sheep from the goats (Matt. 25:32–46).

The way Jesus announced the Kingdom of God shows that it

is the poor who in the first place can receive it with repentance and joy, so that Jesus concludes: "It is easier for a camel to pass through the eye of a needle than for a rich man to enter the kingdom of God" (Mark 10:25). John tells of a rich man, Nicodemus, who sympathized with Jesus, but could not make the conversion that would have allowed him into the joy of the Kingdom (John 3:1–13). Of course all things are possible for God (Mark 10:27); to prove this, Luke tells the story of Zaccheus, a rich man who gave half of his goods to the poor (Luke 19:1–10); and there is mention, without explanation, of the wealthy Joseph of Arimathea (Mark 15:42–7).

These cases apart, the usual pattern is that the joy of the announcement of a new society in which justice will penetrate everywhere bursts out among the poor and is hardly felt among the rich. So much so that at times Jesus declares outright that the good news of the Kingdom is for the poor, thereby discounting the case of the rich whose hearts God is capable of softening.

> Now John in his prison had heard what Christ was doing and he sent his disciples to ask him, "Are you the one who is to come, or have we got to wait for someone else?" Jesus answered, "Go back and tell John what you hear and see; the blind see again, and the lame walk, lepers are cleansed, and the deaf hear, and the dead are raised to life and the good news is proclaimed to the poor" (Matt. 11:2–5).

The sign of the Kingdom of God is life, a life so abundant that lepers are cleansed and the dead raised to life. This is already happening in what Jesus is doing among the poor and outcasts of Galilee. Among the poor, this abundant life for those who experienced deprivation is being received as good news. Those in positions of power, on the other hand, feel it as a threat and accuse Jesus of working wonders in the name of Beelzebul, the prince of devils, an accusation made, significantly, by a delegation of scribes "who had come down from Jerusalem"

(Mark 3:22). In these circumstances, it is perfectly understandable that Jesus should declare the poor and those who weep blessed, and proclaim that those who are rich and have their fill now will find the Kingdom a cause of sorrow (Luke 6:20–26).

Such was the response that Jesus' message aroused among the poor that the people received him at the Passover celebrations in Jerusalem as the representative of "the coming kingdom of our father David" (Mark 11:10). On the other hand, his preaching threatened the social order, or at least was seen as doing so by the authorities: "This came to the ears of the chief priests and the scribes, and they tried to find some way of doing away with him; they were afraid of him because the people were carried away by his teaching" (Mark 11:18).

As events unfolded, just as Jesus had foretold during the early stage of his ministry, his end confirmed that his message had proved one of hope for the poor and had provoked the enmity of the rich. In view of prevailing social class differences, this was a logical outcome, and not the result of the preacher's intention. The message was for everyone: that this society was passing away to give place to a new one that God was preparing to take its place. This announcement brought the need to turn away from ties with the existing society so as to leave room to prepare for the new society of peace and justice. And this brought its own judgment: those who felt at home in a social order that was dominated by the temple and that was under the protection of the Roman empire not only did not receive the message as good news; they saw it as a threat of subversion, even though Jesus and his followers never took up arms. The poor people, or at least a large part of them, by contrast, received Jesus and his message of the Kingdom with joy, since it promised them a better life, an abundant and eternal life.

The proclamation of the Kingdom of God is what the Bible calls "the Good News from God" (Mark 1:14). While Jesus Christ was the foremost preacher of this message, the end of Matthew's Gospel shows us that his followers too were to be bearers of this good news. Early in his ministry, while still in Galilee, Jesus sent his followers out two by two to spread the gospel: "He called the Twelve together and gave them power and authority over all devils and to cure diseases, and he sent

them out to proclaim the Kingdom of God and to heal. . . . So
they set out and went from village to village proclaiming the
Good News and healing everywhere" (Luke 9:1–2, 6).

The nature of the hope they offered must have meant that
the proclamations made by his followers were well received by
the poor and repudiated by the rich. Jesus warned them that
they would meet with resistance and be persecuted; they should
not be discouraged on account of this, for the same had
happened to the prophets before them (Luke 6:22–3). The
effect of judgment and separation was not something in the
preachers' intention, but in the nature of their message, which
is good news for all, but for the poor first. Through his
reference to the prophets, Jesus sends us back to the Old
Testament, so let us now briefly see how God's message there
is indeed good news for the poor and a subversive and
dangerous message for the rich.

## 2.   YAHWEH'S MESSAGE: GOOD NEWS FOR THE SLAVES IN EGYPT

As early as the exodus account, we find the good news from
God, a message of hope for the slaves in Egypt, a message from
Yahweh conveyed by Moses his prophet. In the Yahwist
version of the story (see Chapter 1, section 2 for the different
versions), the message is presented in these terms:

> "Go and gather the elders of Israel together and tell them,
> 'Yahweh, the God of your fathers, has appeared to me—
> the God of Abraham, of Isaac, and of Jacob; and he has
> said to me: I have visited you and seen all that the
> Egyptians are doing to you. And so I have resolved to
> bring you up out of Egypt where you are oppressed, into
> the land of the Canaanites, the Hittites, the Amorites, the
> Perizzites, the Hivites and the Jebusites, to a land where
> milk and honey flow.' They will listen to your words, and
> with the elders of Israel you are to go to the king of Egypt
> and say to him, 'Yahweh, the God of the Hebrews, has
> come to meet us. Give us leave, then, to make a three
> days' journey into the wilderness to offer sacrifice to

Yahweh our God.' For myself, knowing that the king of
Egypt will not let you go unless he is forced by a mighty
hand, I shall show my power and strike Egypt with all the
wonders I am going to work there. After this he will let
you go" (Exod. 3:16–20).

To understand the meaning of this message, we need to know
something of the social structure of Egypt at the time. The king
of Egypt was an absolute ruler. His will, even his whim, was
unquestioned law. Egypt was a wealthy nation, with palaces,
pyramids and cities unsurpassed anywhere in the world. There
was one social class who lived in luxury; these were the priests,
civil servants and military officials of the state. But since the
state was an institution personalized in the king, they were "the
king's servants." The whole of this ruling class were in fact
without personal means and depended entirely on the king's
favour for the means to live in the luxury to which they were
accustomed.

The productive base of society, on the other hand, was made
up of a large peasant population. These peasants lived in
villages, whose internal adminstration was controlled by their
elders. In a formal sense, the whole population of Egypt was a
slave population, since everyone was subject to the absolute
will of the king. The king was the formal landlord of all the
lands of Egypt, and for the peasant villages this meant that part
of their product had to be handed over to the king's agents. It
also meant that the villages had to provide the labour forces for
official constructions. They were slaves in a more literal sense
than the upper classes; however, they could keep their family
and community life; unlike slaves in Rome, who were private
property and could be sold and so separated from their families.
The social structure of Egypt did allow more or less stable
community and family life.

This is why the elders have a part to play in this text. If we
ignore the anachronism of calling the peasants in Egypt "Israel"
and stick to the appellation "Hebrews," which also appears in
the text, its meaning is quite clear. The message of liberation
brought by Moses to Egypt is addressed to a particular group:
all those peasants who might be prepared to recognize

themselves as slaves and to withdraw their consent to the Egyptian system, taking upon themselves the rebellion implicit in calling themselves Hebrews. They could be represented by their elders, since despite their total subjection to the king, they were not scattered bands, but lived in stable relationships in their villages. The message Moses brought from "the God of the Hebrews" would be received as good news by a large part of the peasant population, while for the king this message of salvation/liberation was extremely bad news, since it threatened him with the loss of the work force on which the great country of Egypt depended for its luxury and power.

Of course the text of Exodus as we have it reflects a national consciousness which seeks to push the memory of the class struggle underlying the account into the background. What in historical fact was a spontaneous reaction, with the peasants receiving the hope-bringing message from Yahweh and his prophet Moses enthusiastically, and the king rejecting it as a subversive threat, has been converted into the divine will favouring one nation (Israel) over another (Egypt). But despite the efforts of later scribes to present Israel as a homogeneous unit without class differences, they have not managed entirely to efface the original fact that the message was accepted by the oppressed classes who saw it as one of hope.

## 3.  THE "GOOD NEWS FROM GOD" AT THE TIME OF THE RESTORATION (SIXTH CENTURY)

In the first part of the sixth century BC Judah underwent two Babylonian invasions, one in 598 in the reign of King Jehoiakim, when he and 3,023 of his leading citizens were deported, and the other in 587, when the city of Jerusalem was destroyed along with its temple and a further 832 people sent into exile (Jer. 52:38).[1] The only people left in the country were peasants incapable of mounting a rebellion against Babylonian control, "some of the humbler country people ... vineyard workers and ploughmen" (2 Kings 25:12). This removal of the leadership of Judah's society created the conditions for the hard social struggle that was to ensue when Cyrus of Persia allowed the exiles to return and a group of them came back to re-establish their own way of running the country.

The mouthpiece for the good news from God in this situation was the anonymous prophet whose sayings are collected in Isaiah 40–55, known to exegetes as Deutero-Isaiah. He lived in Babylon, and his message was that Jerusalem would be restored as a city in which the people could live happily. He does not contemplate or mention the presence of either kings or priests:

Go up on a high mountain,
joyful messenger to Zion.
Shout with a loud voice,
joyful messenger to Jerusalem.
Shout without fear,
say to the towns of Judah,
"Here is your God" (40:9).

Thus says Yahweh,
who made a way through the sea,
a path in the great water;
who put chariots and horse in the field
and a powerful army,
which lay there never to rise again,
snuffed out, put out like a wick:

No need to recall the past,
no need to think about what was done before.
See, I am doing a new deed,
even now it comes to light; can you not see it?
Yes, I am making a road in the wilderness,
paths in the wilds.

The wild beasts will honour me,
jackals and ostriches,
because I am putting water in the wilderness
(rivers in the wild)
to give my chosen people drink.
The people I have formed for myself
will sing my praises (43:16–21).

Shout for joy, you barren women who bore no children!
Break into cries of joy and gladness, you who were never
   in labour!
For the sons of the forsaken one are more in number
than the sons of the wedded wife, says Yahweh (54:1).


Oh, come to the water all you who are thirsty;
though you have no money, come!
Buy corn without money, and eat,
and, at no cost, wine and milk (55:1).


With these eloquent calls the prophet evokes the hope of a
people disheartened by decades of life in exile without any
obvious possibility of returning to their native land. The
message is that Yahweh will take charge of their return to
Judah.

What mainly concerns us here, however, is not Deutero-
Isaiah himself, but what happened to his "good news" when
Cyrus allowed all the Jews in Babylon who wished to, to return
to Judah. This happened in 538 BC, when the first group
returned, led by Sanabassar, son of Jehoiakim, the king who
was taken into captivity in 598.[2] This returning group (the *Golá*)
met resistance to their reconstruction plans from those who
were still living in Judah, the descendants of the vineyard
workers and wood-choppers whom Nebuchadnezzar had left in
the country. These "peoples of the land" offered to collaborate
in rebuilding the temple, but the leaders of the *Golá* rejected
their participation, alleging that they were contaminated by
their supposed racial mixing with non-Jewish peoples, and that
their profession of faith in Yahweh did not follow the pure
tradition of the fathers (1 Esd. 5:66–73).[3] The country people
continued to harass the builders for another two years, until
Darius became king, when a new wave of exiles returned, led
by Zerubbabel, nephew of Sanabassar and grandson of
Jehoiakim, and a priest called Jeshua. They succeeded in
completing the rebuilding, despite the continued exclusion of
the peoples of the land and their consequent opposition. This
meant that Judah spent many years in social conflict between

the *Golá*, who claimed legitimacy through belonging to the temple and the city of Jerusalem, and the country people.

This background of social conflict explains the collection of prophecies found in Isaiah 56–66, originating with disciples of Deutero-Isaiah:[4]

> Thus says Yahweh: Have a care for justice, act with integrity, for soon my salvation will come and my integrity be manifest.
>
> Blessed is the man who does this and the son of man who clings to it: observing the sabbath, not profaning it, and keeping his hand from every evil deed.
>
> Let no foreigner who has attached himself to Yahweh say, "Yahweh will surely exclude me from his people." Let no eunuch say, "And I, I am a dried-up tree."
>
> For Yahweh says this: To the eunuchs who observe my sabbaths, and resolve to do what pleases me and cling to my covenant, I will give, in my house and within my walls, a monument and a name better than sons and daughters; I will give them an everlasting name that shall never be effaced.
>
> Foreigners who have attached themselves to Yahweh to serve him and to love his name and be his servants—all who observe the sabbath, not profaning it, and cling to my covenant—these I will bring to my holy mountain. I will make them joyful in my house of prayer. Their holocausts and their sacrifices will be accepted on my altar, for my house will be called a house of prayer for all the people (56:1–7).

This prophecy is clearly polemic: in the context of repression against the peoples of the land, accused of not being pure Israelites, it is directed to all foreigners without distinction, provided they observe the conditions of the covenant. They, and anyone else, whatever their genealogy, will be able to share in the salvation that Yahweh will soon make plain. Again:

> Thus speaks the high and exalted one,
> whose name is holy, who lives for ever:

I dwell in a high and holy place
with him who is broken and humble in spirit
to revive the spirit of the downtrodden,
to kindle the courage of the oppressed (57:15).[5]


Yahweh's message is directed to those who are "broken . . . in spirit, downtrodden." Yahweh has decided to make his dwelling with them and not with those who live well in the restored nation and deny the "peoples of the land" full citizenship.

Days of fasting and lamentation—as the prophet Zechariah tells us—occupied a major place in the religion of Judah at the time of the restoration. The famous oracle of Isaiah 58:1–12 is a harsh critique of this religion so beloved of the *Golá*. The prophet points out that the only sort of worship that pleases Yahweh is "to let the oppressed go free, and break every yoke, and share your bread with the hungry" (58:7). Only then will Yahweh answer the pleas of his people, which he will not do in response to the fasts of Judah.

The popular prophets of the period also spoke out against the project of rebuilding the temple, the *Golá*'s most cherished ambition:

Thus says Yahweh:
With heaven my throne
and earth my footstool,
what house could you build me,
what place could you make for my rest?
All of this was made by my hand
and all of this is mine—it is Yahweh who speaks.
But my eyes are drawn to the man
of humbled and contrite spirit,
who trembles at my word (66:1–2).


Faced with the project of the wise and learned members of the *Golá*, this anonymous prophet addresses Yahweh's message to the humble people who are not allowed to take part in the rebuilding of the temple, telling them that in any case it is of no importance to Yahweh, who neither needs nor wants it. His eyes are fixed on the poor and downtrodden, not on those who build temples and offer sacrifices.

Another famous passage from this collection also displays its full meaning when seen against the backdrop of these social conflicts:

> The spirit of the Lord Yahweh has been given to me,
> for Yahweh has anointed me.
> He has sent me to bring good news to the poor,
> to bind up hearts that are broken;
>
> to proclaim liberty to captives,
> freedom to those in prison;
> to proclaim a year of favour from Yahweh,
> a day of vengeance for our God,
>
> to comfort all those who mourn and to give them
> for ashes a garland;
> for mourning robe the oil of gladness,
> for despondency, praise (61:1–3).

So this collection of messages from Yahweh through the unknown prophets of the post-exilic period is also addressed in the first place to the poor. The good news is in this case for the "peoples of the land" excluded by the *Golá* from full participation in the new Jerusalem they were building. It confirms what has already been established: that the hope of the gospel is primarily for the poor. As a conclusion to this section, we recommend reading the beautiful vision of the new heavens and the new earth in Isaiah 65:17–25, which, more than any other passage in the Bible, delineates the features of the egalitarian society that Jesus was to proclaim in Galilee.

## 4.  THE GOSPEL IS A UTOPIA VALID ONLY IF IT CAN BE BROUGHT ABOUT BY VIABLE MEANS

Reading this account of the new heavens and the new earth, where all will live in houses they have built and eat the fruit of their own vineyards, where those who die at the age of a hundred will be dying young, where the lion will eat straw like the ox, one can be forgiven for asking whether the God of the Bible is not offering the poor impossible dreams. Is the good news from God a vision of a perfect world that does not exist? Can it be true that in the end the religion of the Bible is just another opium of the people, a hope held out with no chance of satisfaction in the real world of history, in which the poor continue to suffer the miseries of deprivation? This is a very serious question: so serious that to try to answer it in advance, without considering the actual hopes and present-day struggles of the poor, would be a mockery. All we can do is point to some signs that an answer must include when the poor are in a position to give an answer in the conditions of the real world.

Indeed, the Kingdom of God is a utopia, a society in which God would be literally the only authority necessary and we should not have to call anyone father or master; a society in which peace would be so secure that there would be no need for armies—the lion could be content with eating straw; a society in which there would be no need to work, where the land would flow with milk and honey. But utopias are not fantasies. It is true that *utopia* by definition cannot be realized; it is no-where, not even in any part of the future. The idea of utopia draws the imagination toward the limits of perfection, in which everything that spoils present society is set aside and everything that is good in it is increased to the maximum. Utopia is a category of mind, and can never be one of empirical reality: to claim otherwise is to confuse categories.

This being so, can a utopia justify realistic hopes, hopes which are not merely flights from reality? The answer to this question is that, while it is true that utopia, as the image of social perfection, is unattainable, nevertheless a valid utopia generates viable historical undertakings.[6] If the Kingdom of God, the God of the Bible, is to be justified as a hope for the poor, it will have to generate viable historical undertakings. This was clearly the case in the history of the biblical people of God, at least on two occasions: the tribes of Israel in Canaan set up a social project based on the rejection of any human king, with laws to organize social life on a more just pattern without state sanction; the community of Christians in Jerusalem, in the years following the death and resurrection of the Lord, organized their life in common, rejecting the "market economy" which leads to the poor suffering want. Let us look a little further at what this means.

In the first case, the goal of the exodus was a land flowing with milk and honey, that is, a land that produces abundance without the workers having to slave for it. It was a utopic vision in the sense defined: the vision of a world that not only does not exist, but that can never exist in actual history. Yet alongside this fairy-tale expression, the text also refers to the lands of the Canaanites, the Hittites and the Jebusites. These were real lands, the sort of lands that with human endeavour were capable of "flowing with milk and honey"—not literally, but as a goal to which the people could gradually draw closer.

The second case, the early community in Jerusalem which practised common ownership, started out from Jesus preaching of the Kingdom of God as a society in which disease and death would be overcome, hunger and thirst would be no more, there would be no division between rich and poor; where it would be more blessed to give than to receive; where the greatest would be those who served their brothers and sisters. This vision was utopic in the sense of being a vision of perfection which, as such, is by definition unattainable. Nevertheless, the utopia Jesus proclaimed generated an endeavour to set up a community in which goods were shared and no one suffered want since whatever was needed was shared out:

> The whole group of believers was united, heart and soul; no one claimed for his own use anything that he had, as everything they owned was held in common.
>
> The apostles continued to testify to the ressurection of the Lord Jesus with great power, and they were all given great respect.
>
> None of their members was ever in want, as all those who owned land or houses would sell them, and bring the money from them, to present it to the apostles; it was then distributed to any members who might be in need (Acts 4:32–5).

This community did not last long. It was the target of persecution by the authorities of Israel, a persecution that led to the death of several of its leaders and the dispersion of many of the faithful. It may well also have suffered from defects in its economic system that contributed to its demise. But these factors cannot obscure the fact that for a time the Kingdom of God generated an undertaking among the faithful in Jerusalem in which the needs of the poor were satisfied.

# PART TWO

# THE THEOLOGICAL ASPECT

Reflection in faith has to progress beyond the purely biblical view of the poor and poverty, seeking to uncover fundamental aspects of the question: its reasons, presuppositions and implications.

This second part looks at three main theological aspects linked to the subject of the option for the poor:

1. The poor as sacrament of God; that is, what relationship exists between the poor and God;

2. The church of the poor; that is, what relationship exists between the church of the poor and the church of everyone;

3. Evangelical poverty; that is, how socio-economic poverty and evangelical poverty relate to one another.

# Chapter V

# The Poor, Sacrament of God

The option for the poor is normally seen as having a prescriptive character: it is a commandment, a commitment, a mission. So it gives the impression of having to be situated, in the first place, in the sphere of ethics and pastoral practice.

Before being a duty, however, the option for the poor is a reality of faith, or theological truth. It has a dogmatic basis, as our examination of the biblical aspects showed in Part One. In fact, before being something that concerns the church, the option for the poor is something that concerns God. God is the first to opt for the poor, and it is only as a consequence of this that the church too has to opt for the poor: "Listen, my dear brothers, it was those who are poor according to the world that God chose, to be rich in faith and to be the heirs to the kingdom" (James 2:5; cf 1 Cor. 1:26–8).

We know that dogma alone gives a sure basis to morality. Only divine truth offers a radical foundation for authentic human action. This is the only way to avoid "moralism"—in this case political activism—both in theology and in everyday life. Without being rooted in the mystery of God, the option for the poor becomes a mere blueprint for action, with no guarantee against the dangers of running out of steam or being distorted.

There is, of course, no need to root the option for the poor in faith in order to justify it rationally. The poor are in themselves sufficient ethical challenge to conscience, summoning us to welcome them and work for justice for them. Their human face is the highest demand of liberation. Yet faith gives

109

the option for the poor its ultimate justification, showing that it is rooted in the very mystery of God, which is precisely love and liberation. This is why human action gains its root meaning and unique motivation when it is inspired by the faith of the gospel.

On the other hand, it is important to resist the temptation to refer to the poor in a purely apologetic sense, pushing the argumentation to its limits out of sheer conviction and thereby falling into a new sort of triumphalism, iconizing the poor and even canonizing poverty. We need, that is, to situate the question of the option for the poor in its proper—high—place within the horizon of faith in order to determine its exact weight and true reach.

## 1. GOD CAME TO US ON THE WAY OF POVERTY

There is a deep theological significance—and this is something we have only recently come to appreciate—in the fact that the social condition taken on by the Word of God was that of a poor person. This is the significance of Luke's "And here is a sign for you: you will find a baby wrapped in swaddling clothes and lying in a manger" (2:12): the clearest sign of the Messiah is the most real form of poverty. The Messiah of the Gospels is a poor Messiah and a Messiah of the poor—and thereby opposed to the usual alienated desires of humankind.

So it was as a poor person that God appeared amongst us. Paul interprets this condition as a specific form taken by the incarnation: "Remember how generous the Lord Jesus was: he was rich, but he became poor for your sake, to make you rich out of his poverty" (2 Cor. 8:9). The incarnation of the Lord took the form of the birth of a poor child. So, looking at Jesus, we can say that the poor are the revelation of the Father and that it was a poor person who saved the world.

Actual poverty was not just an incidental feature of Christ, such as the colour of his skin, his height or physical appearance—things about which the Gospels, in any case, tell us nothing. On the contrary, Christ's condition of poverty was an integral part of the mystery of his self-humbling and self-emptying. So it is not a matter of indifference that the Messiah should have appeared in the form of a poor worker and not that of an emperor; as one of the poor, not one of the rich and powerful.

This fact is of such theological significance that the church has made it a rule of its life, as recognized, for example, by Vatican II in no. 8 of *Lumen Gentium*: "Just as Christ carried out the work of redemption in poverty and under oppression, so the church is called to follow the same path" (see also *Ad Gentes* 5). The Council goes on to say that the poor, all the poor, are a living memorial of Christ: "Indeed, [the church] recognizes in the poor and suffering the likeness of her poor and suffering Founder" (LG 8). So we need to bear in mind that it was a poor person who founded the church. The option for the poor is based, then, on theological (permanent) reasons, not just on sociological (transient) ones.

That God should have chosen to be revealed in the form of a poor person is probably one of Christianity's great originalities. Other religions do not seem to have chosen real poverty as a setting for the revelation of God. The Christian God is a poor God, a poor person—Jesus of Nazareth.

## 2. GOD AND THE POOR: AN INDISSOLUBLE UNITY

Christ himself spoke of the love of God as inseparable from love of one's neighbour (Matt. 22:34–40). And our neighbour is anyone we meet along the road of life, especially anyone in need (Luke 10:25–37). In the Old Testament, Yahweh is the God of justice, the just Judge, the *Go'el* of the poor, the Avenger of the oppressed. The poor and oppressed are those he protects. Jesus, for his part, was born poor, lived and died poor. He loved the poor in a special way and identified with them; they were like the pupils of his eyes.

This being the case, the Christian God cannot be understood without the poor, the defenceless, the despised, all those in need. A God separated from the poor can be anything except the God who has been revealed to us. This is why preaching of the gospel can never dissociate announcing Jesus Christ from proclaiming liberation to the poor. The kerygma of eschatological salvation must include the kerygma of historical liberation,

just as Jesus himself made it do (see Luke 4:18–19), and just as
we see the early church doing, when its leaders, James, Cephas
and John, in approving Paul and Barnabas' mission to the
pagans, insisted only that they should "remember to help the
poor" (Gal. 2:10). This advice to Paul from "these pillars" is
symptomatic: the three leading apostles were insisting that Paul
should remember the poor perhaps because his fixation on the
"Lord of Glory" might make him neglectful of this side of his
mission. But he assures them that helping the poor was
something that "indeed I was anxious to do."

The truth is that, in Paul's vision, the "eschatological
caesura" provoked by Jesus resurrection and the gift of the
Spirit is something he feels with such intensity that it eclipses
all everyday reality. So, unlike the Jesus of the Synoptics, the
Letter of James and the rest of the New Testament, Paul's
writings show little sensibility to the social question of poverty.
His passion for the Lord Jesus is so devouring that it puts all
social questions into the shade. They have practically no
interest for him; he has no time to concern himself with them.
He does deal with community and even political affairs (see
Romans 13), but questions such as slavery and poverty do not
merit much consideration in his writings, or at least do not take
on the prophetic greatness they have in Jesus or James. This is
why Paul always needs to be "completed" with the Synoptics;
without this, it is easy to fall into the sort of "angelism" and
alienation now so typical of out-and-out charismatics.

So opting for Christ means opting too for what Christ chose—
the poor. But why, ultimately, did God choose the poor?

This choice, option, is linked to the very essence of the
revealed God. The God of the Bible is an ethical God, a just
God. The poor, for their part, are those who have injustice
done to them, through being abandoned or even oppressed. In
them, as Puebla says, "the image and likeness of God ... is
dimmed and even defiled" (1142). But God loves them: their
cause is God's cause. Their battered faces, in which the image
of God can no longer be recognized, reveal an objective
situation that is deeply offensive to God. And God then takes
on their defence. So we are not dealing with a question of moral
choice in the first place, but with the divine plan being

objectively frustrated. What moves God to take the side of the oppressed is not human injustice, but the justification of those offended for the sake of re-establishing justice in history. God's anger against oppressors is no more than an expression of love for God's children, the little brothers and sisters of Jesus, the First-born, because they are placed in a situation of humiliation and abandonment. Jesus expressed nothing else in the course of his earthly ministry. He was and always showed himself as the Messiah of the poor and despised (Luke 4:18–21; 7:18–23, etc.).

The option for the poor, it follows, is not something marginal or added-on for Christians; it is rather something central to the church's mission, and is so because it is intimately linked to the very heart of God and so to the very centre of the revealed mystery of God.

## 3. THE IMMEDIATE RELATIONSHIP OF THE POOR TO CHRIST

Though they are not to be confused, there is no separation or distance between Christ and the poor. It is not, therefore, a case of Christ referring us on to the poor, as though they were something outside him. No, we meet the poor in the Lord. The immediacy of the relationship needs to be appreciated: what we do to the poor, we do to Christ. The poor are the living *mediation* of the Lord, his real expression and not just an intermediary between us and him.

It is in this sense that the poor are the sacrament of Jesus: the manifestation and communication of his mystery, the setting for his revelation and dwelling. So there is a coincidence between Christ and the poor, not just in a moral, but in a mystical sense, and so on the deepest level of reality. This does not mean that there is an abstract ontological identity (the poor = Christ), but that there is an actual identification (the poor *in* Christ).

The basis of this sacramental identification is not just Jesus' declaration that what was done to the poor was done to him— taking the poor fictitiously "as though" they were his little brothers and sisters. The Jesus-poor identification is not in the juridical or moral order. It is theological, meaning that, in the

Christian mystery, God and the poor are so intimately united
that there is a sort of family relationship between them. Jesus'
use of family categories—"little brothers and sisters"—was not
made casually. Now this "consanguinity" between God-Christ
and the poor is rooted precisely in the incarnation of the Word
in the form of poverty. The poor alone, of all classes, can glory
in having the eternal Son of the Father among their relations.
Of course this "class" nature of the incarnation does not
exhaust its whole significance. Nevertheless, one thing is clear:
the God of the Bible was never revealed in the shape of an
emperor or a high priest, let alone that of a rich landowner or
a patriarch of the people.

But how does the Lord appear in the sacrament of the poor?
In this sacrament, unlike those of the ritual, God does not
appear directly, in divine power and saving grace. In the poor,
God is met precisely in poverty. God appears here as the poor
God and not as the God rich in favours. The sacrament of the
poor shows us the God they want and not God helping them;
here God is challenge, not consolation; questioning, not
justification. In effect, faced with the poor, human beings are
called to love, service, solidarity and justice. So receiving this
sacrament is bitter to the taste. Yet it remains the *only
"sacrament" absolutely necessary* for salvation. The ritual
sacraments allow of exceptions, and many; this allows of none.
It is also the *absolutely universal "sacrament"* of salvation. The
way to God goes necessarily, for everyone without exception,
through human beings—human beings in need, whether their
need is of bread or the word.

Without going further into the fruitful relationship that exists
between the sacrament of the poor and the liturgical sacraments, particularly the eucharist, let us note that one refers to
the other, just as faith (the sacraments) leads to agape (the
"corporal works of mercy") and as the practice of agape is
expressed and completed in the celebration of faith. This is
why, in the great tradition of the church, the celebration of the
eucharist has always incorporated expressions of love for the
poor, just as work for the poor has the altar as its centre,
beginning and end.

## 4. THE THEOLOGICAL FOUNDATION OF THE OPTION FOR THE POOR

If the Christian community declares itself for the poor, this is because of its faith in Christ. This means that the deepest foundation of the option for the poor is not anthropological (humanist, ethical or political) in character, but theological, and specifically christological.

At root, it is because Christians opt for Christ and for the Father of Jesus Christ that they opt for the poor. Christianity is christocentric, and cannot be otherwise, in the sense that Jesus Christ undeniably occupies the centre of everything for it, as Lord of the world and of history. All the rest, including the question of the poor, is organized and harmonized round this greater reality.

It is just this that makes the difference between the Christian community's option for the poor and that of any other group or social movement. For Christians, their option for the poor is not and cannot be a primary movement, but is derived from an earlier option: their option for Jesus Christ, Lord of history. This means that, for Christians, the option for the poor cannot be an absolute choice. If in some cases it becomes absolute (to the point of having to give up one's own life for the liberation of the poor, for example), this absoluteness is derived rather than basic. The Christian identity of the option for the poor is rooted in christological faith.

There is therefore no reason to oppose opting for Christ and opting for the poor. These are not really two options, but two dimensions or aspects of one and the same commitment. The two aspects are linked in the manner of the roots and the trunk of a tree.

Neither is there any reason to contrast an option for the poor based on faith with one on the political level, nor to oppose *a priori* the Christian option for the poor to a humanist or Marxist option. These are not necessarily different, but different levels of the same basic option. These levels can, in actual practice, find themselves in opposition, but there is no need for them to do so. Faith has the capacity of assimilating, purifying and deepening genuine natural and secular aspirations. Christians can very well find a valid and powerful motive for opting for the poor in the simple human feeling of com-passion in the face of their sufferings. Jesus himself was no stranger to such reactions (see Matt. 9:36 and 14:14, etc.). If beyond this motive, they find a degree of *radicality* through considering the example of Jesus, of his sacramental presence in the poor and so on, this in no way diminishes the greatness and value of that first dimension. On the contrary, it gives it a greater consecration and a unique deepening.

The fact that the starting point or ultimate principle of the option for the poor is to be found in faith in Christ is a statement of theological ontology—considering the thing in itself, objectively. From the subjective or anthropological standpoint (be it logical, pedagogical or political), the option for the poor can be based on motivations other than that of faith. But these, as we have seen, can then be radicalized through motivations of faith. Wherever we start from, there is a dialectic between these two poles—the option (of faith) for Jesus Christ and (political) commitment to the poor. Faith in the Christ of the Gospels leads to the poor, and commitment to and with the poor leads us into the mystery of Christ. Jesus makes us discover the poor and their greatness, and they lead us to Jesus and his Kingdom. Between the two poles there is what Paul VI called a "mutual interpellation" (EN 29).

Then there is what happens in practice: reading the Gospels alerts us to the importance of commitment to the poor, and this in turn sheds light on unsuspected dimensions of the person of Christ and his mystery. In this way, on the level of actual practice (ethical, political or pastoral), what matters is not so much the starting point as the dialectic movement that must always take place between the two terms of this unique and complex relationship. We must always, however, bear in mind that in fact this dialectic has a *determinant* pole, which is precisely (and cannot fail to be) the option of faith.

So far we have considered the theological basis for the option for the poor under its christological aspect. We cannot ignore that it also has a *pneumatological* basis. This is an important subject which does not yet seem to have received the attention it deserves. The Spirit and the poor—what a provocative, even inflammatory subject! And then there is the *mariological* aspect of this option. For both these aspects, we have to refer the reader elsewhere.[1]

## 5. WHY IS IT ONLY TODAY THAT WE SPEAK OF AN OPTION FOR THE POOR?

The observations above do not really add anything new from a theological viewpoint. It is in fact of the very substance of the Christian faith to see God and humanity united and to stress the cause of the poor as forming part of God's cause in history. What theology is doing today is just putting greater emphasis on the consubstantial relationship (in Jesus) between God and (poor) men and women, precisely because of our particular historical context, in which faith, with unprecedented force, is faced with the challenge of poverty and how to overcome it. There has never been such a challenge to faith as there is at the present time: to prove itself not an opiate but a leaven of historical progress.

Here we have to say that the option for the poor is not an absolute novelty, nor a discovery made completely *ex novo*. It has a *substantial continuity* with the great tradition of faith, while at the same time presenting us with a *formal discontinuity*, that is, a change in the tenor of historical expressions of that same faith. As to the continuity: the relationship between God and human beings, especially between God and the poor, has always been seen as belonging to the permanent content of the Christian faith. This deep relationship is clearly recorded in the pages of scripture and is witnessed in the life of the church up till now. Basically, substantially, this option for the poor that is so much discussed today traces its roots way back, in the long history of revelation.

But this does not really explain why the expression "option for the poor" is so prominent nowadays. The very novelty of the expression is symptomatic of the novel nature of its historical setting. In effect, the option for the poor expresses a *new form* of embodying that "love of the poor" that is both ancient and always new. It points to a different way of expressing today the agape of the early Christians. One might say that "option for the poor" is the new name, the modern expression, for the "charity," the love of one's neighbour, that has always been enjoined on Christians.

So what is this new form of agape that we call "option for the poor"? In a nutshell, it expresses the social dimension of charity, or the political nature of evangelical love. To put it another way, the option for the poor is concerned with the structural, collective, liberating and even revolutionary aspect of the living gospel. Or, more simply, it is concerned with social justice, what Paul Ricoeur has called the "love of long-term relationships," and José Comblin "macro-charity." This is what is new, and it does really present a discontinuity from the old love of the poor (which was first "charity," then "aid" and finally "social works" or "development'); the new love for the poor is social or political love.

This dimension of *formal* novelty, still on the basis of the same substantial dimension (the spirit of the option for the poor is the same as always), is linked to the new historical situation of the "social question" produced by the industrial revolution. The poor today do not appear under the same guise as the poor of earlier times. Our historical consciousness now sees them as a *collective*, and at the same time *conflictive*, reality. And the poor have to be loved as they actually are; this is why the option for the poor has had to take on the historical embodiment it shows today.

This is also why, in the cultural world of Latin America, it is becoming more and more outmoded to speak of "aid" to the poor or of "charity." The question has to be one of "opting," committing oneself, which means taking up a social position or making a historical choice which is all-embracing and far-reaching. If Christian love today is to be clear-sighted and effective, it has to take the form of an option for the poor. This is the new face of love: love with one's eyes open and one's hands working; love that is the leaven of history and the seedbed of an alternative civilization—the "civilization of love" in fact.

## 6. THE HISTORICAL EMBODIMENT OF EVANGELICAL LOVE

What were the reasons that led the church to put itself on the side of the poor? And had the church then previously made a sort of "option for the rich"? Whatever the answer to these questions, one thing seems clear: even though it may have had the intention of helping the poor, the church in the past was in practice tied to the rich and powerful. And this could only result in a legitimation of their position and so in a reinforcement of the *staus quo* in society. The church being on the side of the rich was not a matter so much of subjective intention as the outcome of actual practice.

Without engaging in an examination of the historical reasons that led the church to make a conscious and preferential option for the poor, we can just say that it was, on one hand, convinced by the urgent phenomenon of the growing scale of poverty, and, on the other, inspired by the evangelical counsels relating to such a phenomenon. So the option for the poor is the church's response, based on its own—evangelical—message, to the threatening challenge of "undeserved poverty" (Leo XIII). The church no longer views the poor as objects of aid—paternalistically—but in a truly liberating way. So the option for the poor expresses a new historical embodiment of Christian love. And the church has moved into step with the times in which it is living: the *new historical situation* of the poor (collective and conflictive) is now being approached from a *new theological and pastoral standpoint*—that of the option for the poor.

If this option is now the object of critical questioning from both inside and outside the church, if it even arouses polemical opposition from certain quarters, this is just because of the *new form* that Christian faith and evangelical love are taking in our day. This is the *hic et nunc* of the whole question. The problem is not one of Christian love (of the poor) as such, but of the specific form this love has to take at the present time. Nor is there, in general, opposition to the concept of love of the poor today as "social" or "political" love: this is clearly expressed in the documents that make up the social teaching of the church, even if it cannot be said to be the position adopted by most Christians as yet. And the magisterium of the church has already recommended a "political" or "macro-structural" reading of the Bible, especially of the texts that deal with love for those in need: the good Samaritan in Luke 10:29–37; the rich man and Lazarus in Luke 16:19–31; the last judgment in Matthew 25:31–46; and so on.[2]

But as soon as one asks *how* this macro-structural love is to be put into effect, the waters begin to part. And they divide overall into two basic positions: one is the reformist view, content with improving the existing system; the other is the revolutionary view, which seeks the transformation of the existing social order. And each of these viewpoints implies its own pastoral approach, its own political strategy, its own pedagogical methodology, all dependent on the basic outlook.

From what we have seen, the option for the poor, insofar as its essential content (love for those in need) is concerned, belongs to the permanent nucleus of Christian faith and ethics, and here there is no problem; this is a perennial doctrinal truth and moral imperative. When it comes to the specific form the option for the poor should take (love in its political dimension), it is really a question "horses for courses." At this level, we are faced with a practical imperative posed by the historical requirements of agape. The underlying *spirit* of the option for the poor has always been there, felt by most Christians in former times and today. The critical point of discussion is what actual historical embodiment this same spirit of charity should take.

This means that the option for the poor, in its aspect of *a particular form* of embodying love for the poor today, should not be elevated to the status of a basic tenet of faith. This would be falling into an old-fashioned dogmatic approach. What has to be done is to show how the perennial agape of the gospel is better expressed and effected today by the option for the poor than by the methods of earlier times.

## 7. AND WHEN THERE ARE NO MORE POOR?


Will the option for the poor then have become historically superfluous? Once the divisions and class antagonisms in society have been reconciled, will there still be an ethical (pastoral and political) need for the option for the poor?

It has to be said that the emergence of social and historical conscience is an irreversible phenomenon. From now on, it will no longer be possible to ignore the structural dimension of evangelical charity. This being so, even in an egalitarian (never perfect) society, the option for the poor will continue to operate. Of course it will take other forms, in accordance with the specific problems thrown up by each society—defence of minority rights, quest for perfecting new structures, pressure for changes in moral and intellectual values, and so on.

Whatever form society takes, poverty, understood generically as the specific lack of something, will continue to be a permanent dimension of the human presence in history. In this world, human beings will always be *capable* of suffering and dying. Poverty will cease to be a social problem extending over whole classes, masses and nations, as it is today, but it will not cease to appear in one or another form of the vicissitudes to which the human condition is subject. In this sense, Jesus' remark "you have the poor with you always" (John 12:8) is quite true, because it is simply realistic. And in this sense equally, Christian love will always be needed, including its aspect of taking care of poor people in person, the "neighbours" we think of now, to whom we always have to "show mercy."

Obviously, Christians will always know what to do for a poor old person knocked down in the street by a car when crossing without looking. In any future society, Christian charity will always bend over an abandoned child crying in the night. These manifestations of love can never be regulated by social organizations, whatever form society takes; they depend solely on qualities the human heart alone can possess and nurture: affectivity, inventiveness, courage, sacrifice, self-giving. They belong to the order of the spirit and its creative freedom, independent of any state organization or regimentation.

Christian realism contradicts the ingenuousness of those ideologies which, in the words of John XXIII, "fail to take account of the undoubted imperfections of human nature, such as disease and pain—imperfections which cannot be remedied in any way, and obviously not by even the most perfect economic and social systems" (MM 213). There are clearly such things as incurable anthropological forms of poverty, incurable because they belong inescapably to the human condition. But there is a distinction between these and the sort of poverty that can be overcome. Victor Hugo declared, in the French National Assembly in July 1849, to protests from the right wing: "I am not one of those who think the *suffering* of this world can be done away with ..., but I am one of those who claim that *poverty* can be destroyed!"

*Chapter VI*

# The Church of the Poor:
# The Church of All

The previous chapter dealt with the relationship between the poor and Christ. This one looks at the relationship between the poor and the church, seeking to examine exactly what the option for the poor means for the church—its objectives, its actual content, its nature, its practitioners. And to the extent that the option for the poor touches on the question of class, we examine how this affects the catholicity of the church as open to all, asking whether the option for the poor can be equated with a class option, and if so for which class, and whether the option for the poor involves class struggle.

So there is a whole series of questions requiring examination and clarification. Our purpose here is to resolve the main ambiguities surrounding the matter of the option for the poor so as to establish some firm, basic positions.

## 1. THE OPTION FOR THE POOR IS GOVERNED BY THE OPTION FOR CHRIST

As the previous chapter established, the Christian community roots its option for the poor in its option for Christ: the former is securely anchored in the latter, so intimately bound up with it that the two can be said to form one single commitment. The commitment of faith, however, always remains the primary and ultimate source to which the Christian community goes to find the wellspring of the endless energy it devotes to its efforts on behalf of the poor and oppressed. There is not, then, (metaphysical) identity between the poor and Christ, but there is (historical-saving) identification between them. In effect, Christ does not identify *with* the poor; he identifies himself (also) *in* the poor.

The option for the poor comes under the spiritual jurisdiction of faith in Christ. It is on the basis of this that it operates, as well as being judged, so it can never be an absolute for the Christian community, drawing all its force from itself. It must never hypostasize the poor in Christ; this would be falling into idolatry and superstition. Besides, the poor would be the first to rebel against being idealized into a fetish or totem. The primary theonomous reference—"You must worship the Lord your God, and serve him alone" (Matt. 4:10, see Puebla 491)— also goes for the option for the poor.

So the Christian and evangelical option comprises the basic aspect of faith in Christ, and the second aspect is reaching out in agape to our brothers and sisters, those who are oppressed in the first place. How do we move from one aspect to another, given that both aspects, though distinct, are inseparable? Through the mediation of *justice*. Let us explain:

—Opting for Jesus Christ necessarily means opting for justice, and opting for justice means opting for the poor—those to whom injustice is done. Christ-justice-poor form an indissoluble and at the same time structured trilogy.

—For a start, we have to take the option for Christ as the first, foundational stage of the process, because this option is rooted in the essence of God. This is the option for the poor at its theological level, or level of faith.

—Next, we must see the option for justice as the stage immediately derived from the option for Christ, since justice belongs—as we have seen—to the very heart of the God of the Bible and the Messiah of the Gospels. This is the ethical, or political, level.

—Finally, the option for the poor is the stage of concrete embodiment of the option in faith (in Jesus Christ) and the ethical option (for justice). So for example, in the parable of the good Samaritan, following Christ (faith) is "taking pity on" (showing justice to) one's neighbour fallen by the wayside (opting for the poor).

So justice is the middle link intimately and indissolubly connecting the two aspects or dimensions of the single evangelical option: for Christ and the poor. This is why, when the church and its magisterium in particular speak of justice, they are speaking specifically in favour of the poor, since the cause of the poor is the cause of justice. The Jesuits are a case in point: one of their main concerns as laid down by their Congregation is precisely the promotion of justice, which means exactly the same as making an option for the poor.

The dialectical counterpart of this is that the requirements of justice are laid as much on the poor as on those who opt in their favour. This means that it would be impossible to legitimize an option for the poor that identified simply with a morality of class struggle, in which everything that favoured the interests of one class, in this case the poor, would be right and just. We shall return to this in the next section, but it is worth noting here as an illustration of how the idea of justice opens up understanding of the option for the poor, just as ethics opens up understanding of politics.

This observation needs to be completed by taking the reverse side of the dialectic: those who opt disinterestedly for the poor opt for justice and (those who opt for justice opt) for Christ, whether they do so wittingly or unwittingly. So, to follow the dialectic to its conclusion, those who opt for Christ and his cause (justice) are genuinely opting for the poor; but equally it is only by opting for Christ that one can make a true and full option for the poor, Christ's preferred. And so, just as the two aspects cannot be dissociated in practice (of faith), since they form one single movement, neither can they be dissociated— though the reasons for the impossibility of this dissociation are different from those on the level of faith—on the level of theory (theological level). The way that goes up (from the poor to God) and the way that comes down (from God to the poor) are one and the same. The only distinction is in the route taken to follow each way. This is the dialectic that runs through the whole of the New Testament, found at its clearest in the First Letter of John (5:1–2, for example). And there too it is always a "dialectic with a determinant."

## 2. A CLASS OPTION?

We have said that when we talk of the option for the poor today we are referring in a very particular way to evangelical agape for the poor, as they appear today in our social and historical situation: as a collective entity (we are dealing with social groups or classes) and a conflictive entity (they are oppressed or marginalized).

As a requirement of agape (justice), the option for the poor is an essential ingredient of following Christ (see Puebla 476 and 1145) and today, in our historical situation, poses one of the greatest challenges (though not the only one) to the church community. And it is in this new and specific sense that the equally new expression "option for the poor" is taken today in theological reflection and pastoral practice.

From this, it is clear that the option for the poor is not, nor does it claim to be, the whole of the church's mission; if it were, the church would come to be just a social institution dedicated solely to the liberation of the oppressed in history. No, what the option of the poor is is a particular priority for the church, and today certainly one of its major tasks, even a dominant task, at least for the churches of the Third World.

Just because of the priority attaching to it, because it is felt as being of such urgency and responds to such a dramatic situation of need, there is a danger that it can become an *exclusive* commitment, reducing Christianity to a "movement for social liberation." If this were to happen, the option for the poor, uprooted from its soil in the gospel and withdrawn from the wider horizon of faith, would lose its inner force and its radical nature, and, thereby, its identity. So, although the option for the poor can be a dominant factor in certain social contexts and historical situations, it can never become the sole and exclusive option of the ecclesial community. This needs saying, not to set any limits to the option for the poor, but, on the contrary, to maintain the deep source of its vitality and historical force.

Given that it is not an exclusive option, we can now ask: Is it a class option? Here it must be said that to the extent that the poor find themselves objectively forming a class, it is logical for the option for the poor to imply a class option. This is simply a matter of realism and efficacy, since it is not possible to love the poor effectively today without taking account of the social, and particularly the economic, situation in which the poor exist today. This would be loving the poor in the abstract, abstracting them, that is, from their actual social conditions, which in fact constitute the only basis for seeing the poor as poor. Therefore, the option for the poor includes a class option, though this does not exhaust it.

But are these poor for whom the church opts the same persons as the proletariat? If by "proletariat" we understand all manual workers engaged in industry (the urban work force), then clearly they are included in the option for the poor; they cannot be the only class for which the church opts, but as an exploited class, they cannot be absent from the church's preferential love for the oppressed. So there is no point in making a crude contrast between "poor" and "proletariat," trying to show that the church's option for the poor is not the same as the Marxist option for the proletariat. Their methods may be different, but their object is the same. Yet, of course, the poor included in the church's option are a much broader and more numerous group than the urban proletariat, particularly in Third World situations. They include—as we said in the Introduction—the exploited or oppressed rural classes (peasants, tenants, seasonal workers, job sharers and so on) as well as the sub-proletariat (unemployed, occasional workers, outcasts of all sorts) of the cities. The "poor" of the option for the poor are perhaps better described as the "people" or "popular classes."

We also need to recall that the poor who are the object of the option are also individually affected by factors other than their basic socio-economic poverty, factors which aggravate their condition. These can be questions of sexuality (oppression of women, of homosexuals), race (oppression of blacks, Indians, immigrants), culture (ethnic minorities), religion (sects, extreme religious movements), age (children, young people, old people) and so on. Such factors evidently do not define a social class, since they are not directly related to the productive process; they are rather superimposed on the basic class structure, without ceasing to have effects in themselves. So the church community has to take account, in its option for the poor, of these particular aspects—the various shades and colours that fill in the overall picture of a more basic and generalized "poverty."

The church's option certainly has a specific material content: it is concerned with giving bread to the hungry and so on. But this is not the whole of it. As a qualified option—an evangelical option, that is—it is not content with giving just bread, but seeks to give the word as well, as Jesus did (see Mark 6:34ff). It seeks to satisfy not just the hunger of the body, but that of the heart too. This is why Puebla insists that the option for the poor has to be aimed at the "integral liberation" of the poor (1134, etc.); it is a means and not an end, and this in itself should prevent it from being in any sense dogmatized.

The poor, however poor they may be, are always human beings. However crushed by various forms of oppression, they have a spirit stronger than the weight of any oppression heaped on them, a power that transcends all oppression, an energy for liberation and therefore a potential for revolution. Consequently, poor people cannot be reduced to their (material) poverty—the basic fault of "aid-ism" and paternalism. Neither can they be seen as locked into their class situation (and so we question absolutization of the class struggle). In theory and in practice, from moral and analytical standpoints, they have to be recognized as human beings who, however oppressed and repressed, are still worthy of respect, permanent holders of inalienable rights and agents of their own liberation.

We need to have a dialectical understanding of the dimensions that define persons, in this case poor persons, in relation to a social class, and this class in relation to society. While their class includes and transcends individuals physically, they still include and transcend their class spiritually (through their living consciousness). For its part, a class (such as that of the oppressed) is subject to a social system in history, but can also overcome this subjection in history, given certain conditions. So the poor, as individuals and as a class, are at one and the

same time under different aspects, both immanent and trans-
cendent in relation to their social conditions. And for this
reason, the option for the poor involves the question of class
but at the same time goes beyond it. It goes beyond it not by
cutting itself off from it, but by moving through it and on from
it.

In effect, the interests of the poor cannot be reduced to their
(social) class interests. They are also their (human) interests,
including their need for dignity and faith. And this is what one
actually comes to experience through sharing in their lives: the
poor feel hunger not for bread alone, but also, and above all
and undoubtedly, for meaning and mystery. So the option for
the poor is also an option for human beings, and for the Son of
God in them, though *sub cruce et contrario*, in Luther's phrase.

To summarize these last points:

1. From the point of view of its *content*, the option for the
poor is, theologically, a task of the first importance for the
church, particularly today when the question of poverty and
oppression is one of the most urgent and dramatic challenges
the faith has ever faced. Nevertheless, its option for the poor
is not and cannot be the church's only option: it has other tasks,
tied to this option—catechesis, liturgy, ministerial training, and
so on. This means that the option for the poor is *inclusive*.

2. From the point of view of its *object*, the option for the poor
is concerned with actual poor people because of their socio-
economic condition. In this sense, the option is also a class
option, in that its object is the poor specifically making up more
or less defined and conscious classes. But it is clearly not
confined to one class of poor, such as the industrial proletariat.
It embraces *all the poor* (unemployed, manual workers, small
farmers, beggars, and so on) and *the whole poor (person)*, with
his or her individual characteristics as black, minority race,
woman, and so on. Besides this, in that the option for the poor
implies a struggle for justice, it is also open to participation by
the non-poor—as we shall see in more detail later. So it seeks
not to exclude but to include.

3. Finally, from the *formal* point of view, the question of its
nature, we have to realize that the option for the poor is not

just temporal but also spiritual, not just political but also religious. In a word, it seeks to be *integral* or all-embracing; otherwise, it is not a fully evangelical option.

## 3. A CLASS STRUGGLE?

The question is linked to the previous one. Here again we have to say outright that the option for the poor includes, but is not reduced to, a class struggle. This is, in effect, the dialectic (of integrating and going beyond) that always has to be applied to this sort of question.

If by "class struggle" we mean any form of action aimed at defending the legitimate interests of a class (and not just or primarily violent and even bloody struggle), then there is no reason why the option for the poor should not include a class struggle. This is logical: one class is only that in opposition to others, so that speaking of classes immediately involves speaking of class struggle, whether this is something passively borne or actively undertaken.

Here it needs to be said that, on the class level, "struggle" is not directly dependent on human will (aggression), nor can it be explained simply by human nature (aggressiveness). Struggle here is rather dependent on the *economic structure* (as unequal and conflictive) of a given society. It is this economic structure that gives rise to the objective opposition between material interests: capital versus labour, profit versus wage, bosses versus workers. The class struggle is born from and feeds on this structural contradiction, which is something independent of human will.

We also need to be clear that the class struggle is not the only type of social conflict. It is certainly a very special type of conflict, because of its outreach (conditioning other conflicts) and import (relating to the whole social order as such). There are, however, other social conflicts besides those of class: racial, cultural, sexual, religious, between generations, between political parties, and so on. There is really no such thing as a society without conflicts.

Nevertheless, for the poor, the class struggle evidently

represents the basic and decisive struggle, since it refers precisely to their socio-economic condition—that of being poor: that is, either exploited by the system or excluded from it; oppressed in one way or another. Therefore the struggle of the poor, aimed at their liberation from poverty and oppression, has an overall class character. This means that they build a basic solidarity around their legitimate class interests, which run from seeking to improve their living conditions to working to overthrow the system that oppresses them.

Does class struggle have to be struggle *against*? Obviously, the overall objective is not a struggle *against* the ruling classes but a struggle *for* justice and liberation. Also, it is not really a struggle against the persons of the oppressors, though this cannot be ruled out (cf LE 20c), but against the oppressions they perpetrate. Furthermore, the initiative for the class struggle comes from the ruling classes, leaving the dominated no alternative but to fight to defend themselves. Finally, the struggle of the poor includes battling against situations that are simply the result of social backwardness, not directly the outcome of class relationships—illiteracy, lack of basic hygiene, and so on.

So, all in all, the option for the poor cannot be seen as simply a translation of the Marxist class struggle into Christian terms. For Christians, the class struggle implicit in the option for the poor has to be effectively subordinated to the gospel ethic. This is why they cannot have recourse to means that are perverse in themselves, such as calumny or torture. More positively, Christians will engage in the class struggle in the spirit of the Beatitudes: meekness toward the enemy, preference for peaceful means, maximum economy in the use of force, offers of forgiveness and reconciliation, recognition of the dignity and inalienable human rights of one's adversaries, distinguishing between one's oppressor as a member of a class and as a human being, and so on. There is, then, for Christians, an evangelical ethic of struggle and not simply an ideological ethic subject to the political objectives of the struggle. From the standpoint of faith, the class struggle is to be judged by its justice, not merely by its outcome. Here as elsewhere, as Kant said, "politics must do homage to morality."

## 4. WHY A "PREFERENTIAL" OPTION?

The adjective "preferential," added to the phrase "option for the poor" (Puebla 1134, etc.), means that this option cannot be for the poor *exclusively*, i.e. closed to the non-poor. Christian love is love for the poor, but in the first place rather than exclusively. The church is on the side of the poor (through love of neighbour, agape), but not tied only to them (out of excluding, possessive love, eros). Its love for the poor is, then, a love of predilection and not an exclusive love.

This love by preference can be described as having three features; it is affective, practical and dialectical:

1. *Affective*. The Christian community is inclined as it were spontaneously and naturally toward the poor. This special sensitivity to the oppressed is something special to Christianity, as it was to the heart of Jesus of Nazareth: made up of compassion for the suffering of the humble, indignation at the dominance of the powerful, prophetic courage in denouncing injustice, audacity in taking sides in conflicts, a spirit of initiative and creativity in the struggle for liberation . . .

All this means that the church must also love the non-poor, with the aim of their conversion and association with the way of the humble. But they can never claim the bulk of the Christian community's attention.

2. *Practical*. The option for the poor takes shape in actual practices, as we shall see later on; it is not rhetoric, but action. And it is precisely on the levels and in the processes of pastoral and political action that the poor must occupy the very forefront of the stage. As they were for Christ, the poor must be both the first recipients and the prime emissaries of the gospel's message of evangelization. Likewise, the mission of both church and society must make the poor its principal beneficiaries and at the same time its main agents.

These considerations do not deny, but imply, a place for the non-poor also in the way of liberation, but with no other privileges than those of serving.

3. *Dialectical*. Preference for the poor demands that more love and more resources should be devoted to them than to others. We need to recognize that there can be situations in

which the option for the poor ceases to be preferential and becomes exclusive; this is due to the nature of the situations, not to the will of those taking part in them. This happens in cases of class conflict as such; these, as we saw, are not the only ones (the poor being more than their class) but they exist and are often major conflicts. This would apply to strikes and other acute conflicts. Here the option has to be exclusive by its nature, in the sense of excluding the non-poor, that is the oppressors as a class (as a group with conflicting interests), from the struggle. Strictly speaking, it is not the poor and their allies who do the excluding, but the oppressor class who exclude the poor on their own initiative. In this sense the option for the poor excludes on a formal level (that of opposing interests), but is materially (on the level of the individuals involved in the conflict) preferential.[1]

And when the poor are forced to undertake a (class) struggle in order to defend their legitimate interests, they do not do so out of hatred for the persons of their oppressors. Their defensive struggle is a form of love for them: combative love. In effect, through social conflict with those they oppress, oppressors have an opportunity to take stock of the injustices they commit and to be converted from them.

So the dialectic goes like this:

—loving oppressors but not their oppression, rather as a doctor loves the patient but not the disease;

—loving the persons of the oppressors, while fighting their class and illegitimate interests;

—liberating the oppressed, and thereby, as a direct result, liberating oppressors from their conditions and means of oppression.

## 5.   PASTORAL REASONS FOR PREFERENCE FOR THE POOR

The first thing to take account of is that the poor, according to the gospel, have, by right, regardless of their personal merit, the Kingdom of God as their inheritance (Luke 6:20). They belong to the church "by evangelical right" (Paul VI). They are as it were its citizens by birth, or are open to faith in advance, being a sort of road to Jesus.

The rich, on the other hand, are, by nature, outside the Kingdom. To enter into it, they need to rid themselves, affectively or effectively, of their riches. Their situation in relation to the Kingdom is problematic—even dramatically unfortunate (see Luke 6:24–6). Their status in the church is critical: the New Testament always considers their riches a danger to faith and an obstacle to following Jesus (though not as an evil in themselves). So the evangelization of the rich is always prophetic and dramatic because of the separations it requires of them.

The second factor is that, because of the privileged status of the poor in relation to the Kingdom and within the church, they form the good soil in which the seed of the word grows to give more abundant and better fruit. In fact the pastoral fruitfulness of the church has always been greater among the popular sections of the community than among the ruling classes. The explosive growth and effectiveness of the base Christian communities in Latin America today are the most recent proof of this. Jesus' own "pastoral work" illustrates this: he had more "success" with the masses than with those in power. Besides, Jesus knew—and said—that riches are like thorns that choke the development of the word (Mark 4:19).

It is not only in the pastoral sphere that the poor show the greater potential; they do so in the political sphere as well. Without going into this deeply here, suffice to recall that the historical protagonism of the poor rests on their greater numbers and their objective interest in changing a situation that is unfavourable to them. This fact cannot escape the attention of a liberating pastoral practice seeking to change society in the direction of the gospel.

So the option for the poor, being preferential, does not exclude the rich either pastorally or politically, but simply cannot accord them the historical priority and protagonism they spontaneously claim for themselves.

The third and final point is that the church has to prefer the poor for the sake of the rich themselves. This is a paradox that needs explaining. The situation of the rich in relation to the

Kingdom is a frightening one, as we have seen, and the more so the less they show themselves aware of the dangers they run. In this sense the rich, before God, suffer the most frightful form of poverty—poverty of faith and grace, not to mention their frightful lack of humanity. But if this is the case, are not the rich the strayed sheep who need the shepherd's, in this case the church's, special attention? True, but then we come to the second aspect of the paradox: Who can convert the rich? Who can make them aware of the true riches of the Kingdom? In the words of Puebla: "The witness of a poor church can evangelize the rich whose hearts are attached to wealth, thus converting and freeing them from this bondage and their own egotism" (1156). So, poverty alone can proclaim the good news of integral liberation, both to the poor and to the rich, but above all to the latter.

The conclusion is that the option for the poor is indirectly an option for the rich. This dialectical detour, through the poor to reach the rich in the end, is imposed on the church by the problematic status of the rich with regard to grace and by the favourable situation in which the poor find themselves before God and in terms of evangelizing potential. So the one option dialectically unites two poles: the poor directly and intentionally, the rich mediately and by effect. Therefore, opting preferentially for the poor is "doing the rich a favour", even though they may feel themselves abandoned and betrayed (and so they are, as far as their anti-evangelical interests are concerned).

This is precisely what is happening in Latin America today: the poor are evangelizing not just themselves, but the church and especially the rich as well.

## 6. WHO AND WHAT MAKES THE OPTION FOR THE POOR?

The next question is that of the subjects or agents of the option for the poor: Who makes or should make it?

In the first place, the *institutional church*, i.e., the official representatives of the church: pope, bishops, priests, religious and lay ministers. This is how the duty of the church to opt for the poor has been understood and by and large still is. But immediately as we say this, we are faced with the evidence of how far the hierarchy have become distanced from the poor, how much the poor have been living on the fringe of ecclesial life. In this sense, the option for the poor faced the official church with a call to conversion and to redefine its mission in history. This in turn implied breaking its historical pact with the powerful and siding with the oppressed masses.

This option for the poor, put into effect by the church's pastors, was expressed in different ways: by adopting a poor lifestyle, by living or working in close proximity to poor people, by steeping pastoral ideas in the cultural world of the poor, by sharing the life and struggles of the oppressed, and so on. What happened was a vast process of "popularizing" the pastors of the church, and so the church of the pastors.

In the second place, *lay Christians* too must make the option for the poor. In fact, in the course toward the poor taken by the church in Latin America, many lay people anticipated the clergy, or associated with them, particularly those lay persons involved in the pastoral work of the church in some way—Young Christian Workers and suchlike groups. Although such people were generally "middle class" in origin and lifestyle, they ended by taking up a truly "popular" class position.

In the third place, the *rich* are also called to take up the cause of the poor, by joining in their struggle for justice and with them building a new society in which there will be neither rich nor poor, in the manner of the early Christian community (Acts 4:34).

Finally, the *poor* themselves are clearly agents of the option for the poor. They carry it out in terms of solidarity among themselves, of openness to the poorest of the poor, and finally by welcoming the non-poor who seek to become their companions on the way. In fact, the poor in the church became agents of the option for the poor and protagonists of their own process of liberation through pastors working for and with them, arousing their consciousness of their own dignity and encouraging them to take a constructive part in society. In this way, the poor began to opt consciously for their own rights and their own future—which is the future of all—instead of opting in an alienated manner for their own oppressors and their projects.

But at the same time as this movement by pastors toward the base of society, there was another, corresponding movement: that of the rise or emergence of the poor within the sphere of the church. The bottom-to-top movement, explosive in force, accelerated the inverse movement. And it was precisely this convergence of movements, one starting at the top and the other at the base, which characterized the Latin American church's option for the poor and made possible the emergence of a "new way of being church," a way expressed above all in the base communities.

From the point of view of the institution of the church, the process of this new church project was, and goes on being, a three-stage process: church *for* the people, church *with* the people, church *of* the people. And being the church *of* the people means being essentially a church of participation in its inward manifestation, and a church of liberation in its outward manifestation.

## 7.  IS THE "CHURCH OF THE POOR" A CATHOLIC CHURCH?

A church of the poor is a church in which the poor are privileged, a church in which the poor occupy the first rank. This means that there is also room in it for the rich, but only to the extent that they are converted and fraternize with the humble. It is not true that the church of the poor is against the rich; what it is against are the privileges, illegitimate interests and anti-evangelical pretensions of the rich. Therefore, the church "is and wishes to be the church of all, but especially the church of the poor," as John XXIII proclaimed in his radio message of 11 September 1962.

The poor possess a natural openness that makes them a wellspring of true "catholicity," unlike the rich. This means that only a poor church and a church of the poor can be a really "catholic" church. A rich church slanted toward the rich, in which the rich have control, is a closed church and in this sense "neo-catholic," or even "anti-catholic." The poor in this way make up a sort of "universal class," an "overall part," by virtue of the fact that it is around them and their cause—justice—that all are called: this is because of the nature of evangelical faith itself, one of whose basic values is justice—to the poor.

It is important, however, to bear in mind that the strongest bond of church unity is not a social bond but the bond of faith— faith in Christ Jesus. This means that, even if it is divided in class terms, the church is not split apart. Pastors and lay people continue to read the same gospel, recite the same creed and celebrate the same eucharist, even though they may find themselves on opposite sides in terms of class struggle. It is only the bond of faith that can hold politically opposed sectors of the church together in unity.

This gives rise to the question of whether such a unity is just a myth—"the myth of the communion of the faithful," as Althusser called it, in the sense that it covers over and mystifies the deep and painful divisions between oppressed and oppressors within the church. Unfortunately, this is what has happened many times in the history of the church: the dogma of the unity of the church has been used as an ideological cover-up to mask a conflictive and even scandalous situation. If unity in faith is not to perform an ideological function of mystification, it needs to be understood and practised in a *dynamic* fashion. It grows to meet the particular requirements placed on it. In fact, religious unity *tends* to promote political unity, without ever becoming confused with it. Faith is not such an all-embracing bond that it can embrace the most extreme and antagonistic political views. Faith is not a donkey that one can get on and ride wherever one wishes—to use Weber's famous metaphor.

Faith, to the extent that it is made manifest in theory and practice—to the extent that it materializes, that is—can indeed be a powerful impetus in the direction of growing social and political unity. Consequently, when the poor are intimately linked to Jesus Christ, the unity of faith is also built round them. Now this unity will be that much more concrete, and so that much more visible, the more concrete are the requirements of faith in regard to the poor today. Nevertheless, full unity will always be an eschatological event, toward which our ephemeral historical unities point progressively, but without ever reaching.

# Chapter VII

# Material Poverty and Spiritual Poverty

The question of the option for the poor leads naturally to that of spiritual or "evangelical" poverty. This is a point at which discussion of real poverty slips subtly, or polemically, into that of spiritual poverty, which is used to turn attention away from socio-economic poverty and void it of all content. This is giving way to hypocrisy, carrying out an ideological takeover of the actual problem of real poverty in the name of a mystified poverty sheltering under the name of spiritual poverty.

Neither can the question of spiritual poverty be tackled seriously by claiming that it is irrelevant in the face of the enormous and dramatic problem of material poverty. It is a genuine theological question in itself, with undeniable repercussions in the social and historical spheres, as we shall see.

In order to discover and analyze the connections between different forms of poverty, we first have to distinguish clearly what each of these forms actually means. So let us take three clearly differentiated forms of poverty, examining them one by one and trying to see how they interrelate with one another. They are: material or socio-economic poverty, spiritual poverty or poverty of the heart, and evangelical or Christian poverty.

## 1. MATERIAL POVERTY

This is simply being really poor in socio-economic terms—poverty with no need of further qualification. Still on the plane of simple description, real poverty comprises two categories of poor: those who live at subsistence level and those who exist at below this level—the destitute. The boundaries between the two are extremely fluid, due to the very economic instability of the situation of the poor in present-day society. The former are mainly manual workers, the "labouring classes" (what the Bible calls *penes*); they are those who struggle to earn their daily bread. The latter are those who are marginalized in all sorts of ways, who have no guarantee of any sort of work, however impermanent (called *ptochos* in the Bible: the indigent, destitute, starving).

From these two categories of "poor" we exclude "lower middle" classes and those whom welfare or work maintain above subsistence level, even though on a barely decent or acceptable level. Faced with the huge majorities who make up the "poor" of the Third World, they are relatively privileged.

### (a) Material Poverty: Social Sin

How is such a situation to be viewed from the standpoint of faith? Real poverty does not just represent a mere socio-economic fact; it also has an ethical and religious dimension. It is an essentially human, and therefore also theological, pheno-menon. So what is the theological significance of real material poverty?

From an *objective* point of view, material poverty is not willed by God, is not part of God's plan. It therefore represents a contradiction of God's will and this makes it a "social sin" (Puebla 28, *passim*). Socio-economic poverty is a fact that must be condemned in the strongest terms (Puebla 1159). Christian conscience, and even simply human conscience, cannot accept the existence of poor people in this world. This alone is enough to form the basis of a whole Christian ethic and political theology to justify the efforts made to overcome poverty once and for all, to abolish this social sin which is an outrage to the poor and to God.

From the *subjective* point of view, that is seen from the standpoint of the poor who are subjected to this situation, they are clearly not to blame for it. They are the victims of their poverty. And this is what is essentially to be condemned: they are "socially innocent," those to whom injustice is done, who clamour for justice. It is precisely because they are humiliated and downtrodden children of God that "the poor merit preferential attention, whatever may be the moral or personal situation in which they find themselves" (Puebla 1142).

The "*sensus fidelium*" has always intuited the innocence and holiness of the poor. Hence the custom of the people of Latin America, and also and perhaps even more so, those of Russia, to "canonize" the poor and innocent creatures who have been subjected to undeserved suffering by other people. Popular religious feeling, especially in Russia, nourishes a sacred respect for those who suffer injustice. All those who suffer and suffer unjustly are to be venerated.[1] Note that in such cases it is not the suffering that is venerable, but the sufferer. Suffering in this context points to something quite other—the iniquity of those who oppress and cause to suffer.

Even with regard to the moral degradation produced by extreme poverty (destitution), such as prostitution, alcoholism and criminality, we need to understand clearly, theoretically and morally, the actual situation of the poor. This is that they have been "pushed" down the slope of social degradation by the sub-human conditions in which they are forced to live. For its part, the Bible goes so far as to interpret the groans, cries, complaints, shouts of anger and even blasphemies and curses which the poor hurl up to heaven as supplications with a religious value that God will not fail to hear (Ecclus. 4:5–6; Exod. 3:7; James 5:4; etc.).[2]

### (b) Poverty Still a Problem for the Poor

While the situation of poverty has to be rejected without more ado, the poor for their part have to be truly loved, and loved just because of the painful and unjust situation in which they find themselves. To be for the poor and against poverty—this is the only correct approach! Today, rejection of actual poverty has to be unequivocal; there is no longer anything to justify a lyricism or mysticism of poverty: quite the contrary.

Such a condemnation must, of course, not have anything bourgeois about it; it can in no way be a matter of falling into the crass alternative of "get rich"! It is a question of an evangelical condemnation appealing not to riches as the alternative, but to human dignity, the dignity of children of God, who are being disfigured. The alternative offered is not riches but a material condition that will allow the poor to affirm themselves as human beings and develop in freedom.

Love of the poor must not be a paternalist love, love out of mere commiseration ("Poor little things!"). This can lead at best to political and revolutionary Messianism, seeking to liberate the poor in spite of themselves. No, love for the poor is love for subjects and not for objects. It is precisely an "option for the poor" in terms of solidarity with their struggle. "Option" here means the same as "solidarity."

Though the poor are not guilty of their own situation of oppression and suffering, they are at the same time the agents and protagonists of their own liberation. Therefore, condemnation of objective poverty leads to recognizing the historical mission of the oppressed and their political potential. This is why poverty can be described, not morally but politically, as "a problem for the poor," in the sense that it is they who should and can resolve it.

If we speak of the "objective social innocence" of the poor in relation to the state of poverty in which they are sunk, we can still ask whether the poor are exempt from all responsibility for their situation. If we say they are, we are once again considering them as mere objects, ignoring their power and freedom as human beings. Because to the extent that the poor resign themselves passively to their poverty, or seek an egotistical liberation, not one in communion, they change themselves from victims into connivers in the oppression that dehumanizes them.

It is, of course, true that the uncaring attitude of the poor to their own oppression is largely a fruit of the very system of oppression that weighs down on them and literally alienates them right to their hearts. This shows what levels the process of impoverishment of the poor can reach: to the point of depriving them of their own consciousness.

Yet the oppressors will never have the last word; there will always be reserves of consciousness in the oppressed, however much it is stolen from them. Hence the urgent need for, and possibility of, a popular education and an ethic of the poor that will situate as basic values: (1) *Commitment to the struggle* for social liberation (against all resignation and fatalistic passivity); (2) *Solidarity* with companions in the struggle and on the same path (against the individualism of "rising" or "winning" in life). "The noble struggle for justice" and "solidarity among workers and with workers"—those are the same ethico-political principles expressed by Pope John Paul II (see LE 8f).

Away, then, with all false triumphalism of the poor and with all "superstition" of their holiness because of their condition. All such talk is of no use whatsoever to the poor in their liberation and is sensibly rejected by the poor themselves.

### (c) Are the Poor More Open to God?

Is poverty not a social situation specially propitious to the religious spirit and to faith? Are the poor not spontaneously more open to God? And are they not also more open to others in their lives?

We know of the *anawin* of the Bible: really poor and at the same time full of the greatest piety and trust in God, in God's power, providence and justice. Are the poor of Latin America not also a poor and at the same time religious people in the same way?

Now, if there is a real connection between poverty and openness to God and to other people (if not always on an individual level, then nearly always on a social level), how then do we condemn—in the name of faith—a situation that produces such excellent fruits? Religious *because* poor? Is religion then the delicate flower of that barren soil that is material poverty? Is it just the "cry of oppressed creatures" (Marx)? And are the option for the poor and all the social practice of the church not merely religion's last great statement, prior to its irreversible decline?

All such questions are indications that there is a real problem here. In the first place, faith is certainly linked to poverty, but not necessarily to material poverty—rather to "anthropological" poverty (contingency, mortality). Material poverty for its part is just a particular expression and prime embodiment of this more basic anthropological poverty. And this is the soil in which religion and faith take root.

In the second place, "freeing oneself" from God does not really lead to atheism, but to idolatry: the paramount danger of people losing their faith is not that they will be without a god, but rather that they will replace the true God with idols. The radical insufficiency of humanity is such that it always needs an absolute, and when it fails to find one, ends by inventing it. This is why Jesus speaks of riches as an idol: Mammon. Other New Testament passages deal with envy as an idolatry (Col. 3:5; Eph. 5:5; 1 Cor. 5:10–11). The quest for riches is an obstacle to faith (Mark 4:18; Luke 14:18–20; etc.). In effect, the theological status of capitalism today is precisely that of a vast idolatrous cult of the great god Capital, creator and father of so many lesser gods: money, the free market, and so on.

What does all this mean? That liberation from poverty does not necessarily bring liberation from religion. What it can do, in the worst possible scenario, is to substitute one religion for another, idolatry for popular religion; in the best possible scenario, it can replace a religion of liberation with a religion of liberty. Which leads to a reaffirmation of the principle that the true replacement for material poverty is not riches. Because what lies at the root of the problem of poverty is not poverty itself but rather the way it represses and smothers the human and divine dignity of human beings. Poverty is merely the social symptom of a deeper human set of problems. To solve these, we need an adequate economic order. What would this be? The concept of evangelical poverty, which we shall deal with later, can provide a pointer to the right track.

## 2. SPIRITUAL POVERTY

This is a whole new area. The term "poverty"—and the adjective "spiritual" tells us as much—is no longer being used in its proper sense but in an applied or metaphorical sense.

We can, in accordance with this latter sense, pick out a first meaning of poverty: ontological poverty. This is the poverty inherent in every created, or rather contingent, being. Every

relative being is a "received" being and so absolutely dependent
on an Absolute. This makes it an ontologically poor being.

Human beings' recognition of this precarious situation
awakens a "religious sense" in them. When this religious sense
is deeply absorbed and put into practice along the lines of faith,
this is *spiritual poverty*, which is made up entirely of openness
to God, trust, humility, abandonment to the Mystery. In other
words, it is spiritual infancy. In fact, the poor and little children
are typical figures of those who receive, who live by, grace: this
is why it is said of them "theirs is the kingdom of heaven"
(Matt. 5:3; 19:14).

In this sense, spiritual poverty can co-exist with material
riches—in principle. In practice, however, the relationship
between the two is intrinsically difficult, since (and we shall go
into this more fully later) spiritual poverty requires a different
attitude to material things: detachment, freedom, sharing. ...
Nevertheless, spiritual poverty is a concept whose qualities are
relatively autonomous and comprehensible in themselves. So
the publican in the parable (Luke 18:9–14) and the publican of
history (Zaccheus in Luke 19:1–10) are truly "poor in spirit,"
though it is nowhere said that they became poor in reality. So
too Moses is called "poor" (*ani*) in the sense of "humble":
"Now Moses was the most humble of men, the humblest man
on earth" (Num. 12:3). Jesus also declared himself "humble in
heart": "Learn from me, for I am gentle and humble in heart"
(Matt. 11:29; cf also 21:4).

This is being "poor in spirit" according to Jesus as recorded
in Mark 5:3, the "humble of the earth" of whom Zephaniah had
spoken earlier (2:3; cf 3:12–13): "Seek Yahweh, all you, the
humble of the earth [*anawim*] who obey his commands. Seek
integrity, seek humility [*anawah*]." This *anawah* usually exists
in the real poor, but can also not be in them if the poor are full
of ambition or envy, in which case they are no better than the
potentially rich or frustrated rich.

## 3.  ACTUAL AFFINITY BETWEEN REAL POVERTY AND SPIRITUAL POVERTY

*In abstracto*, on the level of the respective concepts, real
poverty and spiritual poverty are two distinct entities. *In*

*concreto*, however, they can go together and even tend to coincide. This means that those who are really poor tend to have poor, humble and open hearts, while on the other hand, those who are rich tend to be more subject to arrogance, self-centredness and envy. The parable of the rich man and Lazarus (Luke 16:19–31) illustrates this clearly, and the common run of experience confirms it. The rich are generally more self-sufficient and the poor more humble; the former more egotistical and narrow-minded, the latter more generous and welcoming. Their relative conditions of life favour one or the other attitude, not in any deterministic sense, but as psychological conditioning. This is not to idealize the poor, but simply to show how the poor relate to the divinity in reality.

This is why the Bible, especially in the prophets, Psalms and wisdom literature, frequently makes the correlation rich-impious and poor-innocent.[3] These equations illustrate what in fact happens in human experience. Poor people perceive the virtue of "spiritual poverty" and live it to the full. This is shown by their use of expressions such as: "I am poor but rich in God's grace." The way the poor see life embraces the idea that the "truly poor" are the "rich of this world" because they are "full of ideas," whereas they, the poor, are the "truly rich in God's eyes" because of their faith and the blessings they see God bestowing on them every day.

Today we are of course aware of how easily this sort of language can be put to ideologically alienating use, particularly when used by oppressors. This does not prevent it from being a pointer to the truly evangelical meaning of "spiritual poverty." In fact, Jesus too used this level of language when he spoke of "making [oneself] rich in the sight of God" (Luke 21:21) or of getting oneself treasure in heaven by sharing out one's possessions and giving them to the poor (12:33 and 18:22). And "rich in [God's] grace" is a properly biblical expression in itself (cf Eph. 2:7; etc.).

All this is valid on the general level; on the particular level, one can of course find money-grubbing poor persons as well as detached rich ones. Which shows that the message of conversion and evangelical poverty is valid for everyone.

## 4. EVANGELICAL POVERTY

What precisely is this ideal of evangelical poverty, as lived and propounded by Christ and his followers (Luke 13:33–4; 14:33; 18:18–30; 19:1–10; etc.), as practised by many saints to the most radical extremes, and professed by members of religious orders?

It might be described as the synthesis of the two types of poverty previously portrayed. Evangelical poverty, the ideal of all Christians, has an inner and an outer face; it is spiritual and material at the same time. It consists of a prior inward attitude that has to be expressed in an outward mode of life. One aspect is as bound up with another as the soul is with the body.

The taproot, or ultimate source and motivation of evangelical poverty, is based in spiritual poverty and what it means in terms of faith, humility and self-abandonment. More specifically, it is the will to follow Christ and to imitate him: *nudus nudum Christum sequi*. Now such a disposition will logically unfold into an equally poor way of life, as the necessary visible expression of this inner poverty. And as a retroactive or dialectical result, this simple and poor way of life, at the same time as expressing the spiritual attitude, completes it and reinforces it. And so on progressively. Yet poverty "in heart" is and always remains the primary and determinant pole, even though in turn super-determined on the basis of its empirical expression.

Obviously, the relationship between these two dimensions of evangelical poverty—the spiritual and the material—should not be understood by way of a mechanical model in which material poverty shows itself just as an automatic reflex of spiritual poverty, like light shining from fire or water flowing from a spring. No, the relationship between the two poles is rather a dialectical one: that of a dialectic with a determinant. In this dialectic, the determining pole is certainly the interior one, since the exterior one, at the same time as being determined, reacts on the interior from its own specific autonomy. So, in actual spiritual practice it is certainly important to reinforce the interior pole—the option for Jesus Christ and the will to imitate him. But this in itself is not sufficient: one has to go on actually to adopt an objective *forma vitae* that will harmonize with this inner determination. This is the way to give shape and strength to the spiritual option itself. In other words: a will that does not take on a visible body is an abstract and impotent will, and consequently an unreal(ized) will.

From this it follows that a "spiritual poverty" which is only spiritual is not enough, but tends to empty itself of content to the point where it vanishes, leaving at most no more than a hollow shell—spiritualist talk of "spiritual poverty," which on its own is a seed that fails to germinate. But on the other hand, exegetical and theological efforts aimed at showing that Matthew's "poor in spirit" (5:3) have nothing to do with "the spirit" are equally mistaken, since any kind of poverty which does not have its prime root in interiority is not evangelical (cf Mark 7:14–23), and so is lacking in authenticity and power.

A true "poverty in spirit" or "in heart," though, will be expressed and realized in appropriate actions and actual practices. For the Bible, in fact, the "spirit"—or "heart" in some texts—is the vital and creative centre of human life and action. So anyone who has really become poor by choice is genuinely "poor in spirit."[4]

Therefore, Christian poverty is something mystical and at the same time something empirical. Furthermore, Christian poverty takes on a community and social character. Vatican II recommends that religious should "aim at giving a kind of corporate witness to their own poverty" (PC 13e). This can and should be extended to Christian communities and even to the whole church (cf GS 8c; AG 5b).

There is no justification today for the existence of huge and comfortable monasteries, convents or presbyteries, especially if they are surrounded by the slums of the poor. The fact that the religious or parish priests who live in them may lead lives of personal poverty does not annul the objective adverse witness given by such a community. Community, social and even architectural structures cannot be divorced from people, any more than people can be from them. While each has its own autonomy, they are equally undeniably inter-dependent. So it is most important that the actual form of religious life and dwelling should preach poverty: poor religious in poor communities—that is what the gospel demands today!

When evangelical poverty has a truly spiritual root, it will manifest itself and embody itself in a number of forms. Let us now look at the actual components of evangelical poverty.

### (a) Three Components of Evangelical Poverty

(i) *Affective Detachment*. The evangelically poor do not have their hearts set on material things. They are not alienated and subject to material goods, but feel and behave freely towards them, with no affective clinging to them. They may live in a palace, but will do so as though passing through, like guests. In this sense, only the poor in heart really possess things, in the sense of being able to dispose of them freely with an open heart, without being possessed by them. They neither adore them nor curse them, but use them in freedom.

This is the inner attitude of complete freedom with respect to the world of which Paul writes: "Those who have to deal with the world should not become engrossed in it" (1 Cor. 7:31). The poor in spirit are above all free when faced with anything life might bring them: "I know how to be poor and I know how to be rich too. I have been through my initiation and now I am ready for anything anywhere: full stomach or empty stomach, poverty or plenty. There is nothing I cannot master with the help of the One who gives me strength" (Phil. 4:12–13). Freedom here takes the form of healthy indifference to either having or not having.

Following the dialectic envisaged (disposition/realization), it is clear that one can achieve such personal freedom only through inner decisions, acts of will, impulses of good intention. And then, without dispensing with these, there has to be an ascesis—practical exercises in effective abstention. Only those who are capable of radical rejection of the world can learn to receive it as grace, to possess it inwardly and rejoice with it in all freedom, free from all dangers (cf GS 37e).

Affective detachment really means liberation from avarice, the root of all alienating appropriation, all enslaving accumulation: "Be on your guard against avarice of any kind," Jesus said (Luke 12:15). And Paul warned in his First Letter to Timothy: "The love of money is the root of all evils" (6:10).

(ii) *Sharing*. Evangelical poverty is also expressed and

brought into being, consists, in sharing one's goods with one's fellow men and women, especially those in need. This is the hallmark of whether one is truly detached and free in relation to things. The calling to follow Jesus always involves distributing one's own goods to the poor. It is not a matter or destroying riches or throwing them into the sea, as the cynic philosopher Crates is reputed to have done. It is a question of destining them to their proper function: sharing. Evil does not consist in riches themselves but in their egoistic accumulation; "Give alms from what you have. ... Sell your possessions and give alms" (Luke 11:41; 12:33).

Generosity is the first concrete sign of freedom of heart in relation to possessions. 1 Timothy warns Christians who are "rich in this world's goods" that they should, first, "not set their hopes on money, which is untrustworthy, but on God," and then tells them that they should be "rich in good works, generous and willing to share" (6:18). Communion in faith needs to be complemented by communion of goods (cf Rom. 12:13 and Acts 2:42, 44).

Today, sharing by means of almsgiving still has its value. However, alms today, if they are to appear free of any patronizing and paternalist connotation, need to take a different form: they have to be "political alms." This means using one's time and position in society in the service of the poor. Perhaps this involves leaving a more highly paid job and taking another that will serve the cause of justice better. It might mean devoting some of one's leisure time to political and social movements that work for the oppressed. It certainly means not accepting favours, privileges and bribes that seek to cover up connivance in injustice. It means devoting one's intellectual powers to the cause of the poor. It means solidarity with the struggle of the oppressed, whatever this may cost in political and economic terms.

Such procedures re-establish the original and rich meaning of "alms"—a word the Septuagint rightly translates *sedaqah*, justice. Almsgiving as an expression of justice is clearly found in the Bible (Matt. 6:1–2, for example) and runs through the whole tradition of faith, especially the Fathers. So if we are to recover the original spirit and meaning of alms, we should say that the best form of almsgiving to the poor today is doing them justice. This means, in a Third World context, associating with them in their struggle for liberation, through direct participation in political practice; for this, material help, such as is provided by agents and agencies in the First (and Second) World, is needed as an essential ingredient.

(iii) *Moderation*. Finally, evangelical poverty is practised through adopting a moderate pattern of life. This means not surrounding oneself with so many things that one is weighed down with them and so loses one's freedom and availability with respect to the gospel. The style of life called for might be described as simple, modest, austere; it means concentrating on essentials, reducing possessions to what one really needs rather than multiplying them for their own sake. As such, it is the opposite of the growing wave of consumerism; it is real and noble asceticism.

Evangelical poverty is something specific; it implies adopting a certain pattern of life. This pattern will be one of neither *opulence*—always a danger to faith and humanity—nor *destitution*, a condition unfavourable to the practice of virtue, as Thomas Aquinas reminds us (*De reg. princ.* 1.5). It consists rather in having what is necessary in order to live with dignity. This is what the oracle of the Book of Proverbs asks:

Two things I beg of you,
    do not grudge me them before I die:
keep falsehood and lies far from me,
    give me neither poverty nor riches,
    grant me only my share of bread to eat,
for fear that surrounded by plenty I should fall away
    and say, "Yahweh—who is Yahweh?"
or else, in destitution, take to stealing
    and profane the name of my God (30:7–9).

Paul echoes the same message in 1 Timothy: "As long as we have food and clothing, let us be content with that" (6:8). And Jesus' criticisms of excessive care for the things of this world follow the same patterns (see Matt. 6:25–34; Luke 10:38–42).

Evangelical poverty does not dispense us from, but imposes,

the "common law of work." Poverty out of idleness is not virtue, but vice. The whole tradition of religious life has realized this from the start. Evangelical poverty requires individual labour—as witness the examples of Jesus of Nazareth, Mary, the apostles, Paul, and as all the great founders of religious orders have demanded: St Francis, for example, requiring that the brothers should learn to work: "he who does not know how to work, let him learn" (*Testament*, 5). Alms for him had the function of supplying what could not be gained through work.

It is only the rich who do not need to work. However busy they may be, the rich are parasites, living, in effect, off the work of others. The poor are essentially those who absolutely need to work in order to live.

The ideal of evangelical moderation is lived in concrete terms today by many of "the more modest members of the middle class" (Puebla 1151), as well as by countless families of workers in cities and the countryside, living in dignified and settled poverty. Both really do live removed from the extremes of luxury and indigence, living a "modest" life. Obviously, this "modest" pattern is not something that can be assessed in the abstract, but has to be related to the society in which people live. Now, society today is worldwide in character. So one cannot just say that people should have their basic needs satisfied: food, clothing, housing, basic health care and elementary education, because the means by which these basic necessities are provided are a function of society and therefore of history and culture. The worldwide character of modern society, based on the internationalization of economies and the communications media, has two contradictory dynamics: one calls for ever higher levels of consumption; the other cries at our doors in the form of the dispossessed masses of the Third World.

From this it follows that one's personal pattern of life has also to be decided in terms of others. This has to be worked out by means of sharing. This sharing, as *Gaudium et Spes* teaches (69 and 88), can extend not only to superfluities, but also to essentials, since its basic aim is the achievement of equality (cf 2 Cor. 8:14), in abundance as well as in penury (why not?).

Today there are groups of Christians, from wealthy backgrounds, who deliberately set out to live the evangelical ideal of poverty in terms of moderation. They adopt a lifestyle counter to the prevailing consumerism: they give substantial portions of their income to social projects designed to favour the poor; they refuse to change their car just because it is out of date; they take jobs which may pay less but produce more in the way of political liberation; they refuse to save more than a certain amount; they choose to live in working-class areas, send their children to state schools, and so on.[5]

As we shall see later, this model of life, adopted on a personal or community level, can also apply to whole societies and so become a historical project. And while a life reduced to essentials is a requirement of the blessedness of poverty enjoined on all Christians (cf GS 72), it is still more so for those who make a public profession of poverty, as do religious. This is the subject of the next section.

### (b) Charismatic Forms of Evangelical Poverty

There have always been, and still are, special forms of evangelical poverty in the shape of radical voluntary impoverishment for the sake of identifying with the poor, and even the destitute, of society. This was the impulse of St Francis of Assisi and many more.

This is the field that traditional theology, with doubtful appositeness, has called the evangelical "counsels," and which would be better called "charisms," since they are concerned with personal gifts and special vocations. There cannot be laws governing this field, since each person has to decide for him- or herself under the free impulse of the Spirit. No one can impose this type of radical poverty on anyone else, not even those who have adopted it so as to give an example.

What is happening in the church today, more particularly in Latin America, is the awakening and growth of a whole, truly charismatic, movement of identification with the poor. Pastors, lay people, and especially men and women religious are moving into the actual world of the poor in order to share in their lives and struggles. The degrees to which they identify with the poor vary, but the movement is widespread and vigorous, operating under the signs of com-passion, *kenosis* and incarnation among the oppressed masses.

This is without doubt a re-discovery of the original impulse behind religious poverty, which from the beginning presented a radical and charismatic face, which had, therefore, to be voluntary (on the level of a "counsel," i.e. something not obligatory for everyone, indiscriminately). With the passage of time, this impulse tended to lose its nerve, its radicality, until, in the best of cases, it came to embrace a lifestyle that could be called merely "modest"—which is a general requirement laid on all Christians (a "precept"). Now, however, the growing number of religious communities that are establishing themselves in poor milieus is rekindling the original impulse behind religious poverty, and is doing so in new ways.

The church will only become poor by force—as Karl Rahner said, adding that it is incapable of being converted through moral exhortations alone; it needs the imposition of "physical factors" if its conversion is to take place with the speed needed today.[6] These "physical factors" can now include the harsh contact and suffering experience of so many religious alongside the poor and oppressed. This is what is dragging the whole church in the direction of the poor. This incarnation, however, is merely the prior condition for something later and greater: redemption. It is an insertion for the sake of liberation.

This truly Spirit-led movement of living communion with the real poor, going beyond any question of rule or duty, represents an irrepressible requirement of evangelical consciousness and a historical imperative in the face of the dramatic situation in which the Third World lives. As Cardinal J. C. Maurer of La Paz, Bolivia, has said: "The church could possess her wealth and her territory in the past with a quiet conscience, but today, in face of the hunger and destitution of so many people, this can no longer be done without sin."[7]

### (c) Evangelical Poverty as a Socio-economic Ideal

The blessedness of the poor, according to both Matthew and Luke, has to be proclaimed to the poor, and to them above all.

It is true that the poor are the "socially innocent," as we have seen, but this cannot be used as a pretext for depriving them of the glowing and liberating message of poverty in heart. This would be a sort of contempt, since it would be like denying them their soul. And it would be the end if we were to want, or rather dare, to deprive the poor, who are deprived of virtually everything, of the good news of radical liberation. The more so as the gospel is addressed to them in the first place. So Puebla is right to say: "The gospel demand for poverty . . . frees the poor person from being individualistic in life, and from being attracted and seduced by the false ideals of a consumer society" (1156).

It is a known fact that, in their struggle to liberate themselves, the oppressed run the risk of seeing their goal in their oppressors, and so of wishing to take their place. This is the phenomenon known as the "introjected oppressor." The real transformation needed, however, is more radical than this: it seeks the suppression of oppression rather than of the oppressors. It attacks not so much the prince as the principle.

The ideal of evangelical poverty should also inspire the socio-economic model of a new society. The dream of the church of the poor cannot be of a rich and opulent society, but must be the dream of a human and communal society, one in which material progress is but the necessary (and ever insufficient) condition for integral development. This was Paul VI's great lesson in *Populorum Progressio*: the quest not to have, but to be, and to have only for the sake of being.

The struggle for liberation will have to find ways of overcoming material poverty and oppression without falling into the, equality alienating, opposite extreme: the quest for accumulation for its own sake. This, whether on the individual level, as in present-day capitalism, or on the collective level, as in existing socialist regimes, is always the materialist ideal, and is unworthy of human beings. The social ideal of Christians is not the cornucopia of affluent societies today. These, with their sad-faced, over-fed people, their hearts emptied of hope and meaning, cannot serve as an adequate model for the utopia of the gospel.

This, however, does not remove the urgent and permanent

need to struggle to obtain the basic material goods necessary to support life. What we have to do is set the right level of material goods necessary for human fulfillment in this world. This level lies at the point of balance between the lack which prevents development of a decent life and the surplus which stifles the impulse of the spirit and enslaves us to things. So it is a question of steering clear of both the deprivation that goes with exploitation, and the excess that brings alienation.

In fact, human nature is made in such a way that it suffers when material conditions are too low, and is harmed when they are too high. So in the parable of the sower, the seed will not flourish if it falls on rocky ground, but neither will it if it falls into thorns, which choke it (Mark 4:16–19). The ideal of evangelical poverty, translated into social terms, indicates the happy medium: that in which economic development functions as the plain material basis for human development, and not as the goal and substance of development itself.

The option for the poor, then, has nothing to do with either individualist or class competition for the sake of pure material gain. If it seeks this, it does so purely in the guise of the means to a culture of equality, freedom, and openness of spirit to all dimensions of reality. To have in order to be, and to have to the degree needed for being. The economic base is certainly necessary, but as a condition not of material riches but of "human riches" (Marx). Only in this way can the economy be placed at the service of human beings and cease to be an end in itself. It is in just this sense that Albert Tévoédjrè speaks of "poverty: the riches of the poor."[8]

So Christian poverty is not just an ideal for individuals, the community and the church; it is also an ideal for humankind and for a society that seeks to operate on the level of human beings and their mystery.

# PART THREE

# THE PASTORAL ASPECT

This final part looks at the more practical and concrete aspects of the option for the poor.

Chapter VIII is a—partial—historical examination of the option for the poor in the history of the church, showing how the church viewed and treated the poor over a thousand-year period.

Chapter IX deals with the church's response to the challenge thrown up by the poor today.

Chapter X shows how the poor struggle for their liberation: the poor opting for the poor, for their life, their future, their dignity.

Chapter XI examines practical pastoral questions raised by the option for the poor, such as: the evangelizing potential of the poor, pastoral care of the non-poor from the side of the poor, and specific consequences of the option for the poor affecting both the church and society.

Finally, we close the book with a look ahead: the tomorrow of history is in the hands of those who are deprived of its today.

*Chapter VIII*

# The Option for the Poor during a Thousand Years of Church History

This chapter looks at the option for the poor as practised in the history of the church during the period when the church exercised the greatest influence on society: the period, that is, from the sixth to the sixteenth centuries, the whole of the Middle Ages. This is also the period that has been most thoroughly studied from the point of view of poverty and care of the poor.[1] So we here leave the first and last four centuries out of account, though drawing lessons for today at the end.[2]

## 1. THE EAST IN LATE ANTIQUITY: THE FATHERS

In the Byzantine world poverty was above all urban. Concentration of land-owning and sub-divisions of holdings forced smallholders into slavery and migration to the cities, where they formed concentrations on the outskirts, reduced to begging, prostitution and crime. The state tried to find work for the "deserving" poor: those with good health and a useful trade, while trying to "cleanse" the cities of the non-deserving.

The church took the latter under its wing. An example was St Zotikos: an aristocrat, he defied the imperial edict by building leper hospitals in Constantinople, for which he was condemned to death by being dragged and torn apart by mules. Rehabilitated after his death, he was hailed as a martyr and known as "nourisher" of the poor throughout the empire.

The social teaching of the Fathers, in both West and East, can be summed up in two basic principles:

(i) The surplus of the rich is the needs of the poor (St Augustine);

(ii) Human beings are merely managers of the goods they possess, never their owners (St Basil).

## 2. THE MEROVINGIAN PERIOD: RURAL POVERTY

Ecclesiastical writings form our only source of knowledge of the condition of the poor during this period (fifth to eighth centuries). The poor were regarded as being victims of natural disasters: plague, earthquake and the like. These were also seen as punishment for sin, as shown by the procession against the plague organized by Pope Gregory the Great in the year 590.

The "structural poor" were in effect the "rustics"—that is, free agricultural labourers; but they were free only to an extent, since they were strictly bound by feudal oaths. Unlike in the East, poverty in the West was mainly a rural concern. The misfortunes of the poor were multiple. Churches put out marble vessels in which abandoned babies were placed. Some of these grew up to become saints, at least in popular legend, such as St Vincentian and St Odilia. The greatest of these was St Martin of Tours, the son of a Roman officer, who became known as the patron saint of the poor because he divided his cloak in two to share it with a poor man. Another example was St Sigiramnus (Cyran), Archdeacon of Tours, who opted for a poor and contemplative life, and is supposed to have gone to live amongst poor agricultural labourers.

## 3.  THE CAROLINGIAN PERIOD: THE "ECONOMIC COUNCILS"

A great contrast of this period (ninth and tenth centuries) was between *pauper* and *potens* (poor and feudal lord). The Second Council of Aachen in 836 made a distinction between the "indigent" (those living below subsistence level) and the "poor" (freedmen of the countryside, though subject to feudal oath).

Kings, and bishops in particular, appeared as "protectors of the poor," meaning of the weak of all kinds. In the early ninth century, several councils took the defence of the *pauperes* against the *potentes*. They denounced the frequent dragging of the poor before courts of law, fiscal exploitations of the poor, unfair pricing and trading methods, raising prices by hoarding in periods of famine, low prices paid for agricultural produce (Council of Paris, 829).

Such measures, however, had little effect. Even saints and wise men, in the ninth century, failed to see structural implications of land ownership. They therefore tried to correct inequalities rather than eliminate them. They encouraged the myths of the "good king" and "rich administrator" of goods to the benefit of the community. So they were left dealing with the results of basic injustice. The great Bishop Hinkmar of Rheims wrote to his suffragan, Bishop of Beauvais: "It is episcopal duty of the utmost importance to receive the poor and pilgrims in suitable hospices."

Yet there was the occasional "good lord": one such was Count Géroud (d. 909). He had always been a *potens*, who never had to work with his hands, only to manage the family estates. But he took real care of the poor, distributing a ninth share (more than a tithe!) of his income to them, and judging their suits with strict justice (blinding thieves, for example!). The people canonized him, long before the first worker was canonized, which happened only at the end of the twelfth century.

## 4. THE BISHOPS AND THE POOR: AN OLD ALLIANCE

Even before the "Economic Councils" of the ninth and tenth centuries, numerous meetings of bishops had revolved round the social problems of the poor. In the year 500 alone, there were no fewer than forty-one councils and synods. In several of these, the expression "*necator pauperum*" was applied to those who despoiled the poor, including ecclesiastics.

Bishops were seen as "*procurator et dispensator pauperum*" (advocate and provider for the poor). The Council of Macon in 585 declared that the bishop's house was the house of the poor. Bishops were forbidden to go out with a pack of hounds, in case these bit poor people and so prevented them free access to the person of the bishop. ....

One quarter of ecclesiastical goods was distributed to the poor, a custom that originated in Gaul in the fifth century and spread to the whole of Europe in the sixth. This portion was held to be theirs *by right*. Earlier, Fathers of the Church such as Ambrose and John Chrysostom had sold church possessions, even precious liturgical ornaments, for the benefit of the poor and prisoners. The Archbishop of Trèves found himself obliged to sell his horses—which represented a treasure for noblemen of the time. Later, in the eleventh century, a new type of prelate, the abbots, began to give away church possessions, including sacred objects, for the sake of the needy. This was done by Abbot Richard of Rheims and Abbot Guillaume of Volpian during a famine in Burgundy.

"*Cura pauperum*" became institutionalized in the early fifth century with the establishment of "matriculations." These were a sort of "deaconry" entrusted with looking after the poor who were "matriculated" (on the public registers) in episcopal sees. They later became assimilated into monastic hospices and were perverted in lay hands by being made into sources of income for the owners and their proteges.

The teaching of the Fathers had been enriched by the contributions, especially, of St Gregory and St Isidore. It now comprised four main affirmations:

(i) Any surplus belongs to the poor by right;
(ii) Possession means management for the good of all;
(iii) Almsgiving obtains pardon for sins;
(iv) Christ is in the poor.

By the end of the tenth century, the power of kings was giving way to that of warrior lords. The distinction was now between the *pauper* without arms and the armed *miles*. The church took on the defence of the unarmed populace with the institution known as "God's truce." This period saw the first instances of armed popular uprisings; the poor were beginning to speak and behave as actors on the scenario of history.

Besides being "providers," bishops became "defenders" of the poor. An example of this was St Caesarius of Arles (470–543). He regularly received poor people at his table, and when the Gothic King Theodoric gave him presents, he sold them to ransom captives deported by the king himself. His homilies (which have come down to us) denounced usury and extortion practised against agricultural workers. He is even known to have kept his sermons short so as not to take up too much of the time of busy workers. . .

Yves Congar has published two important articles[3] which will serve to round out this section. In the first, he examines the tradition of regarding the temporal goods of the church as the "patrimony of the poor." Bishops and fathers were no more than *"dispensatores in rebus pauperum."* This is why the Gallic Councils of the fifth and sixth centuries excommunicated those who withheld goods from the poor—even bishops themselves. This shows the extent to which actual, practical love of the poor was considered essential to church communion. It was not for nothing that gifts for the poor were accepted in the context of the Eucharist/sacrament of communion: they were something sacred. For the same reason, the church of the Fathers refused gifts from those who exploited the poor. In the Middle Ages, the poor even had the right to appeal to ecclesiastical tribunals against rich people who held on to their surplus, which belonged *by right* to the poor; this was known as the *denuntiatio evangelica.* St Thomas Aquinas, for his part, saw almsgiving as an obligation in justice.

Congar's second article looks at the tradition of the church as protector of the poor, starting with the Peace of Constantine, by which bishops, who had become *"illustri,"* were charged with defending the weak and underprivileged. In the Early Middle Ages, bishops were given a function as appeal judges. So canon 26 of the Council of Tours in 567 decreed: "Judges and lords who oppress the poor are to be warned by the bishop. If they do not change their ways, they are to be excommunicated." The same principle was embodied in royal decrees, such as that made on the election of Guy, *rex Italiae,* in 889: "If the Count of the place permits an injustice, or practises it or condones it, he shall be considered excommunicated by the bishop of the same place till he makes due reparation." In the High Middle Ages, St Bernard recommended some poor people to Pope Innocent II with these words: "If you attend to your apostolic duty and ancient custom, you cannot reject the cause of the poor nor flatter the mighty." His successor in Clairvaux, Henri de Marcy, taught that prelates had the duty to "protect the poor from the injustices of the rich, and the rich from the snares of the devil." Sadly, Congar is forced to conclude that, except in the thirteenth century, all this teaching and legislation failed to produce the desired effect. The basic cause of this, he says, is that it remained on the level of personal morality, without reaching the *structures* that produced justice and opposition. It never could have reached them—we would add.

## 5. THE TWELFTH CENTURY

### (a) Monks

Spiritual and historical tradition approximates the voluntary poverty of monks to the involuntary—*invitus*—poverty of the poor. When the focus of poverty shifted from the cities to the countryside, monasteries became the main centres of help given to the poor, taking over from episcopal sees. Aid was now institutionalized, adopting "matriculations" and building hospices. Each abbey supported an arranged number (twelve, eighteen, seventy-two, or whatever) of poor people, devoting the tenth part of its resources to this. In the abbeys, the liturgy of service prevented the bureaucratization of charity. The poor, in fact, were welcomed with the ceremony of the *mandatum*, the washing of feet. This was particularly solemn on Good Friday, when each monk would file out to stand in front of a poor person. At a sign from the abbot, they "bowed, genuflected and adored Christ in his poor," then blessing and promising to serve them. This is what the old rituals ordered.

### (b) Theologians

Theology up to the thirteenth century maintained the tradition of the Fathers, but with one new element: frequent reference to the fifth chapter of the Letter of James—the warning to the rich. This theology appreciated the importance of the poor as those who by their work maintain the fabric of society. So it saw the poor as *workers*. It defended strict equality between rich and poor and sharing of goods as a natural right.

It also recognized the *rights of the poor*, particularly that of "theft arising from necessity." This was proclaimed in the context of the famines and plagues of the eleventh and twelfth centuries, which forced the poor to steal in order to survive. The twelfth-century *Lex Rhodia* absolved in cases of "starvation theft," and by the beginning of the thirteenth century the innocence of thieves who stole out of necessity was generally accepted. The Bishop of Paris, Guillaume d'Auxerre, for example, unhesitatingly declared that poor people in need can, without sinning, take what they need in order to live.

The poor did not defend their other rights themselves; if they did, their self-defence usually ended in disaster. Tradition held that bishops should be advocates of the poor at tribunals, and St Bernard describes St Malachy doing just this in Ireland.

Loved and feared at the same time, the poor were seen as:

—the image of Christ the Judge: *vicarius Christi*;

—the intercessor incarnate: "judge and gatekeeper of heaven";

—a new incarnation of Jesus Christ living and present.

But the myth of personal destiny, sanctioned by the will of God, shut out any prospect of a change in the social order.

### (c) Hermits

Up to the year ten hundred, the general attitude toward poverty was one of contempt. Being poor was an indignity, especially for the clergy. Hence the church's insistence on guaranteeing their standard of living by means of a "benefice." It was said that it was as difficult for poor people to enter heaven as for rich, due to the former's envy and anger. A character in a medieval romance, Aucassin, openly declares that he despises paradise as being full of poor and old people. He prefers hell, where one is likely to meet a better class of person. . . .

The virtues recommended were: for the poor, patience; for the rich, generosity. All that we know about the poor of those days comes from works written by the rich for the rich. The poor were simply objects of charity.

This view changed with the hermits of the twelfth and thirteenth centuries. Generally coming from rich backgrounds, they adopted the way of life of the poor, in dress and work. They sought the company of manual workers, farm labourers, lepers and prostitutes. This also led to a growing cult of St Mary Magdalen. The "*liberalitas erga pauperes*" of the rich changed into the "*conversatio inter paupers*" of the impoverished hermits. This marked the start of the prophetic challenge directed at the church to adopt an effective form of evangelical poverty.

The hermits changed the social image of the poor; they began to be seen from the standpoint of the poor themselves. So one of the hermits, Peter of Blois, said: "It is the poor and the weak who will possess the kingdom of God and the Holy Land, the two Jerusalems, the earthly and the heavenly." But it was above all St Francis, followed by St Dominic, who took a new look at the ever ambiguous phenomenon of poverty, and caused the church to do the same. They accomplished this through their radical choice of life *like* and *with* the poor of the city outskirts.

### (d) Apocalyptic Messiahs

Famines were endemic in the twelfth century, which led to outbreaks of rebellion amongst the poor. These had two main characteristics:

—Messianism: the rebellion was usually led by an apocalyptic prophet;

—Milleniarism: people hoped in the miraculous advent of an era of plenty. Abbot Joachim of Flora was the main influence in this movement, with his proclamation of the coming "age of the Spirit."

These sudden outbreaks of anger amongst the poor led to arson, stonings and various other forms of revolt. The main uprisings are known by the name of their leader:

(i) The Aeon of the Star, in Brittany: the prophet demanded the purification of the church, leading a mass of poor people who were put down mercilessly.

(ii) Durando, in 1182: this led to the revolt of the "hooded," which denounced the extortionate rents demanded by feudal lords, denied all hieracrchy and proclaimed an ideal egalitarian society. Accused of heresy, the whole movement was destroyed.

(iii) Guillaume Longebarbe in 1196: the "saviour" claimed for himself the title reserved to bishops—"protector of the poor." He preached equality and moral conversion. He was hanged and the people attributed miracles to him and venerated him virtually as a saint.

Then there was Foulque de Neuilly, who went about shouting: "Feed those who are dying of hunger, because if you don't, you're a murderer!" He attracted a lot of disciples. But in the end he "quietened down" somewhat, accepting favours from the rich, and so ending up largely discredited. . . .

And the Bishop of Plasencia, Raymund, who led a procession of all the destitute of the town through the streets chanting: "Help us, you cruel Christians, because we are dying of hunger while you are swimming in abundance!" . . .

### (e) Canons and Laity

While there were those who defended the poor (bishops), those who fed them (monks), those who thought about their problems (theologians), those who lived among them (hermits) and those who fought for them (messianic leaders), there were also those who actually worked for them. These were those who devoted themselves to "works of mercy" in the twelfth century.

In the first place came the canons, secular clerics who created or restored hospices for pilgrims and the poor, mainly along roads, in woods and hills. Monasteries were no longer able to cope with the ever-increasing numbers of poor people. In particular, a new class of poor was emerging, consisting of outcasts of all sorts: prostitutes, beggars, vagabonds, petty criminals and the like. This situation was brought about by social changes—the growth of populations, cities, wealth—and aggravated by natural disasters.

Then there were groups of lay people, who did most of all, caring directly for the poor, without delegating this task any longer to monks or clerics. They built bridges over the rivers (*pontifices*); they founded confraternities of charity, such as the Hospitallers, who used the formula "Our lords the suffering," which spread to all hospitals. There was also the Order of the Holy Spirit, to which Innocent III gave a house in Rome to take in babies whose mothers would otherwise have thrown them in the Tiber. ... Another lay order was that of Redemption of Captives, whose members took a fourth vow: to set a prisoner free by taking his place, if needs be. It was also lay people who founded the institutes of *Maison-Dieu*, which became widespread. Such lay people counted royalty among their members: Louis VII, Charles the Good, Queen Mathilda, the Emperor Henry V, and others.

All these works were supported by alms, especially those left in wills.

Some lay people went further. A certain Werimbold, grown rich through usury, became a monk with all his sons and then went to live as a poor man in the midst of the poor in order to serve them, eventually dying as one of them.

### 6. THE THIRTEENTH AND FOURTEENTH CENTURIES

#### (a) Backward Thinking—With Some Exceptions

By this time the contrast was between the poor and the merchants (burghers). A new class of poor was making its appearance: the "labouring poor," the exploited workers of the cities and countryside. But the famines of the previous century did not recur.

In this changed situation, preachers, particularly the mendicant orders, still thought of the poor in a conventional manner: thin, blind, ulcerous, feckless, dirty, begging from door to door. . . . This view helped determine their interpretation of the Lateran Council's recommendations of charity. Their solutions were likewise traditional: patience and prayer for the poor, almsgiving for the rich. There was very little talk of reform, and hardly any that went to the heart of the matter.

But there were some exceptions:

(i) An anonymous Friar Minor, in his *Tabula exemplorum*,

declared that the cause of poverty was human selfishness. The creator has provided everything necessary, and people should share this out equally. The deprivation of the poor is the result of the super-abundance enjoyed by the rich.

(ii) A Polish Dominican, Peregrinus of Opole, compared human society to the Red Sea. In the sea, the big fish eat the little fish; likewise in society the rich eat the poor. Now, blood calls to blood, and selfishness begets rebellion. So the world turns red like the Red Sea. ...

The scholastic theologians reflected little on poverty, but when they did so, they took the side of the poor. They condemned usury, expropriation, speculation in prices, tax abuses, arbitrary judgments, unjust wages, and the like. They upheld the teaching on surplus and need, almsgiving and justice. They tried to clarify the ambiguous nature of poverty, distinguishing between the deserving and the undeserving (lazy and criminal) poor.

### (b) The "Charity Revolution"

The thirteenth century saw an enormous proliferation of various institutes of charity. The main one were:

(i) *Almshouses*: These became widespread: in monasteries, in dioceses, in canonries, in the papal court and the princely courts.

(ii) *Lay Confraternities* run on a mutual help basis: These were opened to the poor.

(iii) *Parish Collections*, or *Poor Tables*: These likewise spread widely. Some parishes, as in Valencia, had an office of "bread for the poor" run by a lay person, whose responsibility was to visit the poor and care for them.

(iv) *Justice for the Poor*: This made progress: some states introduced an "advocate for the poor," while the Council of Vienne is 1311 recalled the ancient tradition of bishops as "defenders of the poor," and ordered that clerics alone should plead the cause of the poor. St Ivo of Tréguier was proposed as the model for advocates and judges for the poor.

(v) *Hospitals*: These were the "estates of the poor," places reserved specially for them. They were originally a clerical responsibility, and the Council of Vienne made the clergy swear to carry this out. They then passed into lay and finally into state hands. Some had as few as six beds, others as many as five hundred. Europe had some twenty thousand leprosaria to care for those suffering from this terrible disease which excluded them from society and left them considered socially and liturgically dead.

All this charity was based on personal generosity. Besides the social status attaching to almsgiving, rich merchants also felt "redeemed" by it, since charity—it was said—covers a multitude of sins and guarantees salvation. Alms were given mainly in the form of cash, rather than "in kind"; this left more freedom to the recipients and allowed help to the "shamefaced" poor, as well as to the destitute. One way or another, the personalization of almsgiving did serve to educate the medieval conscience to human needs.

St Louis of France (1214–70) is a good example of the period, combining the saint—going secretly at night to sleep among the poor (in a bed that was then left unslept-in as "blessed Louis' bed")—with politician. In the latter role he worked to make his subjects conscious of the situation of the poor and set up a whole administration for their benefit: almshouses, leprosaria, schools for ex-prostitutes (the *"maisons des filles de Dieu"*) and several hospitals. Not to mention his personal and direct dispensing of justice to the poor, often against the rich, setting up his court under a tree . . .

### (c) Still Backward—With Honourable Exceptions

The end of the thirteenth and early fourteenth centuries saw changes in the economic structure: higher prices, monetary instability, exploitation of labour and the like. In this situation, the "new poor," the wage-earners of the city and countryside, became more prominent. Their situation worsened with a new series of natural disasters: famine, plagues, floods, etc. Many were forced to become beggars and vagabonds. More than a third of the population of Europe was poor in one way or another.

In the cities, the "new poor" were exploited by the wealthy merchants—patrons of the "arts." They lived in a state of permanent indigence, fell into debt and so became totally dependent on rich people, or drifted into unemployment or under-employment, or beyond the normal boundaries of society in one way or another.

In the countryside, the growth of agriculture worked against the labourers: they were forced to give up their lands or live on small plots (six hectares per family on average). Conditions of life and work, already hard, became worse. Many were forced to work other people's land; this was true of 50 percent of English labourers in 1300. Many fell into debt, and with interest rates at 30–40 percent, they had no hope of ever repaying. Forced to sell their land, they drifted into the cities or into vagabondage and often into suicide.

Reflection on poverty still remained backward. The mendicant preachers in particular still "spiritualized" poverty, persisting in seeing the poor in traditional cliches. They did nothing to encourage workers in the towns or country. Their endless sermons on the poor showed no appreciation of the real nature of work and wage-earning.

There were exceptions, however, and these were most expressive. Bernat Puig, a Catalan Carmelite, caused a scandal in Barcelona Cathedral itself on Christmas Eve 1333, when he spoke out against the city councillors, denouncing their speculation in grain prices at a time of shortage. Tadeo Dini, a Dominican, spoke in his sermons of God hearing the "laments of the poor," of their right to a just wage and of their hope of a better future on this earth.

Besides these, there were apocalyptic movements that were inspired by Joachim of Flora and that, like him, preached a better world; among these was the challenging movement of the poor known as the *Apostolici*, who denied any right to private property. Political utopias were devised by various writers; two of the principal exponents being:

(i) *Arnaud de Villeneuve:* His *Dialogue* (1309), addressed to King Frederick II of Sicily, suggested that he transform the royal treasury into a divine ministry in favour of the poor, who were oppressed by the rich, laws and court officials. He recommended the king to ride round his kingdom on horseback getting to know and listening to the poor, devoting a weekly audience to them alone, and several other measures, some of which Frederick II actually went some way to putting into effect. ...

(ii) *Ramon Llull*: His *Blanquerna* (1300) was addressed to the whole church. He proposed that the church should actively take the side of the poor, helping them against the rich. He imagines his protagonist walking down a street, gathering the poor outside the houses of the canons, from which emerge defenders of the oppressed. The first of these is the "canon of poverty," who, like a choirmaster, leads the group, chanting "Justice, justice!," a cry which is echoed by the people. In this way they reach the house of the arch-deacon and finally the bishop's residence. Here the second defender of the poor, the "canon of mercy," appears: as advocate of the oppressed, he denounces injustice and dishonesty, threatening to lead the mob into the streets. Finally, the "canon of persecutions" arrives on the scene, which seems to threaten open rebellion, but elsewhere Llull is more cautious and recommends traditional almsgiving. . . .

### (d) The Anger of the Poor and Those Who Took Advantage of It

Inbuilt poverty, aggravated by natural disasters, led to a number of popular uprisings from the second half of the thirteenth century on. In Siena, for example, the mob took to the streets shouting, "Death to the dogs who are making us die of hunger!" But these popular uprisings were exploited by wealthy people for their own ends; they used the poor as a mass force to further their own power struggles. And in the end it was always the poor who paid in the violent repression that followed.

This happened in country rebellions, such as that of the *Pastoureaux* in France in 1251. Led by a typical "Messiah," known as the Master of Hungary, they invaded Rheims Cathedral during a session of the Synod. Repression was not slow in following; nor was it after their next uprising in 1320. In the towns, the story was much the same. There were endless uprisings throughout Europe in the late thirteenth and early fourteenth centuries. In 1328 the poor people of Flanders rose up in a rebellion that lasted six years before they were finally defeated. They were led by burghers who were vying for power with the church and the local counts. The rich may have seemed to side with the poor, but this was only to take advantage of them; their basic contempt for them remained the same, expressed by the Florentine Caffo degli Agli: "These workers? They're shit!"

### (e) After the Black Death: Support for the Workers

The great plague known as the Black Death decimated Europe in 1348, killing one third of the population, two thirds of those dying being, naturally, poor people. And then the poor had to live with the suspicion, sometimes even the outright condemnation, of being the cause of the plague. . . .

With the Black Death past, the whole of society needed to reorganize itself. As a first step, all wages were raised, by 150 percent in the towns and 100 percent in the country. Then the cost of living rose to meet the increases, and the workers lost their purchasing power. A new element was increased state intervention in the economy. This affected the workers adversely, by setting a maximum wage and taking measures to prevent the able-bodied from begging. So the poor rose up once more, and this time in greater numbers. But again they were seduced by demagogues and their aspirations frustrated. A well-known example was that of the French peasants, known as the *Jacqueries* (*Jacques* being a generic name given to labourers), in the second half of the fourteenth century, against the lords and knights.

The specialization of textile manufacture made the craftsmen more dependent. The introduction of clocks to regulate working hours led to new revolts all over Europe. In Italy, the urban working classes formed associations known as *Ciompi*. In Siena, three hundred people formed their association illegally, in 1371, to fight for higher wages. The *Ciompi* of Florence ran through the streets in 1378 shouting, "We have nothing to eat!" Shortly before, a Franciscan prophet had foretold: "The little will exterminate the great—those worms of the earth!" In Florence, the organized workers actually seized power and set up their own city council—which lasted but one summer.

The revolt of the French artisans known as the *Tuchins* spread through Languedoc and the whole of the South, lasting six years, till 1384. Their cry was: "Let us kill, let us kill the rich!" Revolts spread everywhere: the textile workers of Ghent in Belgium, the peasants in England and Germany, the *Remensas* in Catalonia (autonomous organizations of farm labourers set up in 1400 to shake off the yoke of serfdom).

The greatest popular struggle of the time was that of the Hussites. The movement embraced both peasants and artisans; its ideal was communistic, and its adherents tried to live up to this ideal by setting up communities, such as that of the Volunteers of Mount Tabor. These communities lent strength and discipline to the whole movement, which withstood five crusades sent to crush it, finally succumbing only in 1434.

### (f) Workers' Organizations: Problems of Leadership and Aim

Social upheavals provoked by the poor were mostly urban, and their aims were always the solution of a pressing problem: to stave off hunger, to shake off serfdom, to raise wages or reduce taxes. Their aspirations were generally to share in the advantages enjoyed by the rich: only the Hussites were truly revolutionary; the rest always showed respect for the monarchy. Nevertheless, they engaged in destruction and arson, all sorts of cruelty and even murder.

Solidarity among the poor took various forms. In Portugal, peasants helped one another with their work in the fields; in Ravenna an association of the "shamefaced poor" was started in 1311; in Barcelona and Valencia associations of the blind were formed. And the weavers of Bruges received their rebelling co-workers from Ghent on 3 May 1382 with the cry "All one!" But links among the poor were generally weak. There was a corporate consciousness, but no class consciousness. Their strength was based on their numbers and the concentration of their actions, but they possessed little inner cohesion or continuity. This meant that the leadership of these popular uprisings rarely rose to the occasion. Only Hussite Bohemia produced genuinely messianic leaders, drawn from the ranks of the poor and placed by them at the head of the movement. Most other movements were led by puppets, by poor people who soon allowed themselves to be bribed, or by petit-bourgeois, or by outright demagogues. An example of the latter was Silvestre de Medicis, who renounced his aristocratic title in favour of that of "knight of the poor" in order to gain the support of the *Ciompi* of Florence and so assure himself a private army. The utopian aspirations of the poor made them an easy prey to unscrupulous manipulators of their movements, who usually led them to the scaffold.

The front line in these uprisings was occupied by the working poor. They often demonstrated a good strategic sense: so, to avoid being accused of theft, the *Ciompi* of Florence burned the houses and possessions of the rich. Beggars and vagabonds followed behind, their presence always compromising the movements with their get-rich-quick dreams and their selfishness. In the revolt of August 1378 in Florence, one of their number declared: "We'll turn this city upside down, rob the rich and kill them... we'll be the lords of the city, we'll rule it as God tells us, and we'll be rich."

The church played a major part in these popular movements. It provided their "prophets," such as Taddeo Dini in Florence, and the preachers who spread the church's official teaching on poverty. Above all, it opened the doors of its sanctuaries—churches, monasteries and convents—for the poor to organize their mobilization. In Florence, for example, the *Ciompi* worked out their proletarian programme during night-time sessions in the church of San Lorenzo in July 1379.

### (g) The Driving Ideas behing the Popular Movements

These might be summarized as:
   (i) Straight affirmation of *happiness now in this world*. One

of the *Ciompi* declared: "The time will come when I shall be rich for the rest of my life."

(ii) The sacred right of the oppressed to the *use of force*. They saw themselves as the "people of God" and compared themselves to the exterminating angel. So in Flanders those in revolt thought of themselves as Israel fighting against Pharaoh, or the Maccabees against the foreigners. This was furthermore what the Friars Minor called them at each of the seven masses said for them every Sunday.

(iii) A vision of the *labouring poor as Christ*, as expressed in Langland's *Vision of Piers Plowman*, where Christ is incarnate once more, but this time in the poor. He describes the image of Christ the worker and of the worker as Christ, so the figure of the artisan appears with the instruments of the passion or the halo of the redeemer. . . .

(iv) *Communion of goods*, as proposed by John Wycliffe, who saw poverty as the sign of predestination (the exact opposite of Calvin). John Ball, self-appointed "announcer of the apocalypse," preached common ownership of goods and social uprising, so that there should be "neither villeins nor gentlefolk." Jan of Zeliv, a disciple of John Hus, after describing the "return of the poor," incited the people to armed rebellion and communal poverty.

Faced with these aspirations, the rich and powerful of the time levelled two accusations against the poor: that of *envy*—"revolutionary sin"—for wanting to be equal to the rich; and that of *heresy*, for preaching the reign of God on earth and insubordination to the authorities. These accusations had the effect of confusing many people. An instructive case is that of the Benedictine Thomas Brinton, Bishop of Rochester at the time of Lollardy and the Peasants' Revolt. Before the revolt, his sermons were full of the virtues of poverty and charity. But after the revolt with its violence, looting and assassinations, when its perpetrators were accused of both subversion and heresy, Brinton was a member of the tribunals which condemned them, including the synod of Canterbury in 1382 which condemned Wycliffe. And from then on he never preached another word on poverty.

# 7. THE CLOSE OF THE MIDDLE AGES

## (a) Still Ambiguity on Poverty

With the growth of pauperism at the end of the fourteenth century and the popular uprisings this provoked, the poor increasingly became an object of fear: this on account of their numbers, their anonymity and their potential for revolt. The ruling classes were not wrong in re-evaluating the latter, and so increased their repressive measures. Though the poor may have ended up crushed, they could still make their voice heard and shout: "Present!"

By the fifteenth century, the poor were more and more the workers. There was a net distinction between the idealized poverty of the mendicant orders and the material deprivation of the very present and noisy real poor. Hence the criticism made of the mendicants throughout the fifteenth century: that they should earn their living by working and not beg for alms.

There were two contrasting tendencies during this period. On one side, material poverty was devalued. In effect, it always had been: by feudal lords as a sign of weakness; by burghers as a sign of laziness. But now humanist contempt for poverty took a new and subtle form: poverty was unworthy of human beings. On the other side, the sufferings of the poor were sublimated: they had always been associated with Jesus Christ; now they began to receive the title *"pauperes Christi,"* previously reserved for the mendicants. This ambiguous view of poverty forms part of its long history, but the differences have never been so accentuated as at the close of the Middle Ages.

In theology, St Bernard of Siena and St Antoninus of Florence, archbishop of that city from 1446 to his death in 1459, were prominent in renewing reflection on the basis of the new social problems. Antoninus, son of a Florentine notary, opted for the poor in becoming a Dominican. Besides producing theological treatises on traditional lines (surplus-need, etc.), he put forward the thesis that *the need of the poor imposes an absolute obligation*, whatever poor are in question. The only exception is proper use of one's own bequest. In this scheme, almsgiving is rooted in justice and aid to the poor is given a collective form. In this way Antoninus opened the way for new thinking on organized charity.

### (b) And Still Almsgiving

Even though the face of poverty had changed radically, becoming the inbuilt poverty of the working classes above all, the old remedy of almsgiving was still being applied. People gave directly or left money in their wills to support the "aid agencies" of the day, in particular the almshouses of all kinds: lay, monastic, diocesan, princely.

Hospitals no longer attended to the poor, and the Hospitaller orders were in decay. The rich began to make use of what had been the "estates of the poor," proposing to spend their last days there or place their dependents in them. So for lack of space the poor were put out into the streets or simply never brought to the hospitals. By the close of the Middle Ages, the fourteenth and fifteenth centuries, charitable institutions were unable to cope with the various forms of poverty, especially the widespread poverty of the labouring classes.

### (c) New Charitable Institutions for the New Poverty

By the end of the fifteenth century, a definite process of laicizing charity was under way. The state, which was steadily growing, began to take over the work of the church and private institutes. The process of evolution was a smooth one: in the first place, church and state officials were the same people; in the second, the prince was seen as responsible for justice and as guardian of the common good. It was also in the interest of public order for the state to take on responsibility for care of the poor. King Pedro of Portugal declared, in his *Virtuosa Benfeitoria*, that the state had duties toward the poor. Other rulers, such as Charles V and Richard II, thought the same. The anonymous German author of the *Book of a Hundred Chapters* wrote: "If sovereigns do not take responsibility for establishing a harmonious social order, then the Lord will loose the reins of the poor, who will become instruments of his anger and artisans of his liberation."

This process gave rise to various types of new institutions to remedy the new poverty:

(i) *Confraternities*: These were administered by lay people and subsidized by municipalities. In Geneva they came to care for between two and three thousand poor people.

(ii) *Poor Tables* or *Poor Dishes*: Lay people also operated these, though helped and overseen by church and state officials. Their purpose was to distribute food, clothing and the like to the poor. They also helped workers in difficulties: to pay a doctor, repay a debt, buy a house or a coffin, and so on. They also acted as credit banks and warehouses for the distribution of essential goods.

(iii) *Montepios* (friendly societies): These appeared at the end of the fourteenth century and spread mostly in Italy in the fifteenth. They usually came into being through a preacher denouncing an act of usury; public opinion was roused, and a collection made to set up a fund for the poor. A council was formed to administer the fund, and money from it was lent at 5 percent (levied to cover administration costs only, compared to the 30, 40 or even 50 percent then charged by money-lenders). Bernardino of Feltre, who preached more than three thousand sermons throughout Italy, was a great propagator of *montepios*, and at the beginning of the sixteenth century they were formally approved and blessed by the pope.

(iv) *Reformed Hospitals*: St Antoninus inspired lay people to take charge of the care of the sick, and the state began to take a part in administering lay and church hospitals, initially just through providing subsidies. This evolution provoked tensions in Italy, but in Germany it was regarded as normal for the state to administer hospitals, and wrong for bishops to intervene. Hospitals became larger, and began to specialize: there were hospitals for the blind, for the insane, for syphilitics, for prostitutes, the old, orphans. ... They came to be seen as places in which to recuperate and not simply as places to go to die in, as they had been. For abandoned babies, some churches clung to the old practice of providing an altar or a bed where babies could be brought and left.

(v) The beginnings of *"Policing" the Poor*: After the Black Death, when the state began to play a growing role in society, it was considered that charity had to be deserved: it should be extended only to those who were incapable of living by their labour. So the state turned to repressing beggars and vaga-bonds, who were imprisoned, manacled and put to forced labour in the fields and galleys. Those poor who were genuinely infirm were transferred to asylums in which their subsistence was assured.

## CONCLUSION

Throughout history, the face of the poor is constantly changing. First come the traditional poor: sick, infirm, old or bereaved; then the weak—who have to depend on a powerful protector; then the outcasts: parasites or vagabonds; finally, there is the advance of the "labouring poor": those who cannot earn a living from their work. All these have the common characteristic of being unable to overcome their state of material and moral dependence unaided.

Although during the years we have been examining the number of these "labouring poor" was never very large, this group did acquire increasing social importance: the 40 percent of urban workers in the fifteenth century who were poor were more of a social force than the 80 percent of agricultural labourers who had been poor in the tenth century. From ten hundred onwards, the poor began to find their voice; by the time of the Peasants' War of 1524–5, this had become a mighty clamour.

As for development in the church during the thousand years we have been looking at, it has to be said that Western consciousness of the need to liberate the poor from their poverty was a product of the church. This came far more from what the church actually did—in lives of the saints, charitable institutions, miracle stories, homilies from the Fathers—than from its laws or learned treatises. And yet the church failed to eliminate poverty, not so much through its fault as because new problems continually arose. At the close of the Middle Ages, it lost the material resources for dealing with the new forms of poverty that had arisen, while retaining its moral resources. The state generosity of the sixteenth century was the direct successor of the medieval works of mercy: charity endures as long as poverty.

## Ten Lessons from Ten Centuries

(i) Concern for the poor has been constant in the church. One cannot simply define the time since Constantine as "betrayal of the gospel." The spirit of an "option for the poor" has a long history and is ultimately rooted in the gospel itself. And demand for this option has grown whenever individual Christians or groups of Christians have made the gospel their own, such as monks, religious (particularly the mendicant orders), theologians and especially bishops. These last have an impressive tradition of understanding their function as supporting the cause of the poor, both in maintaining them (*procurator*) and in defending them (*defensor*).

(ii) It is equally impressive to see how the whole history of the church is studded with shining examples of Christians from all walks of life who practised love of the poor to a heroic degree: Zotikos, Caesarius of Arles, Gregory the Great, Martin, Louis IX. . . . No other movement in history can point to such a comprehensive gallery of outstanding figures in this respect.

(iii) The contribution made by the hermits and mendicants to changing the image of the poor within the church must be given its due. By going to live *with* and *like* the poor and no longer just *for* them, they helped foster a better appreciation of the state in which the poor lived and the need to rescue them from it. Another great step in the affirmation of the poor was taken by messianic and apocalyptic leaders, who, not content with living with and like the poor, put themselves at their head in a process of struggle, thereby moving from a mysticism of poverty to a politics of poverty.

(iv) There has always been a notable ambiguity affecting both the image of the poor and of poverty (swinging between rejection and veneration), and of the actual struggles of the poor (with social movements strongly marked by alienation, ineffective strategies and unreliable leaders). This ambiguity is linked to the actual historical settings in which the thinking and practice of the church moved.

(v) The church made a tremendous effort to "solve" the problems of the poor, but failed to see what we can see today: that all this generosity, effective and affective, produced for the poor mere "crumbs" of society's total production. Economic mechanisms and social systems worked in favour of small minorities—among which we have to include the hierarchy of the church. During the Middle Ages, people did not—and could not—see the underlying structures of society, so could not see poverty as a structural problem. They were tied to the idea of society as a static system: people could change their status within this, but what made up the different levels of status— the social system—could not be changed. So the history of the church up to the close of the Middle Ages is the history of poor Lazarus and the *good* rich man.

(vi) Probably the greatest contribution the church made to the liberation of the poor was in educating the conscience of men and women; it made them sensitive to the state in which the poor lived, awakening feelings of mercy and generosity to, and solidarity with, the poor. In this sense the Christian mysticism that saw the poor as the image and incarnation of Christ had an immense influence. Its effects, however, remained on the personal (saints) or institutional (works of charity) level, without ever penetrating to a truly structural level. Nevertheless, one can ask whether the ethical and religious sensitivity to the poor nourished by Christianity was not one of the necessary conditions for the growth of revolutionary consciousness and the science of history. In other words: Christianity may have been the father of Marxism, so that there is a sort of continuity between them going beyond their differences. The relationship between the two is in any case a dialectical one.

(vii) The process of secularization of charity, moving from the official church to the laity and finally to the state (and now to the poor classes struggling for their own liberation), can be seen not as a perversion of Christianity or even as a breaking away from the church, but as a logical development of Christianity in the historical world. If the process is one of emancipation from the church, it is so only in a relative sense.

In any case, it is possible to understand this process theologically as part of the dynamic of faith and the plan of salvation.

(viii) How do we explain the fact that the church's "preferential option for the poor" appears so new today? Such an option is not new: history shows that the church has always been, or at least tried to be, concerned with the poor. This has always been true at least in intention, a principle never denied as such, so why does the "option for the poor" seem like a new phenomenon today? It is because today it has taken a new form, that of a *strategic* option; it is now a matter of opting for the *struggles* of the poor, of working in solidarity with them, of associating with them as the protagonists of history. It is no longer a matter of bending over them full of mercy, like the Samaritan; it is now a *political* question: that of walking along the way of the oppressed. Therefore, it is no longer a question of devising and establishing a whole new network of charitable institutions, one that would finally be adequate in the contemporary situation, continuing the church's long practice in the ten centuries we have been examining. It is rather a question of challenging the system from the standpoint of the popular struggle, of dissociating oneself from works on the social-institutional level and moving to works on the popular-organizational level. This is the *formal* novelty of the "option for the poor" today.

(ix) When one sees how far the church has been involved in social and political questions, it seems strange that we should have to justify such presence and intervention theologically today. It is symptomatic that we have to speak of "political" or "liberation" theology to demonstrate the close links between faith and politics—something that in the past went without question and so without the need for a specific theology to explicate it. . . . We need to see when and why it was first thought strange and unsuitable for the church to engage in politics. This is a recent phenomenon, and is certainly due at least in part to the politically revolutionary stance taken by the church on some questions. This began to be seen as something inappropriate and even perverted when it started contradicting the ruling ideology and system, particularly that of the bourgeois class.

(x) With all this, it is frightening to observe how church

thinking has always lagged behind reality—though there have always been personal exceptions. This may appear normal, but surely it is dreadful that even today sectors of the church still adopt a mentality and practice totally out of touch with the real historical interests of the poor. So there are those who still give primacy to works of charity and almsgiving—things that were shown to be out of date by the end of the Middle Ages. Nevertheless, such attitudes are receding in direct proportion to the advance of a more gospel-guided mentality and practice. At last, we can begin to say *"autres temps, autres moeurs."*

# Chapter IX

# The Churches and the Poor Today

## 1. NEW AGE REQUIRES THE CHURCHES TO RESTATE THE PRIMACY OF THE POOR

The consolidation of capitalist societies in Europe and the United States in the nineteenth century led to a polarization of society into antagonistic classes. New millionaires like the Morgans and Rockefellers owed their position in society to their wealth alone. At the other end of the social scale was a new working class made up largely of people who had been expelled from their land to swell the ranks of an urban proletariat which barely earned enough to live on, in cities such as London, Manchester, New York and Milan.

In the latter part of the century, the working class developed an increasing realization that their survival depended on organizing themselves to defend their vital interests. "Scientific socialism" came into being, combining the milleniarist dreams of earlier radical Christian movements with the militant trade unionism of the factories, and aspiring to make the working classes the standard-bearers of a new classless society. The *Communist Manifesto* of 1848 had pointed to the existence of a deep conflict of interests between labour and capital, a conflict that could be overcome only through the defeat of capitalism. Karl Marx's *Kapital* of 1867 proclaimed violence the harbinger of a new social order already in gestation at the heart of European society. The Communist Internationals which followed took a militantly anti-Christian line, proclaiming that proletarian science required the destruction of religious myths, used by capitalists to cover up their exploitation of the working class.

This situation faced the churches with a powerful challenge, since their mandate from the gospel has always required them to accord a privileged place to the poor. Now poverty was increasing dramatically in scale, with the new element that the poor were forming a class that made up an integral and essential part of world society. The poor, now workers, no longer organized in order to ask for charity, but in order to demand the power needed in order to abolish structures of oppression. This threatened the churches, which socialist workers saw as allied to their class enemies. The organized workers were demanding justice and saw this justice as implying the destruction of social structures that controlled the modern world and systematically impoverished them. If their appreciation of the root causes of their poverty was correct, this faced the churches with a new situation: the evangelical primacy of the poor could no longer be assured through works of charity, but demanded an option for the poor as a social grouping, an option which, while not excluding the rich, would necessarily oppose their interests.

The Roman Catholic Church responded with a "social teaching" expressed in a series of papal encyclicals, beginning with Leo XIII's *Rerum Novarum* in 1891. In this, Rome recognized the legitimacy of the workers" interests, and their right to organize in order to defend these interests, but rejected the socialist demand for the abolition of private property. The root of the problem, according to Leo XIII and the popes who followed him, lay not in private property itself, which is in accordance with God's plan and is a safeguard of human dignity to which workers too should aspire, but in the abuses and lack of honesty and sensitivity shown by the rich and powerful. The pope asked that they should love the poor and deal honestly with their workers, and asked the poor to deal respectfully with their masters in a common quest for solutions to problems affecting them both in the workplace. The general lines laid down by Leo XIII were repeated, confirmed and developed in the encyclicals issued to mark anniversaries of *Rerum*

*Novarum*: Pius XI's *Quadragesimo Anno* of 1931 and Paul VI's *Octogesima Adveniens* of 1971.

In its social teaching, the official church recognized the existence of the poor as a social class with a right to its own organizations. This was still not a clear *option* for the poor, though moves were made in this direction, such as worker priests, John XXIII's pronoucements on the "church of the poor" and the efforts of the Belgian bishops at Vatican II. The difficulty in Europe, however, was that the churches had "lost" the working classes, whose organizations were generally atheistic and they themselves secularized. This made it impossible for the church to make a clear option for them. It was only in Latin America, where the oppressed classes were also believers, that the bishops pronounced clearly in favour of a preferential option for the poor, at Puebla in 1979.

The social teaching of the church in fact served to buttress capitalism, though not uncritically. Its support was conditioned by its critique of the liberal ideology which the bourgeoisie used to overcome traditional barriers in the fields of science, politics, morality and the like. For the Catholic Church, the sticking-point in the debate was the attempt to subject the Bible to the new principles of historical and literary criticism. A series of papal pronouncements by Pius X (1903–14) placed the church firmly on the side of the traditionalists in biblical criticism, and his *Pascendi Dominici Gregis* of 1907 was a sweeping condemnation of modernism. As the twentieth century progressed, the church tried to come to terms with modern thought. In 1943, Pius XII issued *Divino Afflante Spiritu*, which opened the doors for Catholic exegetes to study the Bible using the tools of literary criticism. But it was not till the Second Vatican Council (1962–5), convoked by John XXIII and closed by Paul VI, that the Catholic Church truly came to grips with the modern world of liberal thought.

By this time, however, the ruling classes had begun to move away from this ideology. In "establishment" circles, traditionalism had ceased to be an enemy and was becoming an ally in their defence against the rising tide of socialism. Since the late 1970s we have been witnessing an effort by the elites of wealthy nations to reaffirm traditional values, along with a resurgence of conservatism. The Vatican too is beginning to reconsider its acceptance of the spirit of the modern age.

The same forces have been at work in countries where Protestantism has been the dominant form of Christianity. Germany embraced liberalism rapidly and profoundly: by the end of the nineteenth century, leading church circles were supporting the new "higher criticism." Theological schools submitted the scriptures to a radical historical and literary examination, at times verging on scepticism. Meanwhile, the working classes drifted away from the churches, which found themselves being maintained by a bourgeois state in order to serve the interests of the bourgeois and middle classes.

Liberal ideology also triumphed in United States Protestant-ism, though with more resistance from traditionalists. Anti-modernist forces organized as "fundamentalist" blocs within denominations, and all the churches experienced a power struggle. This was generally resolved in favour of the liberal wing during the inter-war period, with the result that Baptist, Presbyterian, Methodist and other fundamentalists split off into separate groups in order to continue their struggle against modernism. Fundamentalism lost its prominence but did not disappear.

At the same time as the main denominations were embracing a liberal rather than a traditional ideology, they had to face the challenge of the organized poor of the working classes. The result was the same as in the Catholic Church, even though Protestantism replied from a liberal rather than a traditional theological standpoint. The Protestant response to the workers' challenge was the "social gospel." Major representatives of this current were Josiah Strong, Secretary-General of the Evangeli-cal Alliance and author of *Our Country: Its Possible Future and Its Present Crisis* (1891), and Shailer Matthews, Dean of the Theology Faculty of the University of Chicago and author of *The Church and the Changing Order* (1907). The social gospel proposed a programme of service to the poor, particularly the working poor, designed to win them over to the churches and, incidentally, rescue them from the danger of being swept along by currents of revolutionary socialism. A secularized working class was seen as a threat to the churches as well as a danger to the state. In England, the Salvation Army was formed in the late nineteenth century, with a command structure organized on military lines, whose single purpose was to serve the material needs of the working classes and win them for Christ. There was also a (non-revolutionary) socialist current of the social gospel school, whose main spokesman was the Baptist theologian Walter Rauschenbusch, author of *Christianity and the Social Crisis* (1908) and *Christianizing the Social Order* (1911). He was later followed by Reinhold Niebuhr (d. 1971), author of *Moral Man and Immoral Society* (1932) and other works, who had a wide influence on the spread of critical liberalism in political and cultural circles in the United States.

Recent years have seen a resurgence of fundamentalism in the United States, through its alliance with the Reagan administrations and Bush, a new phenomenon in a country where the establishment has always been liberal. This alliance is launching a combined political and religious attack on the main denominations in which the social gospel has prepared the ground for an opening out to popular liberation movements in the Third World.

It is in this context of a society polarized into classes, and a growing poverty linked to exploitation, that we have to see the efforts made by Christian ecclesiastical institutions to turn the primacy accorded by the Gospels to the poor into a "preferential option" for the poor. Latin America has been the first place in which this has been achieved. The background to this has been, in broad outline:

The Second Vatican Council's Dogmatic Constitution on the Church, *Lumen Gentium*, took the image of the church as the people of God as the principal among various images drawn from the Bible. In this document, rather than treat the hierarchy and the laity separately, the bishops dealt at length with the overall composition of the people of God, the whole of which represents Christ in the world (LG 9–17).

It might seem that once this concept of the church had been established, there would be no difficulty in the church making a preferential option for the poor in Latin America, since there the majority of this people of God was poor and oppressed. But the fact is that, for historically understandable and theologically justifiable reasons, churches are also institutions. And all institutions need authority structures to be responsible for preserving their unity and ensuring their growth and institutional wellbeing. With the institutionalization of the people of God, however, the way is opened up for pathologies of power; these come about when the authorities cease to act for the good of the whole and begin to identify this whole with power and the wellbeing of the authorities themselves.[1] So a permanent tension develops within the church, between its nature as the people of God, of the God who loves the poor first, and instincts for preservation, not of the people of God as such but of the institution, or, worse still, of its hierarchy. In this way the church, made up mostly of poor people and confessing itself the representative of the God who made a preferential option for the poor, discovers within itself—once it takes shape in ecclesiastical institutions—tendencies towards self-preservation that pull it in the opposite direction.

In view of this problem inherent in the institution, it is greatly to their credit that the bishops of Latin America, at their Third General Conference, held in Puebla in Mexico early in 1979, should have made a commitment to a "preferential option for the poor."[2] There were differences of opinion among the bishops, and some tried to water down this commitment (as can be seen from the less courageous statements in other parts of the "Final Document"), but nevertheless, the value of the commitment entered into should not be underestimated. It was made at a time of furious conflict in Central America, when Somoza seemed ready to smash the popular movement in Nicaragua in a terrible bloodbath, and when the cost of solidarity with the poor was plain to see.

Previously, at their Second General Conference, held in Medellín in Colombia in 1968, the Latin American episcopate had recognized that the poor were suffering from "institutionalized violence."[3] In the light of this recognition, making a preferential option for the poor inevitably implied entering into confrontation with the ruling powers of society. Faced with institutionalized violence against the poor, denunciations are not enough; an option for the poor must include action to transform unjust structures. Naturally, it is too much to hope that any institutional structure, even those of ecclesial institutions, will always follow the strict logic of its pronouncements, especially when this would threaten the peaceful existence of that institution....

Looking at the position of non–Catholic Christianity in Latin America, we are faced with the difficulty that the Protestant churches have not had any organ with the institutional weight of CELAM (the Episcopal Conference of Latin America) to articulate an official position on the gospel and the signs of the times in relation to the systematic violence wreaked on the impoverished masses. The Latin American Council of Churches (CLAI), an organ of consultation and co-ordination among several churches on the model of those existing on other continents, came into being only in 1982. At its November 1982 meeting in Lima, CLAI sent a brief "Message from the Churches to the Poor of the Continent," which is the most authoritative statement from the non-Catholic churches in recent times.[4] The core of this message is the advancement and defence of life; it condemns torture and "disappearances," "new forms of slavery" imposed on the indigenous peoples, and recourse to policies of "national security" to justify policies of death. All these declarations are good, but the theme of the poor as such is not developed, which means that the official bodies of the Protestant churches on the continent failed to reach the kernel of the gospel requirements as they affect a world marked by the use of systematic violence against the poor.

## 2. THE HISTORICAL WITNESS OF THE CATHOLIC CHURCH IN LATIN AMERICA

The Christian faith came to America with the invasion of these lands by European powers which boasted a far higher military and technological level than the indigenous population. The Spanish and Portuguese invaders were Catholic Christians; the English invaders Protestant Christians. Neither thought of the conquest as a secular endeavour. The English believed they were appointed by divine providence to found a new Israel in a new Promised Land, which they would rule and subject to the

Lordship of the true God. The Iberian *conquistadores* conquered America in the name of the Catholic Monarchs in order, at least in part, to convert the pagan inhabitants.

Spanish domination over the native population of America received ecclesiastical sanction with the bull *Inter coetera* promulgated by Pope Alexander VI in 1493.[5] In this Rome authorized the Catholic Monarchs to conquer the lands of America in order to evangelize their inhabitants. Theological faculties did not lag behind in devising a theology to justify this enterprise. Juan Ginés de Sepúlveda (1490-1573) declared that it was just to wage war on the Indians, since they were inferior beings born to serve; if they could not be made to submit by peaceful means, then it was justified to wage war on them. More cautiously, the Salamancan theologian Francisco de Vitoria did not allow war against the Indians as the objective of the conquest, but allowed it in the event of their resisting the free proclamation of the gospel.

It was inevitable that the light of the gospel should have been dimmed by its insertion in an enterprise of conquest. The dead weight it carried was augmented by papal backing for the evangelization to be carried out by the same powers as were undertaking the conquest. Under such circumstances, the gospel preference for the poor could only be expressed outside official circles. And there were many missionaries who devoted their lives to trying to incarnate the gospel among the Indians. Given the context of conquest and exploitation of the Indian population, this meant that they had to devote a large part of their efforts to defending the Indians against the Christians who were exploiting and killing them. This was the case with Fray Bartolomé de las Casas, and Bishop Antonio de Valdivieso, who was murdered in Nicaragua in 1550 for defending the Indians. In New Spain, Vasco de Quiroga devoted his efforts to creating a craft-based economy which would give the Indians some measure of independence from the *encomenderos*. St Toribius of Mogrovejo, Bishop of Lima, travelled ceaselessly among the indigenous peoples of Peru, trying to give shape to an American church.

It would not be right to interpret all these missionary endeavours as evidence that there was a church based on the poor, since the power of the church came from the same king who authorized the exploitation of the Indians. Nevertheless, in their sermons and in their lives, these missionaries bore witness to the gospel preference for the poor. It is a tribute to their efforts that the poor of Latin America look to the gospel today as a support in their struggle for survival in desperate situations.

The wars of independence waged against Spain in the nineteenth century were a cause of divisions within the church. Many priests identified with the creoles in their struggle for freedom from Iberian domination: outstanding among such were Fr Miguel Hidalgo y Costilla and Fr José-María Morelos y Pabón in Mexico, both of whom took their stand on the gospel, and both of whom were repressed by the church authorities. The Spanish crown enjoyed the right to appoint bishops, and the colonial bishops who owed their appointment to the crown sided unanimously with Spain. The leaders of the independence struggles were certainly not Indians or even *mestizos*, but in comparison with metropolitan Spain they were the "weak" who are favoured by the gospel. The pope and the bishops were impelled by the interests of the institution to take the opposite side.

During the last twenty-five years there has been a growing awakening of the poor in Latin America. Through local groups, indigenous organizations, trade unions, *barrio*-based groups in the cities and even guerilla groups, they have been taking stock of the disadvantages they suffer from in a society based on inequality, trying in various ways to take part in the creation of a new and more just society. Unlike Europe in the last century, this new class consciousness is not a working-class one: the working classes in Latin America are often a very small sector. A greater strength is often found among peasants and indigenous peoples, who have borne a weight of exploitation unlike that of industrial workers under European capitalism. They are also the sectors least affected by modern secularism. This means that the challenge of the organized and combative poor in Latin America presents a very different aspect from that of European socialism as far as the ecclesiastical institution is concerned.

Today the Catholic Church is in a better position to make an evangelical response to this challenge than it was in the earlier periods of conquest and struggles for independence. The Catholic Church is largely made up of the poor. A significant number of its clergy exercise their ministry among the poor, living in conditions that identify them with the cause of the poor. And even its existing alliances with ruling classes are with local bourgeois groups who are seeing their position crumble in relation to those who work for the transnationals.[6] This has also been the period when the influence of Vatican II has worked to promote a greater democracy in institutional church structures. All these factors help to enable the institutional church, at least sometimes, to give a positive response to the demands of the poor as an organized class. One of the best expressions of this was the document entitled "On Justice in the World" produced by the bishops of Peru in August 1971, from which this is section 7:

> Building a just society in Latin America and in Peru requires liberation from the present state of dependence, oppression and deprivation in which the great majority of our people live. This liberation will be, on one hand, a break with everything that holds people back from the possibility of self-fulfillment, on both personal and community levels; on the other, building a new, more human and equal society.
>
> The salvation brought by Christ is not confined to political liberation; this finds its place and true significance in the complete liberation ceaselessly proclaimed by holy scripture....
>
> For the ecclesiastical community of Peru, this implies opting for the poor and marginalized with a personal and community commitment. This option excludes no one from our love, but opting for those who today experience the most violent forms of oppression is for us an effective way of also loving those who, perhaps unconsciously, are oppressed by their own situation as oppressors.

In the huge country of Brazil, where the church has a great deal of influence in society, it took on the defence of those tortured during the harshest years of repression by the military regime. Bishops publicly spoke out in favour of peasants who were being impoverished and repressed, and of native tribes whose ancestral lands were being seized by huge corporations. The church in Brazil gave its martyrs in the cause of their defence, and througout the country a new way of being church sprang up, the base church communities. In these, small groups of the faithful met regularly to reflect on the Bible in the light of their local situation, and on their situation in the light of the Bible. When all forms of popular mobilization were suffering stringent repression, the base communities provided a space in which the people could prepare to defend themselves. The same happened on a smaller scale in other countries, particularly under the military dictatorships of Central America, where through the base communities the Christian presence became a major factor in the popular struggles.

This was the context for the courageous stand taken by CELAM at its 1968 Conference in Medellín. There the bishops as a body declared that the root cause of the destitution suffered by the peoples of Latin America was an oppression built in to the societies of the continent. They bravely took on the task of finding forms of pastoral ministry appropriate to this unacceptable situation of destitution and "institutionalized violence."

The bishops' declarations fell on well-prepared ground in churches across the continent. With apparent suddenness, there sprang up a current of theological and pastoral thought which had in fact been in preparation for some time, and now felt free to flourish in the open. So Latin America gave the universal church its first native theological contribution: liberation theology. Its pastoral reflection based on accepting a ministry with the poor, and its Christian reflection made from the standpoint of the poor who were becoming conscious of their oppression, provided the poor with a theological instrument to use in their liberation struggles. This meant that Marxism was no longer the only theoretical support for the struggle; it provided a local and religious counterweight to a revolutionary theory originating with an industrial, secularized, European working class. There were those who tried to show liberation theology to be a simple Christian appropriation of Marxism, in order to repress it more easily. There are of course points of similarity, since both recognize the poor as a social group systematically impoverished by mechanisms of exploitation. But the differences are quite plain to see: the oppressed of Latin America are not industrial workers, and Marxist analysis cannot be applied satisfactorily to the state of peasants and indigenous peoples. Furthermore, Christian struggles take their inspiration from the exodus, not from the USSR; from Jesus' rebukes to the scribes and Pharisees rather than from the writings of social science. Nevertheless, the poor of this continent whose inspiration comes from their faith do share with their Marxist counterparts the conviction that deep conflicts of interest exist, and that these cannot be resolved except through commitment to justice.

As the poor increasingly used the gospel as a support for their revolutionary struggle, so the honourable company of those who gave their lives as Christians in solidarity with the poor grew. Some fell in actual combat against inhuman and repressive regimes, such as Camilo Torres in Colombia and Gaspar García Laviana in Nicaragua; others died at the hands of assassins because of their pastoral commitment to the poor, such as Bishop Enrique Angelelli in Argentina and Archbishop Oscar Romero in El Salvador. The numbers of lay people, religious and priests who have given their lives in Christian witness are now beyond count. This mass of witnesses gives the option for the poor a power that puts pressure on the hierarchy and helps to explain how CELAM found it possible to overcome the fear dictated by its institutional responsibilities and declare its option for the poor.

## 3.  THE HISTORICAL WITNESS OF NON-CATHOLIC CHURCHES

The Protestant churches in Latin America sprang up in the second half of the nineteenth century. They came from two different movements. The first was the mass emigration of poor communities from central and eastern Europe in quest of political refuge and economic opportunity in the vast unpopulated spaces of Argentina and Brazil. Many of these were Protestants, for whom the gospel acted as a spur to their hopes and also a nucleus of identity guaranteeing their cultural survival in a foreign continent. They felt no need to evangelize the Indians or other poor peoples of the continent. These communities contributed little to the subject that concerns us here.

The other movement that provided the context for the rise of Protestantism in Latin America was the rise of capitalism and its liberal ideology throughout the last century, stimulated by the expansionist policies of England and the United States. As liberals came to power in successive countries, they felt the rooting of Catholic traditions in the masses to be a hindrance to the formation of a liberal culture that would give social acceptability to the economic and political institutions of modern capitalism. Seeing the important place held by Protestant Christianity in Anglo-Saxon societies, they encouraged Protestant missionaries to come from those countries to evangelize and educate the poor. So whether they wished to be or not, the Protestant missions formed part of U.S. expansionism.

While they might objectively have formed part of a new wave of imperialism, however, many missionaries from the United States lived lives of heroic self-sacrifice in commitment to the poor. Protestant mission schools fulfilled their aim of providing a true service to the poor, while embodying the tension between gospel and institution already discussed. While the missionaries at the grassroots devoted themselves to the poor, the stategies behind the mission institutions had other aims: the schools were to form non-Catholic cadres from among the poor who would later become the leaders of a new, open and liberal society in which a Protestant minority was to occupy leading positions in society, and in turn support the grassroots churches. So their preferential option for the poor found expression alongside the institutional aim of using the poor to spread and legitimize a form of Christianity better suited to the needs of capital than traditional Latin American Catholicism.

In the first half of the twentieth century, a new branch of

Protestantism sprang up on the continent: the Pentecostal movement. Though Pentecostalism had originated in the United States, its implantation in Latin America, with the exception of Brazil, was not carried out by U.S. missionaries. It was introduced partly by Latin Americans who had emigrated to the United States, returning later after experiencing the charismatic impact of Pentecostalism. Another factor was growing divisions in the mainstream churches, often in protest at the increasing influence of U.S. missionaries in them. Authority in Pentecostal churches is exercised by local leaders, usually pastors from the ranks of the poor with an empirical theological formation, who use the church as a means of establishing new forms of control over the poor themselves. They use anti-Catholicism as a natural form of self-defence, with the unfortunate result of making this movement a source of division among the poor and preventing it—with some honourable exceptions—from producing the fruit it originally promised as a Christianity of the poor.

The Protestant churches of Latin America have given rise to a number of institutions which live on the fringe of official churchdom, with the support of world Protestant bodies, and have in this way made a valuable contribution to popular struggles inspired by Protestantism. Such are FUMEC (the Universal Federation of Student Christian Movements), ISAL (Church and Society in Latin America) and CELADEC (the Latin Ecumenical Commission for Christian Education). Such bodies have helped to break the ecclesiastical siege laid to the churches in Cuba as part of the blockade mounted against the Cuban revolution, and have produced martyrs in popular struggles against military dictatorships in the South of the continent. They have also helped to develop Latin American liberation theology, which is a theology that moves over confessional boundaries to give expression to Christian faith from a non-sectarian perspective.

Recent years have seen the growth of two opposed strands among the non-Catholic Christians of Latin America. The first of these, with the hesitations to be expected of any institution, is seeking to make a life commitment in the form of an option for the poor; this organized around CLAI (the Latin American

Council of Churches), launched at an assembly of Protestant churches from all over the continent held in Oaxtepec in Mexico in 1978, and ratified in Lima in November 1982. It is a confederation of churches supported by the World Council of Churches.

The opposing strand to this ecumenical openness to the poor is made up of an alliance of those who hold that preservation of the purity of Christianity requires a solid front against any Marxist contamination. They suspect any commitment to the poor as a Marxist front. This movement is institutionalized in CONELA (the Evanglical Council of Latin America), formed in Panama in 1982 and enjoying widespread support from outside the continent, based especially in the "Bible belt" of the South-eastern United States. Even though it claims to represent large number of the impoverished, its ideological characteristics prevent it from making a true evangelical option for the poor.

Both these movements are competing for the loyalty of the non-Catholic Christians of Latin America.

## 4.   IS THE ENEMY OF THE GOSPEL ATHEISM OR IDOLATRY? THE CASE OF CENTRAL AMERICA

Both Catholic and Protestant Christians in Latin America, then, have in the last few years witnessed an increasing polarization revolving around this preferential option for the poor in a society in which the poor are oppressed. This dilemma is experienced in its most dramatic form in Central America, a region convulsed by struggles for liberation from military dictatorships or, at the present time, from equally repressive "Christian Democratic" regimes. Theologically, there have been two different and opposed ways of viewing these struggles. One side sees them as a struggle between faith and atheism, while the other understands them as an expression of a struggle between the God of life and the false gods who demand the death of the poor.[7]

Archbishop Oscar Romero, that courageous witness to a gospel that gives pride of place to the poor, has become the saint of those Central American Christians who see the struggle against the military as one against a false and death-dealing god; this god demands that subversives must die if Christian civilization is to remain alive. Those who kill in order to preserve an oppressive social order become idolators by claiming to do so in the name of God. In Nicaragua, CEPAD (the Evangelical Committee for Aid in Development), an organ which embraces forty-three evangelical denominations, supports the Sandinista people's revolution because it sees it as fighting for the interests of the poor. It interprets the struggle against the contras as a struggle against the idol that needs to kill in order to live.

Pope John Paul II's visit to Central America in 1983 seems to have given expression more to the view of the second camp, which sees the struggle primarily as defending the faith against the atheism of a totalitarian-tending Marxism. From this side, theological interpretations like those of CEPAD run thè risk of letting Marxism into the bosom of the church. The fact that he came with this outlook explains the pope's failure to heed the pleas of the Nicaraguan mothers who asked him, at the open-air mass in Managua, to pray for their sons recently killed in defence of their country. He was afraid of being used by those who were opening the Christian churches to influences which, from this second viewpoint, seem very dangerous. It received even clearer expression in the openly anti-revolutionary pronouncements of the Catholic hierarchy of Nicaragua, who have vigorously condemned abuses of human rights by the revolutionary government against the Miskito Indians, but have remained strangely silent on the subject of the deaths perpetrated, often with inhuman brutality, by the contras. Neither did they condemn the mining of Nicaragua's ports by U.S. agents. Only their understanding of the faith as being attacked by an insidious atheism can explain such extreme partisanship.

Despite everything, no sector of the Christian churches can fail to concern itself with the primacy accorded to the poor in God's eyes and with the resulting obligation on Christians to follow Jesus in solidarity with the poor. What is being debated today is not the principle of this gospel imperative as such, but the way to respond to it faithfully. Over a hundred years ago, we moved into a new phase of history in which poverty is being produced by systematic oppression built into the social structures of our countries. In this situation, the evangelical primacy of the poor becomes the need for a preferential option in their favour, an option which has to cost the institution dear. Although it was not the eccelsiastical institution that first made this option, it has, as we have seen, made valiant efforts to take it on board. There is no doubt that, for the foreseeable future. Christians will continue to face up to this evangelical obligation which faith tells us will lead to our involvement in conflicts that the poor know are to defend minimal conditions of life for them.

# Chapter X

# The Poor and Their Liberative Practices

Who is responsible for carrying the option for the poor into effect? Ideally, everyone, the poor themselves included. The poor called to opt for the poor—is this social egoism? Not at all, since opting for the poor means opting for justice and liberation for all.

Besides, the option made by the non-poor has the final aim of enabling the poor to opt for themselves, to become the living agents of the process of their own liberation. More than this: this option for the poor seeks to have the poor as the protagonists of a liberation that embraces the whole human being and all human beings.

This chapter sketches the actual practice of self-liberation being carried out by the poor of Latin America. It looks first at the new concept of liberative practices which is emerging on the continent; then analyzes the different forms or types of these liberative practices. It explains next how these practices develop in the ethical and political dimensions, and finally lists some of the practices that are ends in themselves, together making up a "culture of freedom." The features described in this chapter are new, and are therefore set out on the basis of personal observation, not taken from learned studies of the subject—which have yet to be made.

# 1. A NEW CONCEPTION OF LIBERATIVE PRACTICE

What does the process of liberation of the poor by the poor consist of? It consists of an integral process, as integral as its objective: liberation. But is it not really a political process, properly speaking? Yes, it is that, but a different sort of political process.

When one looks at the popular movements (those grounded in pastoral practice, trade unions, political parties and so on) that have arisen in Latin America over the past twenty years, one sees that something new in history is taking place. The following comparative table is an attempt to schematize this emergent historical novelty. It tries to enumerate its characteristics, dealing with them in their pure or abstract form, leaving the contradictions and troubles that inevitably accompany them out of account for the moment.

### Concepts of Liberation

| *New (Latin American)* | *Classical* |
|---|---|
| 1. *Politics:* social life in general | *Politics:* power struggles |
| 2. *Agent:* organized people | *Agent:* party and/or class |
| 3. *Leadership:* internal and autonomous to the people | *Leadership:* by intellectuals outside the people |
| 4. *Type of leader:* animator<br>–a centre articulating the dynamism of the base<br>–with transitory and passed-on functions<br>–with shared powers | *Type of leader:* chief<br>–source of all dynamism: sets objectives and gives orders<br>–professional politician or revolutionary<br>–with power concentrated on himself |
| 5. *Methodology:* from bottom to top<br>–passing from practice to theory<br>–spreading from base to summit | *Methodology:* from top to bottom<br>–passing from theory to practice (application)<br>–spreading from summit to base (orders) |

*(a) The Idea of Politics: Social Life*

The new groups among the people are becoming used to seeing politics as the totality of their life in society. One often hears said: politics is everything—educating one's children, organizing a meeting or a strike, or even hearing mass. Politics thus becomes life in society taken on consciously. In this way, politics re-acquires its oldest meaning, that of living together in society, or human inter-relatedness within the *polis*.

This goes beyond the strict interpretation of politics as something that is the business of governments, political parties or revolutionary movements. Rather, it embraces any form of participation within the ambit of civil society. And this participation is not only through existing organizations—schools, unions, churches, and the like—but also through any other type of spontaneous and autonomous activity—meetings, neighbourhood schemes, etc.

Still more: politics is everything that touches social life, whether directly or indirectly. In this sense, politics is more than an activity: it is an all-embracing *dimension*. So, politics can be found as much in a celebration of mass as in an election—each in its own way, naturally.

So the idea of politics has been enormously broadened. But this is not to say that it has simply become identified with the whole of human life. This has levels of reality which politics still does not touch. So horizons of individuality or human transcendence remain. To say that the political and human are interchangeable would be giving way to totalitarianism, consciously or unconsciously.

This is one danger: pouring all that is human into the realm of politics. But there is another danger: widening the concept of politics to such an extent (pouring everything political out into the realm of humanity) that one no longer cares about actual organization of popular forces, even at the level of political parties.

In the base communities, it is worth noting, the people talk not so much about "politics" as about "life"; so, for example, they speak of the "religion-life" relationship. "Life" here is a richer concept than politics, whether the latter is understood in its modern or classical sense. It includes these understandings of politics and goes further, embracing dimensions that cannot be reduced to politics, such as spiritual experience and the final destiny of humankind and history.

### (b) The Agent of History: The People Organized

Note that the language of popular movements in Latin America uses the term "people" rather than "class." This is first for an analytical reason: social classes in our societies still do not possess definite outlines; second, because social change is the concern of all the people, understood here as the sum total of the oppressed or "subordinate classes." All these are related to the ruling system—capitalism—either through integration or exploitation or exclusion from the system, with the consequent results of unemployment, lack of consumption, etc.

So it is that each oppressed social group (exploited or excluded) possesses a specific political potential. This is also true of the great and largely unorganized masses on the periphery of the system among whom much of the church's work is done contributing to their acquisition of better-defined political form and organization.

Of course one still needs to see how the various popular forces (classes, sectors of classes, etc.) relate to each other within the overall struggle: vanguard or front groups, support groups, etc. But we need to do this without losing sight of the overall unity supplied by the oppressed people, concerned as a whole in overcoming the system that exploits or excludes them. Therefore any specific organization within the people (union, party, armed movement) has to be placed and defined within this greater historical unity. In particular, political parties are not suppressed, but rather redefined: they are the oppressed people organizing themselves in parties.

This is also how we should see all the other forms of oppression which, though basically conditioned by economic (class) oppression, are more than that since they each possess their specific character: racial, sexual, religious, cultural, and so on. These in turn produce a rich variety of historical agents, as of their projects and their struggles.

In the same way, "people" is here not such a broad concept as to encompass the whole nation indiscriminately, except as a "projective concept," in the sense of something providing an ideal pointer to such an identification in the future. In the past, the nationalism that identified people and nation served (and still can, in specific circumstances such as revolutions) to mobilize the masses on a broad front, especially against foreign forces and their internal allies.

### (c) Leadership: from Within

This is probably the first time in the history of our peoples that popular movements have been generated and led by the people themselves and not from above or outside—as happened till recently with populist movements.

In the most self-aware and active popular circles there is a growing instinctive rejection of leaders who come from outside and claim to "guide the people" or "lead the process." There is a greater awareness that only those who are "of the people" can really be representative of them, so that there is a social homogeneity between represented and representative. In this way, representation becomes representation-from and not representation-to. In party circles one hears "workers vote as workers" and "people represent people."

### (d) Type of Leader: Animator

The type of people's leader emerging is not one of the *caudillo*, *duce* or *führer* sort. He or she is simply and more humbly an animator of the community, a co-ordinator or catalyst of the dynamic coming from below and existing among the people. Not a creator of social life, but an organizer and articulator of it.

In this the new type of leader of the people is a far cry from the classical political leaders of the past, both from the liberal type (whether oligarchical or populist) and the Leninist model ("vanguard," "professional revolutionary" or "democratic-centralist"). And the new type of leadership is not authoritarian, as can be seen from the following points:

(i) The new leaders are true *servants*: they occupy a subordinate position as promoters or articulators of movements that precede them and come from the bottom. They are not "heads" of groups, dictating objectives and giving orders. This means they are chosen by the people at the base and not co-opted or simply imposed.

(ii) They *pass on* direction among themselves and so exercise it in a transitory fashion *(ad tempus)* and not a permanent one *(ad vitam)*. So there is no way they can become fixated on power and this in itself removes the abuse of it.

Finally, they exercise power *collegially*, that is, sharing their responsibilities with others, so as to prevent any abusive concentration of power.

So, this new form of power among the people is permanently subject to three control mechanisms: choice by the people, revocability and division. These mechanisms are supplemented by other measures taken so as to safeguard the exercise of authority as service: absence of reward, periodical and public rendering of accounts of their stewardship, direct and general consultation with the bases on important matters, and so on.

### (e) Methodology: From Bottom to Top

Those who lead present-day popular movements always start from reality, that is, from the problems and struggles of the people, and not from already established theories or doctrines. This means that they value practice above theory. Not that theory is dispensed with, but that it is always placed at the service of practice and created and re-created in function of practice.

New leaders are different in this from the old "cadres" of the Leninist type, who always seemed first to be "appliers" of ideas or programmes worked out in advance (on the grounds of the "scientific" nature of Marxism), thereby showing themselves more doctrinarians or ideologues than realistic discerners of the historical process.

Furthermore, these new leaders differ from the Leninist type (still active in classic left-wing movements) in giving priority to the base rather than the summit, to the people rather than the apparatus of leadership, to class rather than party. So the people can never be treated as a mass to be manipulated, but are treated as a historical agent to be awakened, called together and mobilized.

## 2. WHAT ARE THESE LIBERATIVE PRACTICES?

What, specifically, are the struggles in which the poor of Latin America are engaged? What collective actions are they taking part in so as to express their option for a new world?

Two types of practice can be distinguished overall: the first more diffuse and diversified, the second more defined and organized.

### (a) Diffuse and Diversified Practices

These are carried out on what some call the "pre-political" level; but these practices are, in the new understanding of politics as living in society, fully political, though in their own way. They comprise all acts of community participation and popular organization which could also be called "grassroots democracy," and which express the ideal of autonomy: the autonomous adminstration of life together in community.

They include:

(i) *Ways of resisting* social exclusion and rejection. These really form a way of life rather than a series of specific actions. This is made up of the whole psychological, moral and religious, but also economic, political and cultural, reaction that the most oppressed people oppose to the continual assaults of mechanisms of domination and marginalization. This generalized resistance can have manifestations ranging from a religious pilgrimage to an economic boycott or squatting in defiance of an eviction order.

(ii) The *cunning devices* poor people use to "get by" in life, the "knack" they have for getting out of "messes," the "schemes" they devise for resolving complicated situations. All these make up a real "underground politics," a labyrinth navigable only by those who spend a long time in the most submerged sectors of society, and which they employ to frustrate all the stratagems of dominant thinking. How do these people survive on what they earn? How can a widow bring up ten children on a domestic servant's pay? How can a whole family live in a one-room shack? The questions are endless, and unanswerable by normal reasoning.

And it is not only in the field of economics that the poor surprise us with their "mysteries"; it applies in the wider political field too. How does a mother loaded down with children find the time to act as community leader? Why does a candidate who has done everything legal and illegal to win not get the people's vote? Why has a particular subject put on the agenda for discussion been boycotted by a wall of silence? And so on and so on. It all amounts to a fine "know-how," a sophisticated cleverness that can be learned only from life and that enables the weak to mock the strong, frustrate their endeavours and affirm their own social being.

(iii) *Autonòmous actions*: All sorts of personal initiatives in the sphere of self-help are taken by the poor—lending money or something needed, looking after a neighbour's baby, lending a hand to build a house, telling someone where to go for a loan, where work is available, visiting someone who is sick, and so on. All these build up to a fine, self-contained network of little gestures woven by the people among themselves to give each other strength to "carry on." Some actions in this category are more definable, if still spontaneous: joining forces to build a school or a road, organizing a religious festival, getting up a petition, and the like.

### (b) Defined and Organized Practices

Besides the types of action outlined above, the poor also know how to commit themselves to courses of action with a more definite social and political content:

(i) *Acts of protest or challenge*: These are the actions through which the poor put economic and political powers under pressure to recognize their rights. They include marches, strikes, rallies, sit-ins, boycotts and so on, which, even if they cannot eliminate oppression, may at least make it more bearable.

(ii) *Action to organize*: It might be starting a local group or cell for political purposes, reclaiming a trade union from the hands of venal "delegates," setting up a co-operative, starting a base community in the district.... Since the 1960s Latin America has seen an impressive multiplicity of these autonomous people's associations spring up.

(iii) *Party politics*: The poor of Latin America are discovering the importance of political parties for their effective liberation. And so they are showing an increasing interest in party politics at all levels: voting, canvassing and even leading. This is an excellent field in which to judge the degree of political consciousness acquired by the poor, seeing how far they vote for their own interests or for those of their oppressors. Furthermore, here and there on the continent, parties or embryonic parties are beginning to appear whose origins are really from the people, parties or projects for parties generated and led by the people themselves and therefore different in kind from others. The option of the poor for the poor is also and in a very particular way being expressed along this historical route.

(iv) *Armed resistance*: When their own lives are threatened, the poor do not hesitate to take up arms in justifiable self-defence. More than anyone, they regard this as a last resort, to be adopted only in exceptional circumstances. But there are circumstances in which, against their will, the poor are forced to use legitimate violence to assert their rights. Such circumstances would be if their land were invaded, or an armed uprising occurred against a prolonged and bloodthirsty tyranny, like the uprising in Nicaragua, in which many Christians took part and which was legitimized by the bishops (31 July 1979). The poor sometimes also resort to acts of violence in order to survive: armed robbery, kidnapping and other sorts of social criminality. These are doubtless pathological reactions to situations of institutionalized violence, which really need to be countered by more positive and effective forms of action.

## 3. HOW LIBERATIVE PRACTICES ARE CARRIED OUT

*A new ethic of struggle* is taking shape alongside and as part of the new concept of politics among the poor of Latin America.

By "ethic" we understand the way an action is carried out, a way of acting, a basic mode of behaviour. For the sake of simplifying, this term can be taken to include what comes before action, a mystique, and what comes after, a strategy.

These, briefly and deliberately idealized, are some of the main characteristics of this new political ethic:

### (a) Preference for Peaceful Means

Our people are not natural extremists, prone to act from sudden passions. They have the good sense to prefer rational means: persuasion, dialogue, negotiation. . . . Being polite and conceding can be a definite sign of political intelligence. Nevertheless, the weapons used in the struggle can move in a *crescendo* from dialogue, through strikes or public demonstrations to violent confrontations. Even so, face-to-face combat as a principle of political action does not correspond to popular instinct. Only when incited or induced by thoroughly indoctrinated external agents (such as the *enragés* of petty-bourgeois intellectual bent) will the people "go it alone" and embark on violence.

As a rule, the people believe in the power of truth and justice. They have the conviction that, sooner or later, reason will out. This conviction is deeply rooted in religion. So they have sayings such as: "When God delays, it means he's coming soon," and "Human justice fails; God's never does."

### (b) Respect for the Rights of Adversaries

Politics is subject to rules. Not everything goes. The people believe this, know it instinctively. This is why they go on giving those who oppress them, taken individually, credit for good will. They believe that they may give in, change their attitudes, even though they know that a "class conversion" is an illusion.

The people know the ethical limits of struggle in a practical sense. They are for example capable of going to the funeral of an oppressor and praying for his "eternal rest." They will also sorrow over family misfortunes of notorious exploiters, and observe a sort of truce when they find themselves alongside their bosses at a football match, festival or carnival.

In this sense, the people have a wider and more generous social outlook than other classes. The new society they seek to install is decidedly all-embracing, with a place in it for their old adversaries. It will provide the opportunity for all to live in fellowship with their brothers and sisters. Nor, it is commonplace to observe, do the poor "damn the rich to hell," as the middle classes—more resentful and therefore more implacable and impious—tend to do.

### (c) Openness to the Non-poor

The people will welcome anything that helps them to live and struggle on. Only a dated class outlook—typical of petty-bourgeois extremists—will refuse to allow agents who are not from the people to participate in the people's struggle. There is a movement called "workerism" that thinks like that.

This openness of the people to those who are not of them also applies to larger groups of the non-poor, such as those sectors of other classes who seek to attach themselves to the people when their interests coincide—in overthrowing a dictatorship, changing labour laws, and the like.

Nevertheless, the most aware popular groups know that such alliances are always dangerous and need to be subject to the control of the people themselves if they are to be fruitful. Otherwise they are merely being duped.

### (d) Realistic Expectations

In social and political terms, the people are not usually utopian. They do not ask for the impossible. They do not feed the ambitions that their oppressors lay on them. What they really want is to satisfy their basic needs: food, shelter, clothing, basic health care and elementary education. This might be called their "little utopia," a sensible, reasonable utopia. If a system—capitalism in the case of Latin America—cannot bring this about, it is because the system is unreasonable, anti-human and absurd. Therefore it has to be replaced.

This is when the horizon of the "great utopia," that of an alternative historical project, opens up—democratic socialism, for instance. But such a utopia can be established only on the basis of the real advances made by the people on the level of awareness and struggle. This "great utopia" has now been awakened in the consciousness of the most mature popular groups and from them is being more widely spread among the people.

### (e) The Greater Utopia: Integral Liberation

It should not be thought that the people are content with the "little utopia," since the people cannot be judged by the standards of husbandry. They want to be more than a well-nourished and healthy flock. Yet the popular spirit cannot fully be satisfied even with a "great utopia," made flesh in a historical development. What they are looking for is in fact "a full life," that is, integral liberation. This is what can be called a "greater" or "greatest" utopia.

This is expressed on various levels, from general desires: "Oh, if only everyone could eat as God wishes. . .," through historical hope: "Once the people have power in their own hands. . .," to eschatological hope: "But that will only happen in heaven. . . ." The one thing that is clear is that full liberation will only come about "in heaven," beyond history. This is absolute utopia. Such is the religious conviction of our religious people. Only secularized intellectuals can put forward and cultivate the idea of a "paradise on earth" as the sum total of human hopes.

And yet, this (ultimate) eschatological hope still ferments in the hearts and between the hands of the people. It is in the name of the ultimate utopia that the foundations of an absolute future can be laid in this world, in the shape of an egalitarian society.

### (f) A Positive Struggle, Free from Resentment

It has often been noted that the people do not take on the strident tones of voice and modes of behaviour associated with petty-bourgeois militants, those whom Nietzsche castigated: "Preachers of equality, to me you are tarantulas thirsting for secret vengeance" (*Thus Spoke Zarathustra*, Part II). The militants among the people have a more integrated social posture; they have interiorized their feelings, can be indignant without rancour. They act *with* passion, but not *from* passion. They know how to combine social indignation with human gentleness.

This is why they struggle *for* rather than *against*. Theirs is a struggle for life and dignity rather than a struggle against the "bosses." This is an element in it, but the *against* has been integrated in a greater *for*. So the militants of the people keep their humanity in their struggle. In the "teeth of the storm" they can talk about their wives and children. Not for them the tensed face, clenched fist and snarling teeth; they won't let the political struggle descend to an animal level. If you're fighting monsters, there's no need to turn into a monster yourself. They really are convinced that "the meek will inherit the earth."

### (g) Permanent Conversion

The poor do not usually have an idealized or fetishistic view of themselves. The poor people who make up the base communities know themselves to be sinners in need of grace and salvation like everyone else. So they too feel themselves called to conversion. They realize that the oppressors they are fighting are prisoners of their own consciences.

This means that the struggle is not confined to the political sphere; it is also a struggle against oneself. Along with the liberation of society, there is also—above all, even—a need for the liberation of hearts and minds—from fear, from corruption, from selfishness, from the will to power, from unfaithfulness, from ambition. Liberation *from* goes with liberation *for*: for grace, for love, for freedom, for life.

From which the struggle for liberation will be seen to be a *self-involving* process. It is not just a question of liberating others, but also and even more of liberating oneself. So liberation can be compared to a tree, thrusting its branches with their flowers and fruits up into the air, but at the same time burying its roots in the deep bosom of the earth. For these new fighters, conversion and revolution go hand in hand: revolution

is the outcome of conversion, just as the tree is the outcome
from the seed sown in the soil.

In conclusion, one might say that the new ethical-political
type emerging among the poor of the base communities in Latin
America is a mixture of the serpent and the dove, of historical
intelligence and human goodness. It is what Nietzsche called
"the soul of Christ in the body of Caesar," the learning of Marx
with the conscience of Gandhi.

## 4. THE CULTURE OF FREEDOM

It would be a great mistake to suppose that the poor live so
submerged in the "sphere of need" as to be totally estranged
from to the "sphere of freedom." Of course their whole lives
are marked with the "struggle for survival." "The life of the
poor is an endless battle," the people say expressively. For a
large part of the population of Latin America, the destitute or
*lumpen*, the conditions of existence are so tyrannical that life is
degraded on every level: psychic, cultural, social and moral.
Yet even so, among the great majority of the poor—those who
live at or just above survival level—and even among the
destitute, one can find an impressive feeling of dignity and a
vigorous expression of a positive and joyful taste for life.

There is no space here to go into the whole richness of
popular culture, just to emphasize what can be called the
"culture of freedom" as expressed by the popular classes in
Latin America. This "culture of freedom" forms something like
an atmosphere in which the struggles of the poor for their
liberation are carried on and which gives this struggle a quite
special touch. This atmosphere is made up of life-affirmation,
of the will to move forward, of hope ("Tomorrow, God willing,
all will be better"), of a sort of existential vibrancy.

Anyone who has been in contact with the people knows their
intense life style: the crowds of children running about all over
the place, "ghetto-blasters" on full volume, people singing or
chanting as they work or walk, the noisy laughter coming out
of the bars, and so forth. This is a whole atmosphere that lies
beyond politics, that cannot be defined in any category, but
represents their life itself, their way of being. Rather than

something indeterminate on its own, it is what informs all their actions. It typifies the poor in their humanity. It expresses the "transcendence of the oppressed." It shows that the life of the people cannot be reduced to work (on the economic level), but also includes dance; that it is not just a struggle (on the political level), but also play; that it is not just theory (on the cultural level) but also poetry and creativity. Thus the poor combine the sphere of need with the sphere of freedom. But what characterizes this "culture of the freedom" among the poor? Let us look briefly at its components:

### (a) Cultivation of Beauty

Flowers and greenery around their houses, or inside them, designs on walls, a whole variety of ornamentation; the impression made by a sickly little girl "treating herself" to the luxury of plastic bangles on her skeletal arms. The poor love adorning themselves: from out of the most miserable hovels come girls with painted nails, scented and decked-out with jewelery. Whatever their ambiguities, such scenes prove that the poor try to use beauty as a way of transcending the state of oppression they live in, of stating that they are not just creatures of need, but creatures of freedom too.

### (b) Human Love

Love always puts people at a certain distance from economic considerations, though it is strongly marked by them. But there is no doubting the fact that maternal tenderness, loving friendship, passionate desire and erotic love are deep human experiences which the poor feel with special intensity. One would have be very narrow in one's outlook to be surprised by the fact that the poor too can love.

### (c) Conviviality

Simple people enjoy being in crowds: the more people at a mass, in a procession or at a festival, the better! The poor have none of the aristocrat's *odi profanum vulgus*. There is nothing more lively than the chatter that goes on in various groups: men in a café, women washing clothes on a river bank, neighbours in front of a house at the end of a day, friends and relatives on a visit to someone's home. The talk flows fast and free. It will touch on the difficulties of life, no doubt, but also covers the past, fantastic stories and . . . "the beyond." Jokes are told and this or that person gossiped about, while time rolls by. Time is not really money.

### (d) Humour

This is another way in which the poor can transcend the harsh conditions of their lives. There are tricks to be played on each other, ingenuous jokes made at the expense of friends, ironic comments passed on the great and pretentious, and a host of other sources of comedy and laughter. The most serious situations can be relieved by a sudden witty sally; everyone laughs and the struggle goes on refreshed. Humour is a recourse to which the poor turn their hand to put distance between themselves and the harshness of life, to "get a jump ahead."

### (e) Festivals

The poor throw themselves into festivals—weddings, birthdays, saints' days—with rowdy intensity. This is where you can find the one feature of any good festival: *excess*—excess of food, excess of drink, of light, flowers, music, people and everything else.

### (f) Leisure

One only has to think of the great manifestations of popular entertainment: football matches, carnivals, summer festivals and the like. Here the people are the subjects and the players, relegating the others to the role of spectators. Here too, whatever "ideological use" is made of these occasions cannot rob them of their basic function, which is to be a form of freedom and creativity.

## (g) *Popular Religion*

Popular religion is certainly a "religion of affliction," and
therefore a "religion of resistance." It is this because it
represents the sacred language of a life that is both oppressed
and irreducible at the same time. And yet popular religion is
more than this; it is also a special way for the people to express
their freedom and greatness. This can be seen particularly in
the doxological expressions (praises) of popular piety: festive
hymns, litanies and interminable refrains. And with these go
the profusion of flowers, the decked-out floats, the painted
statues, the fireworks, the brass bands—the whole fringe, or
rather solid nucleus, of human and spiritual greatness that
cannot in any way be reduced to economic terms, but which
rather proves the fruitful, self-directed dimension of existence.
All this gives life the grace and enchantment the poor
experience more fully than anyone else. It is from this
"ontological excess" that the struggle for existence gains its
ultimate meaning and depth.

# Chapter XI

# Practical Aspects of the Option for the Poor

## 1. SPECIFIC CHARACTERISTICS

The option for the poor, as we have seen, is one form—and today the decisive one—of Christian love. To define it better, we now need to look at some of its specific characteristics. These are that it is:

    (a) Practical or effective;
    (b) Participatory, in solidarity;
    (c) Political or structural.

### (a) A Practical or Effective Option

Opting for the poor involves specifically liberative action. Here we have to beware of two temptations: resting content with mere feelings, or with mere words.

    (i) The option for the poor is more than *feeling*. True, it involves feeling: of compassion in the face of suffering and of indignation in the face of injustice. These feelings were characteristic of the heart of Jesus of Nazareth (Mark 3:5—compassion; 6:34—indignation).

    But if we remain on the level of feelings alone, we fall into sentimentality and treating the poor as "poor little things." True compassion, on the other hand, overflows into action: it is active. So was that of Jesus, as shown from the passages referred to above. Nor was the good Samaritan's reaction any less active: "But a Samaritan traveller who came upon him was moved with compassion when he saw him. He went up and bandaged his wounds, pouring oil and wine on them. He then lifted him on to his own mount, carried him to the inn and looked after him" (Luke 10:33–4).

So opting for the poor is not just feeling sorry for the poor or distress on their account. It is this and much more: it is a love that activates and liberates.

(ii) The option for the poor is more than *words*. If the first temptation is that of the ordinary run of men and women, this is that of intellectuals and leaders, who are easily satisfied with words and ideas. The option can be reduced to these on two levels:

(a) On the level of *argument*. Making pronouncements and issuing declarations, signing petitions, writing impassioned letters to the newspapers, giving courses and lectures, writing books and articles, and the like: all this can be necessary in terms of the option for the poor. But on its own it is far from being enough. Nothing can take the place of specific action in a given situation. Poverty is above all a (real) problem, not a (theoretical) question; it is a concrete situation and not a subject for study. Being content with words, ideas and essays is falling into rhetoric and academia. Faced with the endless studies economists and now theologians have produced on poverty, we always need to ask: Who are the historical subjects of the questions raised in them? What are the real poor—those really interested in and concerned by poverty—like? Only this can point up the historical relevance of such studies, which means the actual *threat* they pose to the *status quo*.

(b) On the level of *prophecy*. Denouncing injustices and proclaiming a new world, the messianic Kingdom: this is the bounden duty of every prophet. But, again, it is not enough on its own. Prophets can be heard to rattle on to the point where they become boring and annoying; then their words lose their effect and even become counter-productive. At some stage they have to move to action, and then words cease.

So it is clear and accepted that the option for the poor must, above all, be a *practice*. Of course this practice may be a cultural practice, such as taking classes. But this practice in turn has to open out to concrete practice and lead to it. Because only concrete practice can change an actual, real situation.

### (b) A Participatory Option

The very phrase "option *for* the poor" can lead to a paternalistic understanding of its object: that of some people fighting on behalf of others and, in particular, the church taking the side of the poor. Here the poor are reduced to the status of *objects* of Christians' love. This puts them in a position of dependence, like children in need of instruction.

To avoid this understanding, today we speak of working *with* the poor rather than of working for them. So Puebla spoke of an option "expressing . . . solidarity with" the poor (1134). In this view, the poor are truly subjects, agents: "our" relationship with them is one of symmetry or equality; they are our brothers and sisters, our friends, our companions, our partners in joint action.

If we start from this understanding, we can then see an option for the poor as including working *for* them, in the sense that such work is a first step in the process of autonomization, a process leading from "for" to "with." In fact this process is part of the pedagogical or socio-political reality of working with the people in general. There are times and situations in which one can only work *for* the poor, when it is not yet possible to work *with* them. This is true above all when dealing with those who are defenceless or abandoned. But we have to bear in mind that our "for" is always inspired by its finality in a "with." *Opta aequalem*, says St Augustine: meaning, struggle so that the poor may become your equals—and you theirs.

The same logic requires a true option for the poor to set aside all idea of paternalism or permanent tutelage. But to do this we need to unmask the various guises in which paternalism comes.

The logic of paternalism starts from "in favour of," and moves through "in place of" to end with "on the pretext of" or "without"—when it does not end tragically in "at the expense of," or even "against" the poor. This contemptuous treatment of the oppressed, seen as "things" to be defended or favoured, is in evidence both in the economic paternalism of the Right and the political paternalism of the Left.

The economic paternalism of the Right is the stuff of liberal technocracy. This seeks to save the poor without their cooperation and ultimately at their expense. Its political embodiment is populism, the classic expression of an option for the poor as substitution, speaking in "their name," taking on their representation, while actually gagging their mouths and tying their hands.

The political paternalism of the Left, though plausible in its aims and intentions(!), is dangerous and even deadly in its methodology. Like the methods of the Right, it seeks to liberate the poor without involving them, or by manipulating them. It is paternalistic in that it seeks a revolution in which it is for "us"—the Left—to solve the problems of "them"—the poor. The Left may free itself of the vice of technocracy, but it still sees itself as the vanguard, the motive force of history. And if the people—reified once more—resist its proposals, they are regarded and treated as "backward," "reactionary," "conservative," in need of education, which means domestication (by police violence or ideological or even therapeutic conditioning. . .).

To sum up: the option for the poor means putting ourselves on the side of the poor, in solidarity with them in their cause and their struggle, not to make them our allies, but to make ourselves their allies.

### (c) A Political Option

This is perhaps the most obvious characteristic of the option for the poor as a new form of love—precisely "political love." It certainly rejects "aidism," but not aid in the shape of charity or disaster relief. It certainly rejects "reformism," but not reforms and other improvements that mark steps forward on the way to liberation. It seeks the real-life transformation of social structures, a new society without whole classes or masses of people living in poverty.

All this makes the option for the poor a political option. It even includes a class option, though it cannot be reduced to this. In this sense, it involves the conscientization, organization and mobilization of the poor and those who ally themselves with them. The impressive "works of charity" carried out by so many saints (Vincent de Paul, Elizabeth of Hungary. . .), by innumerable religious orders (particularly in the last century), by so many great humanitarians (Schweitzer, Ramakrishna, Mother Theresa. . .), despite all their mysticism and heroic abnegation, have not succeeded in their desired aim: to abolish poverty and social marginalization. Because they depended more on individuals than on structures, they proved ultimately incapable of overcoming poverty on the scale we know it today.

Poverty today is in fact an endogenous phenomenon: it is a by-product of the capitalist system itself. So if we are to overcome poverty, we have to change the system. And this can only be done through appropriate political action.

All this means that the option for the poor, if it is to be genuine, has to move beyond all forms of aid mentality, as expressed in works of charity and campaigns of "social work" or "advancement" for the poor and needy. It is rather a matter of awakening the poor to their rights and the "noble struggle for justice."

So, to sum up this section: the option for the poor is a *praxis* in the strict sense of the word, in that it is:

—objective (practical) action;

—collective (participatory) action; and

—transforming (political) action.

Its praxis is therefore:

—effective, against all ineffective sentimentality and verbosity;

—in solidarity, against all harmful paternalism and *dirigisme*;

—structural, against all forms of dangerous aid mentality.

## 2. THE EVANGELIZING POTENTIAL OF THE POOR

We take for granted here that the poor too are in need of evangelization: more, that they are the primary recipients of the gospel, as shown in Jesus' words and actions (Luke 7:22). But the poor also, as Puebla states (910 and 1147), have an "evangelizing potential." What does this mean? How can the poor be agents of evangelization, how do they proclaim the gospel? In various ways:

## (a) Through Explicit Evangelization

This is the most evident and direct way in which the poor evangelize. It happens wherever the poor act as agents of faith and the church:

—In the first place, within the family. Here the simple mothers of the people transmit the heritage of their own faith;

—In a special way, in the base communities. Here, through reading the gospel in community, the poor—who make up the majority of community members—"continually evangelize themselves" (Puebla 450);

—In the practices of popular religion. This is clearly carried on and often generated by the people themselves. It mediates genuine evangelical values: love of Jesus Christ, the Virgin Mary and the saints, a sense of the sacred, trust in divine providence, a feeling of penitence, a sense of community with the faithful departed, an appreciation of the importance of prayer, and so on (cf Puebla 454).

## (b) Through Witness to the (Religious and Human) Values of the Gospel

The most impressive thing about the people is their faith in the divine, their deep trust in the power of God and the saints. For them, God is the supreme evidence, the *reale realissimum*, the *concretum concretissimum*. All this is really touching, moving, edifying and evangelizing. A pastoral worker who had recovered his faith through contact with a peasant community declared: "You don't put yourself in touch with the people with impunity."

Many priests and religious have also felt their own vocation and mission strengthened by contact with the people and their religion. And not only priests and religious: the great Russian film director Eisenstein was deeply impressed in Mexico by the sight of Indians dragging themselves on their knees across stone floors, muttering their prayers and sorrow. Though an atheist, he left his tribute to them in his posthumous film *Mexico*. The English novelist Graham Greene has told how the faith witness of these same Indians marked a decisive step on his road to conversion.

The poor impress not only through the intensity of their religious life, but also through the deep human values they embody, linked to their religious life. A list of these might go like this: generosity and mutual sharing, solidarity in suffering, hospitality to strangers, resistance in the face of hardship, patience to obtain the necessities of life (look at the long queues at hospitals); common sense and realism, usually saving them from the extremes and sectarianism to which the lower middle classes are liable; ability to communicate with all sorts of people. . . .

And so one could go on, with another list of virtues characteristic of the people, such as: simplicity, lack of affectation; charity, as shown in tenderness and goodwill to their neighbours; straightforwardness in dealings, with no pretence; personal affection, especially when grateful; their unshakeable hope that, as they say, "Tomorrow will be better"; their care for children, sick people, old people and the like. All these qualities could be summed up in the word: *openness.* Material poverty favours and even induces this openness to God, to others and to things. Puebla is right in claiming that the "evangelizing potential" of the poor consists in, among other things, the fact that "many of the poor incarnate in their lives the evangelical virtues of solidarity, service, simplicity and openness to accepting the gift of God" (1147).

### (c) Through Their Clamour, Mute or Out Loud

What do the oppressed want? What are they crying out for? They are crying out for recognition, justice and equality. This cry makes itself heard in various ways:

—As a community asking the official church for guidance, support and solidarity;

—As a trade union calling a strike to demand respect for workers' rights;

—As the silent but pressing waiting of the inhabitants of a shantytown threatened with demolition, looking to the church to take a courageous and prophetic stand on their behalf;

—As, finally, all the petitions the oppressed make of the church and society in general for their needs and rights.

Puebla sums up all these cries in a single vision: "From the depths of the countries that make up Latin America a cry is rising to heaven, growing louder and more alarming all the time. It is the cry of a suffering people who demand justice, freedom and respect for the basic rights of human beings and peoples" (87). Who can deny that these cries have a true evangelizing power? They have this precisely in the measure that they unmask a situation of injustice and force the church and society to conversion and change.

### (d) Through Their Mute Presence

The pervading panorama of poverty is in itself a denunciation of society. The sight of beggars in the streets and street urchins dodging through traffic for coins is upsetting and ethically disturbing. The sight of workers streaming out of a factory at the end of an exhausting day's work arouses pity and even fear. If they are seen at a stormy meeting called to discuss their rights, this fear is greater. So the rich avoid seeing the poor: besides spoiling their view, the poor disturb their conscience and fill them with terror—the terror of seeing their privileges threatened.

The mere fact of poverty is in effect an accusation of failure to carry out God's plan in the world. This makes the sight of the poor, just the mere sight of them, evangelically destabilizing. The actual poor are a demand for justice. The New Testament points to the questioning power of this "seeing": "when he saw the man, he passed by on the other side" (Luke 11:31); "If anyone wants to borrow, do not turn away" (Matt. 5:42); "If a man ... saw that one of his brothers was in need" (1 John 3:17), and so on.

People cannot bear the sight of the poor for any length of time without being challenged to conversion. They are the court in which the church and society are judged, as evoked in Matthew 25.

So, through their mute presence, as well as through their

vocal demands, the poor not only evangelize but call the rest of us to be converted and to practise justice.

## (e) The Basis of the "Evangelizing Potential of the Poor"

Having seen how the poor evangelize, we now need to ask why the poor have a greater potential for evangelizing than the non-poor.

It is because the poor provide the proper *locus a quo* for the word of the gospel. In other words, it is only from the situation of the poor that the gospel appears as good news, leaven, light and salt. Seen from the situation of the rich, the gospel loses its power: it becomes a muddied, alienated and dark "good news." So Jesus sent his disciples out to evangelize in poverty (see Matthew 10:9–10), because poverty alone can preach the gospel. Those who evangelize, then, have to be poor or adopt the viewpoint of the poor. They have to be really poor or poor in spirit, which—as we saw earlier—also involves a degree of material dispossession.

The history of evangelization is very instructive in this regard. Every time the gospel has been presented as the accompaniment of political power or military might, it has been open to all sorts of ambiguities. This has been the rule since Constantine and is seen at its clearest in the whole colonial endeavour that lent cover to missionary expansion, in Latin America and elsewhere. It meant that the gospel ended up being imposed from top to bottom, contrary to what happened in the first three centuries, in which it spread from bottom to top, starting precisely from the poor.

Who, then, do the poor evangelize? In the first place, the poor evangelize the poor. Then, the poor evangelize the rich (and are perhaps the only ones who can do so—see Puebla 1156). Finally, the poor evangelize the church itself. How? By calling it to conversion, to the practice of justice, to evangelical poverty, to solidarity with the oppressed, to prophetic courage. The "evangelizing potential of the poor," besides being shown in the witness of their lives, appears in the fact that "the poor challenge the church constantly, summoning it to conversion" (Puebla 1147). They also evangelize the church by making it discover forgotten dimensions of the gospel, especially the liberating dimension of faith in history.

## 3. SO WHAT HAPPENS TO THE NON-POOR?

### (a) Legitimate Pastoral Care of the Non-poor

The option for the poor is carefully called "preferential." This means it is not exclusive (in favour of the poor alone) nor excluding (leaving the non-poor out of account). The non-poor are and always will be included in the evangelizing mission of the church.

So pastoral care of the non-poor is legitimate, as is "pastoral care of elites," in the words of Medellín (Doc. 7), or of "those who have decision-making power," those who "are collaborating in the construction of society," as Puebla puts it (1228). Together with pastoral action on behalf of the poor, then, and in association with it, there can be pastoral action on behalf of the non-poor: the middle classes, the rich, intellectuals, politicians, those working in the communications media, doctors, university professors, and so on.

This pastoral action, however, can never take the first place in the church, can never require the bulk of its resources. The church's pastoral action has to be like that of Jesus himself: it has to have a dominant motif; it has to show a preference. And this preference today falls without equivocation on the poor. This has to be seen both in the quality of the church's apostolic commitment and in the quantity of persons, time and resources it devotes to the poor. This will emerge even more clearly from the degree of decisive and decision-making participation the poor can have in various aspects of church life: liturgy, catechesis, religious life, seminaries, lay ministries, theology and the like.

What Puebla says is true: "Our pastoral effort is one single effort" (1215). Yes, and it has one single objective: to convert, to evangelize, to create new men and women, sons and daughters of God. Nevertheless, because social situations differ, particularly in terms of class, pastoral methods also need to be different. That great master of pastoral teaching, Gregory the Great, taught "how to speak to the poor and to the rich" (*Reg.* III.2), though starting from and aiming at the same gospel. Christ acted no differently: he sought the salvation of all, poor and rich, but in accordance with the social status of each. So he said to the former: "Blessed are you who are poor; yours is the Kingdom of God," and to the latter: "But alas for you who are rich; you are having your consolation now" (Luke 6:20, 24).

One can, then, speak of a legitimate "pastoral pluralism," provided the unity of purpose to which all pastoral effort must converge is kept. The option for the poor must of absolute necessity have a place in this convergence. This is the criterion for judging various new movements in the church, affecting mainly the middle classes, such as the charismatics, *Comunione e Liberazione*, *Opus Dei* and suchlike. Only to the extent that they succeed in incorporating the option for the poor do such movements have a right to a place in the church of today.

Does this mean that pastoral approaches to the poor and the non-poor need to be antagonistic? Not necessarily, and certainly not in everything: insofar as they deal with questions transcending those of class, and insofar as the non-poor respond to the requirements of justice and solidarity with the poor, pastoral work with the middle and upper classes is not opposed to that with the poor, but rather complements it through the contribution these classes can make to the cause of liberating the poor themselves.

On the other hand, when the rich persist in injustice toward the poor, upholding and even strengthening oppressive structures, then the church can only be against the rich—or rather, against their unjust practices. In doing so, the church is actually working in favour of their persons ("souls") and for their salvation. Here the pastoral approach to the non-poor can only take the form of prophetic challenge and call to conversion. This will be made in the ambit of the specific struggle in society known as the class struggle, which, while not the only form of social conflict, is undoubtedly the most important and pervasive one.

## (b) Ways of Evangelizing the Non-poor

How, then, should pastoral care of the non-poor, the rich and the middle classes, be organized? Leaving the more practical aspects aside for the moment, the overall answer has to be: the main objective of pastoral care of the non-poor has to be to associate them with the cause of the poor. This is to place them on the way to following Christ, taking on all the demands made by this following. Now, one of these demands is clearly detachment from and sharing of goods: "Go and sell everything you own, and give the money to the poor" (Mark 10:21).

The non-poor, therefore, have to *be converted to the poor Christ in his poor*, they have to make their option for the poor, by virtue of their option for Christ; they have to take on the cause of justice, to adopt the viewpoint of the poor, to show solidarity with their struggle, be their companion: "Use money, tainted as it is, to win you friends. . . ." (Luke 16:9). To show the various ways in which rich people can be Christian, the Gospels give us the two figures of Matthias and Zaccheus as the two poles of a broad spectrum. All share something in common: the struggle for justice, or solidarity with those who suffer injustice.

It is of course false to reduce the Christian faith to the option for the poor: opting for Christ implies opting for the poor, but is not exhausted in this. It goes beyond this, making fresh demands. On the other hand, we deceive ourselves if we think we can opt for Christ without opting for the poor and the justice they seek.

To the rich, the voice of the gospel speaks of the need for conversion. So rich people's encounter with the word is a dramatic, if not a tragic, affair: they are forced to choose between God and Mammon, with no half measures. This does not apply only to unjust and exploitative rich people; they are clearly not on the way to the Kingdom (cf 1 Cor. 6:9-10). It applies simply to rich people as such. These, according to the Gospels, are in a dangerous situation, on the slippery slope that leads to perdition. If salvation is impossible for the unjust rich (as long as they remain so), it is difficult for the rich as such. Jesus' strongest words are addressed to them: "Alas for you who are rich . . ." (Luke 6:24); "It is easier for a camel . . ." (Mark 10:23-4); "The rich man also died . . . in his torment in

Hades . . ." (Luke 16:22-3). From a political point of view, the situation of the rich is not much better: they are destined to betray—either their class or their people.

The situation of the middle classes confronted with the gospel is a little different. For them, the word is also a call to conversion, but it is a conversion that is more a sort of *decision*: either to follow the plan of Mammon (accumulation), or that of God (freedom and sharing).

The gospel of course also demands conversion from the poor. But for them, it is clear that they lack the objective constraints which make the rich particularly impervious to the gospel (cf Mark 4:19; Matt. 22:1-10).

Although evangelization of the non-poor takes place subjectively from the gospel and in favour of the rich and middle classes (for the sake of their conversion and salvation), objectively it starts from the poor and for the sake of the poor. Therefore, it is from the poor that the church addresses its word to the non-poor. Just as Jesus did.

Now, inasmuch as riches are oppression and oppression is a relationship between the rich and the poor, it is clear that the conversion of the non-poor requires a change in their relationship to their riches and to the poor—it requires an option for the poor. So pastoral care of the non-poor concerns the poor as well, and not only from the standpoint of faith, but also from a political point of view. We need to bear in mind that the transformation of the relationship of oppression, which involves oppressors and oppressed, brings, from the pastoral point of view, a double dialectic into play: the dialectic of the *power of the word*, by which the gospel is proclaimed to oppressed and oppressors, summoning both to change and, therefore, to equality; the dialectic of *the word of power*, by which historical" conflicts themselves serve to awaken and change the consciences of those involved in them—something that is certainly not foreign to God's plan.

## 4.  PRACTICAL IMPLICATIONS OF THE OPTIONS FOR THE POOR

We are now in a position to set out the practical implications of the option for the poor. They can be divided into three sections:

(a) implications on the level of spirituality;
(b) pastoral implications;
(c) political implications.

### (a) Implications on the Level of Spirituality

The following implications can be picked out under this heading:

(i) *Conversion*. In the first place, the option for the poor is a challenge to all in the church to make a personal commitment to the poor Christ and his poor. Puebla makes several references to this concrete and personal commitment (1134, 1140, 1157 and 1158). It also speaks of "following of Christ" in place of conversion (1140 and 1145), which is not very different in meaning. The fact is that both conversion and following Christ are not so much implications as presuppositions of opting for the poor. But it is still true that, if it is to be radical, the option for the poor demands a new life and an evangelical faith. We cannot love the poor well except with the heart of Christ.

(ii) *Evangelical Poverty*. We have already seen that the option for the poor has an intimate connection with evangelical poverty, understood as an austere life style (Puebla 1158). In reality, the poor can only be served in poverty.

(iii) *Communion with the Poor*. This is a matter of being close to and sharing with the oppressed. This is not so much a political attitude as a deeply human one. It is an attitude inspired by compassion, love and a solidarity that seeks no reward. Its effect is to make one appreciate the life and culture of the poor, accepting them as persons, treating them as sharers in one same destiny. This supposes a reciprocal dialogue in which we speak, of course, but also and above all listen and learn.

(iv) *Readiness for Martyrdom*. The surest results of opting for the poor are incomprehension, persecution and even martyrdom. "Those who concern themselves with the lost are lost," said Bertold Brecht. If the poor are the oppressed and exploited, those who join with them also take on their oppression and the persecution that results from their struggle against oppression. So poverty and oppression normally go together. Jesus was not wrong in making the same promise to the poor and to the persecuted (Matt. 5:3, 10), as Puebla recognized (1134 and 1138). This readiness for martyrdom also applies to the inevitable tensions that opting for the poor creates within the church itself, with concomitant suspicions and even accusations of distorting the faith (see Puebla 79 and 1139).

(v) *Humility*. Christians who opt for the poor cannot make this a title of personal glorification, coming to despise those who are not "into it." Nothing, then, of the arrogance of those who consider themselves "enlightened," "convinced you can guide the blind and be a beacon to those in the dark" (Rom. 2:19). No, opting for the poor should be seen rather as a grace, one which, furthermore, we shall render an account of. To use the poor for self-advancement, whether this be in politics, pastoral work, theology or even spirituality, is to place oneself outside the gospel, the exact reverse of the spirit of "humble service" in the parable (Luke 17:7–10).

(vi) *Love*. The most radical attitude with regard to the poor is that of love: loving them as persons, not just as an abstract cause; loving them for their own sake, not for political purposes, however just; loving them from the heart and not just from the head; loving them deeply, without reserve and without reward, loving them to the end as Christ did (see John 13:1; 15:13; 1 John 3:16; 4:11), as if they were Christ (Matt. 25:31ff).

### (b) Pastoral Implications

This heading relates mainly to the institutional church, particularly to its ministers. Of course the spiritual implications outlined above apply also and even more so to ministers. They too need to: be converted to the poor Christ and his poor; become poor, setting aside their anti-evangelical trappings and titles; commune with the poor in humble listening and lively presence among them; have the courage to speak out and suffer on their behalf; serve them in the humble spirit of those who do no more than their duty; and finally, love them with a fatherly and brotherly love.

But besides all this, the "hierarchical church" has some particular responsibilities with regard to the poor. For it, opting for the poor means, among other things:

—Redefining all sectors of its activity: liturgy, religious education, economic administration and so on, in function of a preference for the poor;

—Evangelizing the poor as the prime recipients of the good news (Puebla 1145). This means specifically preaching Jesus the Christ as integral liberator and saviour of the human race. The poor expect this of the church and the church cannot betray them in this without betraying God's plan;

—Feeding the hope the poor place in a better world, above all at times of their greatest suffering and despair. The church is not the institution of faith and charity alone, but also that of hope;

—Denouncing injustices committed against the poor, particularly when the poor themselves have no voice or chance to do so (Puebla 1138, 1159, 1213);

—Raising the consciousness of the poor, explaining the mechanisms and structures of oppression that bear down on them and making them aware of their rights and duties;

—Acting in solidarity with the poor and supporting them in their rightful struggles (Puebla 525, 1162);

—Offering them moral and material sustenance, including placing ecclesiastical resources (money, buildings) at their service and disposition;

—Initiating and supporting autonomous organizations of the poor, whether this means creating, reviving or renewing them (Puebla 711, 1163);

—Involving the poorest among the poor, the "littlest," in the route to liberation, so that no one might feel left out or excluded to the advantage of those economically or politically stronger;

—Praying for the poor, and celebrating their struggles, hopes and all signs of the divine presence in their midst, with them;

—Appreciating the values of popular culture, especially popular religion, trying to evangelize it and release its potential for liberation;

—Summoning the poor not just to come to church but to be

church, through the creation of base communities, the setting-up of new forms of ministry and general participation at all levels, so that a real "church of the poor" can emerge;

—Distancing the church from the powerful so as not to compromise the clarity of the gospel message and to avoid scandalizing the "least";

—Excluding notorious and unrepentant oppressors from sacramental and even ecclesial communion.

And so on: the list could be longer, but let us leave it at these indications, drawn from the actuality of putting the option for the poor into practice.

### (c) Political Implications

These are the particular, though not exclusive, concern of lay people in the church. Putting the option for the poor into effect on a political level involves one's whole political approach. This is where the practical implications of the option for the poor are most in evidence, since politics means nothing if not action. It involves making choices between different possible courses of action. So what does choosing the poor, placing oneself on their side politically, mean? Among other things:

—Taking care to learn, through critical study and direct contact, what the situation of the poor and its causes are, so as to be able to adopt a clear and effective stance (cf Puebla 1159);

—Being aware of how historical initiatives—parties, political structures, government plans, ideologies—look from the stand-point of the poor. So, for example, if it is a question of deciding which political party to join, ask which is the one that is most concerned with the poor. The same applies to ideologies and models of society, particularly when they involve open social conflict: which side includes the poor and their interests?

—Allying oneself with groups that favour the liberation of the poor and distancing oneself from those that oppress or manipulate them;

—Adopting strategies and tactics that not only favour the poor, but are also within their reach; i.e. those that enable the poor to act as protagonists. This involves the question of non-violent means (see GS 78e and Puebla 531–4);

—Working for the various levels of autonomous organizations among the poor: trade unions, local parties and associations (cf Puebla 1163).

Again, the list could go on, but this is enough to show the principle of making the poor the key criterion in everything that involves political choices in society (Puebla 525, 792). We are not, of course, counselling demagogic or ingenuous support for everything the poor may be or do, since the poor can deceive as well as be deceived. It is rather a question of lending effective support to whatever contributes to their genuine liberation, and this is a matter that calls for critical discernment.

For Christians, liberation is not confined to the social sphere; it has spiritual and eschatological dimensions as well. This establishes the qualitative difference between the classical Marxist conception of "liberation" and the Christian one. Also, opting for the poor in Latin America means following the "logic of the majority," so opting for democracy in its truest sense.

This ends our reflections on the practical implications of opting for the poor. Those that have been put forward are, in our view, what the very process of living our faith in history is demonstrating. This in turn means that numerous other perspectives will undoubtedly emerge in the future—"unto the glory of God, the confusion of the devil, and the happiness of man" (LG 17)!

## Chapter XII

# Looking Ahead: The Future of Humanity Depends on the Preferential Option for the Poor

We began this book, which is a Christian theological reflection on our faith, with an Introduction examining who the poor are. This was right, since both biblical revelation and Christian faith claim to guide believers in their life in the real, concrete world, which they share with non-believers. When speaking of the preferential option for the poor, we have taken care from the start to speak of the real poor in the real world. All biblical, theological and pastoral thinking would be devalued from the outset were it not to concern itself clearly with the actual living conditions of the poor in this world where believers and non-believers live together.

In Part I, on the biblical aspect, we saw how the God of the Bible, through the prophets and finally through the incarnation of the Son of God, made a preferential option for the poor— the actual poor living at the time in Canaan and Egypt, and later in Palestine under the Romans. This option was made in terms that the nature of that world in the distant past demanded, in the conditions imposed by that world on the defenceless of the time. Parts II and III examined the preferential option for the poor in Christian tradition, then the pastoral demands made by this option and the difficulty

237

Christian institutions have in responding to them. This has brought us back to the world of the present where we all live together, rich and poor, believers and non-believers.

The final reflection we have to make brings us back to these real poor people as they live in the world of today. At this stage we know what position faith must take in relation to poverty. We now need to ask what relevance this has in a world in which the majority of inhabitants are not Christians to whom we might appeal in the way we have done in this book on the basis of our Christian spiritual tradition: how relevant, then, is our preferential option for the poor to those who do not share our tradition of faith? Does a preferential option for the poor make any sense if it is divorced from faith in the God who opts for the poor? Are the demands made by our faith opposed to those imposed by the world we know through the social sciences, or is the God of the Bible also made manifest mysteriously through dispassionate and not necessarily believing analysis of the world?

If we look at the world situation in this late twentieth century, it can only be said to be alarming in the extreme. The major cause for this alarm is hunger, the fact that millions of people, most of them children, die of starvation every year. Of those that survive, thousands upon thousands have their intelligence or sight impaired through malnutrition and lack of essential ingredients in their diet. We do not need socio-scientific instruments, which might be suspected of ideological bias, to tell us of the remorseless advance of desert across vast tracts of Africa, forcing huge numbers of people and their animals to migrate from land that can no longer support them. And part of the picture, a part we cannot ignore, is the fact that this is happening at a time of great advances in agriculture and husbandry. We can, through irrigation and artificial fertilization, produce many times the previous quantity of grain per hectare, even in terrain once considered marginal. Experts agree that, from the purely technological point of view, there is no need for such widespread hunger in the late twentieth century. Our present technology would enable us to feed the world's population several times over. And yet mass hunger persists.

Hunger is simply the gravest aspect of the situation in which the majority of human beings live in our day. There are also enormous lacks in such areas as health care and housing provision. Illiteracy is on the increase, even in traditionally cultured countries such as Argentina. Today most people are not only completely shut out from culture and the means of making their own culture, but are fed an alien culture through radio and television. Even this conformist culture, however, cannot hide the reality of starvation and malnutrition affecting large sectors of humanity. It is against the demands arising from these sectors that the forces of "order" have ever-increasing recourse to repression.

We in Latin America have, sadly, a very wide experience of repression. In some countries, such as Chile, Argentina and El Salvador, this has been directed mainly against trade union and political leaders. In others, such as Guatemala, Peru and Bolivia, indigenous peoples have been the main victims. Those tortured or assassinated, or those who have had their houses burned, are always the poor and those who have thrown in their lot with the poor. This is to be expected: social systems that cannot satisfy the peasants' minimum needs for land, the labourers' minimum needs for work, the indigenous peoples' desire to have their ancestral traditions respected, have no way of guaranteeing social order other than by repression.

This state of affairs is *morally intolerable*, for those who do not believe in the God of the Bible as much as for those who do. But it is also *politically unsustainable*, because any order buttressed by repression with no social consensus must always be unstable.

Let us now look at the global situation of humanity in the closing years of this twentieth century from another angle, that of relations between the nations of the world. Even limiting ourselves to governmental points of view, without making ideological judgments or considering how representative these governments are of the people they govern, there is broad agreement about the existence of a number of major problems. For a start, everyone agrees that no good can come of the arms race. For the first time in history, humanity has the capacity to annihilate not only itself, totally and finally, but most of the animal and vegetable species of the world with it. Despite the evident lunacy of continuing to update arms that already have total destructive power, the superpowers continue to do so, and other nations with the capacity to imitate them also do so. Even if the wisdom and prudence of the small group of people who hold all our fates in their hands succeed in holding off the final holocaust, the cost of the arms race is already aggravating the wants from which most people around the world are suffering. This too is a generally accepted fact, and yet still the arms race goes on.

There is another problem recognized by the world's statesmen: Third World debt, owed to the banks and governments of the richest nations in the world. The interest payments on this debt mean that the poorest countries are adding to the wealth of the richest. It is years since we passed the point at which interest payments exceeded the original investments plus new loans to the poor nations. So new loans are made simply to enable the poor countries to pay the interest due on earlier loans and not to help them in meeting their basic needs. This has reached the point where even some superpower leaders have been discussing the possibility of writing off the debts, since there is evidently no way in which they can be repaid. Yet in the meantime poor countries such as Jamaica and the Dominican Republic have draconian conditions imposed on them, which serve only to worsen the plight of the worst-off among their populations.

Together with the weight of international debt, the poor countries also suffer from unequal terms of the international trade which is their only means of earning hard currency with which to pay the interest on their debts to international banks. The price of the goods the poor countries export is determined by conditions in the rich countries, so that there is no guarantee that an increase in production of, say, coffee or sugar will bring a corresponding increase in hard currency earnings. Furthermore, the rates of interest charged by the banks on their loans vary, so there is no way in which poor countries can budget accurately for the amount they have to repay, even in the short term. The United Nations and other bodies have debated this problem, but the rich and rich nations lack the will to make the changes that the establishment of a new international economic order requires.

Within this somewhat bleak overall picture of human life in the late twentieth century, there are certain sectors of the population who suffer additional disadvantages to those suffered by all the poor. These are women, blacks and native tribes. The world is still governed, from international organizations down to the nuclear family, by men, and women still have to please the men who hold power in order to find an acceptable place in society. There are places where women are very seriously oppressed and others where they are less so, but till now there is not a single society in the world in which women enjoy equal power with men. To change this situation would require basic changes in all social bodies, including the churches. There is a growing recognition of the unacceptability of one half of the world's population dominating the other half in this way, but there is still not a general willingness to make the changes needed if the situation is to be altered.

With regard to blacks, we all know the history of their exploitation and enslavement in the past. Today South Africa stands out as a symbol of that exploitation, with its power structure that legitimates the crassest oppression of a black majority by a white minority. International bodies have produced a broad consensus that apartheid is both immoral and unsustainable, but there is still not the general will to take measures that would put an end to it. In Latin America racial discrimination is not so obvious, but is still something built into the system.

Native peoples complain that laws passed in recognition of their rights are simply not being observed, even in the more progressive countries and even where these rights are nominally upheld by trade unions and other forms of workers' organization. Nearly all claims made by native peoples to their right to land cannot be satisfied with individual titles, such as peasants in general find to be their best protection. So they demand the right to control the lands reserved to them and to administer them according to their ancestral customs. These claims make themselves heard even in the wealthiest countries: the United States, Canada, Australia. These are precisely the countries in which their rights to land have been enshrined in solemn treaties, treaties which have since been broken and which the courts today will not uphold.

All these aspects which make up the overall picture of the state of humanity in the late twentieth century have one common name: oppression. They all, including the hunger suffered by millions of human beings, result from the oppression of some human beings by others. The impotence of international bodies in the face of generally recognized problems, their inability to effect solutions, stems from the self-interest of those who stand to benefit from their oppression of other human beings. In each major problem there is broad recognition of both the moral intolerableness and the political non-viability of the existing situation, coupled with a lack of capacity to respond. If the problem is (or the problems are) a conflict of interests, then the energy to find the solution can come only from the oppressed themselves. Wherever there is oppression, there will be struggles to win life-sustaining conditions—struggles between classes, between races, between nations, between the sexes. This is simply an observable fact, not a moral imperative or a scientific conclusion. We can see the just struggles of the oppressed going on around us, and we cannot see any other way out of the vast problems that afflict humanity at the close of the twentieth century.

We have seen throughout this book that the God of the Bible is with the poor and oppressed. This God is with the oppressed even when they cannot find any other course than struggle to defend their lives, as the case of the slaves in Egypt showed. We have also seen that those of us who believe in this God of the Bible have our instructions to follow Jesus Christ in his solidarity with the poor and impoverished of this world. We are now seeing that the very future of humanity depends on achieving conditions that are genuinely those of life for the mass of people. Out of sheer instinct for survival humanity has to make a preferential option for the poor! If it does not succeed in doing so, all the indications are that we shall all perish, rich and poor alike.

There are symbolic events that concentrate the whole problematic in themselves. One such was the revolution in

Nicaragua. What is being decided in Nicaragua is the possibility of creating acceptable conditions of life for the poor, for the peasants, for the indigenous peoples, for women, and for a small nation dependent on agricultural exports in a world dominated by arms and the economic and financial might of the rich nations. Besides this, the people of Nicaragua are a Christian people. For Christians and non-Christians alike, the preferential option for the poor has to take a course that must involve defending events and situations of which Nicaragua is the best exemplar today.

# Glossary

AGAPE—Love in the form of giving and forgiving such as is put forward as an ideal in the New Testament. The best English equivalent is probably "solidarity."

APOCALYPTIC—Referring to the end or consummation of the world. A literary genre employed before and around the time of Jesus, as exemplified in the Book of Revelation.

CANONICAL—Serving as a rule (canon) of faith. The "canonical Gospels" are those found in our Bibles, while "extracanonical" or "apocryphal" Gospels are those not held by the church to be normative for faith, and so not taken into the "canon" of the New Testament, established in the third century.

CHARISMATIC—Used of a gift or vocation given to someone in particular by the Holy Spirit for the sake of the common good. Also of a movement composed of Christians who emphasize the primacy of the Spirit.

DIALECTIC—Movement, in actuality or in the mind, between two confronting poles. "Dialectic with determinant" indicates that one of these poles has greater priority.

DEUTERO-ISAIAH—Unknown author of the "Book of Consolation" written at the end of the Babylonian exile and added to the Book of Isaiah (chs. 40–55). There are other "deutero-prophets" whose works were added to those of other major prophets in the same way.

KERYGMA—Proclamation of the message of salvation. The Christian kerygma is the proclamation of the crucified and risen Jesus as God's final and definitive act of salvation.

PNEUMATOLOGICAL—Relating to the *pneuma*, the Greek term for the Holy Spirit.

244

SYNOPTICS—The first three Gospels (Matthew, Mark, Luke), a term used because they can be placed in parallel and "seen as a whole" (Greek *syn-optikos*).

TRADITION—Used (in the context of Bible studies) of the different literary and theological currents in the Old Testament: Yahwist, Elohist, priestly and Deuteronomic.

ZEALOT—A Jew who took part in a movement of armed uprising against the Roman occupation of Palestine at the time of Jesus.

# Notes

## CHAPTER I: THE OPTION FOR THE POOR IN THE OLD TESTAMENT

1. Biblical quotations are taken from the *Jerusalem Bible*, adapted occasionally in accordance with the authors' own references to the original Hebrew and Greek.

2. J. Severino Croatto, "Yavé, el Dios de la 'presencia' salvífica: Exod. 3:14 en su contexto literario y querigmático," *Revista Bíblica* 43 (1981), pp. 153–63.

3. Though there are antecedents on the insurrectional theory of the origins of Israel, the definitive work is N. K. Gottwald, *The Tribes of Yahweh: A Sociology of the Religion of Liberated Israel* (Maryknoll, N.Y., 1979).

4. For a detailed examination of the texts, see J. V. Pixley, *On Exodus: A Liberation Perspective* (Maryknoll, N.Y., 1987).

5. See Judg. 8:22–3, and for an interpretation, J. V. Pixley, *God's Kingdom: A Guide for Biblical Study* (Maryknoll, N.Y., 1981).

6. A good reading of the Pentateuch in the light of lack of land for Israel can be found in J. Severino Croatto, "Una promesa aún no cumplida. La estructura literaria del Pentateuco," *Revista Bíblica* 44 (1982), pp. 193–206.

7. Much has been written on Hebrews/'*apiru*. See G. E. Mendenhall, "The '*Apiru* Movements in the Late Bronze Age," in *The Tenth Generation: The Origins of the Biblical Tradition* (Baltimore, 1973), pp. 122–41; M. L. Chaney, "Ancient Palestinian Peasant Movements and the Formation of Premonarchic

Israel," in *Palestine in Transition: The Emergence of Ancient Israel,* ed. D. Feedman and D. Graf (Sheffield, 1983), pp. 39–90.
8. The classic work on the Psalms is H. Gunkel, *Die Psalmen,* 2nd ed. (Göttingen, 1968). There is an excellent work by S. Mowinckel, *The Psalms in Israel's Worship,* 2 vols. (Oxford, 1962). See also the notes in H. Oosterhuis et al., *Fifty Psalms* (London and New York, 1968).
9. We omit here a phrase from the masoretic (*masora,* accepted text from which variant readings and inconsistencies had gradually been excised over the centuries—*Trans.*) text which seems to be a diptography (erroneous repetition of the same phrase by the copyist).
10. The masoretic text does not make good sense here: "He will strike the land with the rod of his mouth." We follow (as does the JB) a conjectural emendation that the masoretic *'eretz* is an error for *'aritz.*
11. There is no good up-to-date study of the prophets of Israel. The best is still J. Lindblom, *Prophecy in Ancient Israel* (Oxford, 1962).
12. D. L. Petersen, *Late Israelite Prophecy: Studies in Deutero-Prophetic Literature and in Chronicles* (Missoula, Mont., 1977).
13. A. Monteiro de Oliveira, "Miqueas, profeta revolucionario de los campesinos," *Taller de Teología* 12 (Mexico City, 1983), pp. 31–51.
14. The translation of terms describing the "wicked" and the "just" in the Psalms will always be debatable, perhaps because there is an intentional ambiguity in the original. On this point, see J. Porfirio Miranda, *Marx and the Bible: A Critique of the Philosophy of Oppression* (Maryknoll, N.Y., 1974), and E. Támez, *Bible of the Oppressed* (Maryknoll, N.Y., 1982).

## CHAPTER II: THE OPTION FOR THE POOR IN THE NEW TESTAMENT

1. This argument is pursued in phenomenological terms by Paulo Freire in his classic *Pedagogy of the Oppressed* (London and New York, 1972, now available as a Pelican Book).
2. For this geographical account I have relied on H. Zorrilla,

*La fiesta de la liberación de los oprimidos. Relectura de Juan 7:1–10, 21* (Costa Rica, 1981).

3. Luke's Gospel has been the subject of special interest in Latin America. In Mexico alone, three good books on it have appeared: G. Hirata, *Pobres y ricos. Estudios exegéticos sobre el evangelio de Lucas* (Mexico City, 1972); M. Villamán, *Leyendo el evangelio de Lucas* (Mexico City, 1982); V. Leñero, *El evangelio de Lucas Gavián* (Mexico City, 1980), which is a very Mexican novelized version of Luke's Gospel.

4. The best discussion of this subject is J. L. Segundo, *The Historical Jesus of the Synoptics*, vol. 2 of *Jesus of Nazareth Yesterday and Today* (Maryknoll, N.Y., and London, 1986).

## CHAPTER III: SOLIDARITY WITH THE POOR: BASIS OF THE BIBLE ETHIC

1. There is an excellent account of the biblical setting in G. von Rad, *Theologie des Alten Testaments*, vol. 1, 3rd ed. (Munich, 1966), pp. 302–8.

2. See J. V. Pixley, *On Exodus* (Maryknoll, N.Y., 1987).

3. I follow the analysis made by A. Alt in his "Der Stadtstaat Samarias," *Kleine Schriften* 3 (Munich, 1959), pp. 258–302. On Baal of the Omrides, see F. Fensham, "A Few Observations on the Polarization between Yahweh and Baal in 1 Kings 17–19," *Zeitschrift für die alttestamentliche Wissenschaft* 92 (1980), pp. 227–35.

4. For discussion of the exegetical alternatives, and a defence of the view adduced here, see J. V. Pixley, "Jesús y el siervo de Yavé en el Déutero-Isaías," *Servir* 85 (1980), pp. 9–47. This shows that it is not suffering that defines the minister of God, as exegesis since Duhm would have it, but mission. Suffering is the result of mission.

5. Heb. 18:3. A very good book on the social and evangelical significance of manual labour is R. F. Hock, *The Social Context of Paul's Ministry: Tentmaking and Apostleship* (Philadelphia, 1980).

6. See J. L. Segundo, *Jesus of Nazareth Yesterday and Today*, 5 vols., but esp. vol. 2 (Maryknoll, N.Y., and London, 1986).

7. An example could be the experience of the people's

movement in Colombia in 1984–5, when President Betancur established a pact with a wide spectrum of armed movements, including M-19. The people's movement made a great effort to change into a political movement to pursue its claims through democratic means. In the middle of the truce, Fr Alvaro Ulcué Chocué was assassinated, and rebel groups going to pre-arranged meetings with the government were ambushed. In May 1985, M-19 decided to revert to the armed struggle to defend the people's right to minimum conditions that would ensure their survival.

## CHAPTER IV: THE POOR: FIRST RECIPIENTS OF THE BIBLE MESSAGE

1. There are wide variations between the number of deported given in Jeremiah 52 and 2 Kings 24–5, but Jeremiah can be taken as more probable.
2. According to the apocryphal 1 Esdras 2, which seems to preserve an older version of these events than the canonical Esdras, or 2 Esdras in the nomenclature of the Septuagint. See F. Moore Cross, "A Reconstruction of the Judean Restoration," *Journal of Biblical Literature* 94 (1975), pp. 4–18. The Davidic genealogy can be found in 1 Chron. 3:17–24.
3. Correcting the mention of Zerubbabel in 2 Esdras with that in 1 Esdras 5:66–73.
4. There is an excellent study of the collection of prophets known as Trito-Isaias in P. D. Hanson, *The Dawn of Apocalyptic* (Philadelphia, 1975). Though I do not agree with his thesis in all details, his general line of enquiry and sociological knowledge have been very useful in reaching my conclusions here.
5. Modern translations of the Bible have nullified the harsh meaning of this text by unjustifiably translating *dakka'* as "contrite/humbled," when its meaning is "downtrodden/oppressed." (The version given here is an adaptation of the NEB, whose version of the last two lines—"to revive the spirit of the humble, to revive the courage of the broken"—is an example of what the author is complaining of, but not as bad as the JB's: "to give the humbled spirit new life, to revive

contrite hearts"—*Trans.*) The problem of modern translations dodging references to oppression in this way is very general. See E. Támez, *Bible of the Oppressed* (Maryknoll, N.Y., 1982). (The *Biblia Latinoamericana*, of which an English version, *The Christian Community Bible*, is now available, redresses this tendency, more positively in the Spanish than in the English—*Trans.*)

6. The subject of utopias has been much discussed lately. See R. Vidales and L. Rivera Pagán, eds., *La esperanza en el presente de América Latina* (San José, 1983); F. Hinkelammert, *Crítica a la razón utópica* (San José, 1984).

## CHAPTER V: THE POOR, SACRAMENT OF GOD

1. Cf J. Comblin, *The Holy Spirit and Liberation*; I. Gebara and M. C. Bingemer, *Mary, Mother of God, Mother of the Poor* (both in this sense, 1989). Cf also on Mary and the Poor, Puebla 297, 299, 302, 1144; John Paul II, *Mariah's Cultus*, esp. A. 37.

2. For example, Pope John Paul II's address to the UN, 2 Oct. 1979: "We need to translate the parable of the unjust rich man into economic and political terms, into terms of human rights, of relations between the First, Second and Third Worlds."

## CHAPTER VI: THE CHURCH OF THE POOR: THE CHURCH OF ALL

1. Cf J. B. Libanio, *Pastoral na sociedade de conflictos*, (Petrópolis, 1982), p. 214.

## CHAPTER VII: MATERIAL POVERTY AND SPIRITUAL POVERTY

1. L. Bouyer, *La spiritualité orthodoxe et la spiritualité protestante et anglicane* (Paris, 1965), pp. 14–15: Eng. trans., *Orthodox Spirituality and Protestant and Anglican Spirituality* (London and New York, 1969), p. 13.

2. J.-M. González Ruiz, *Pobreza evangélica y promoción humana* (Barcelona, 1966), pp. 33ff.

3. Cf J. Leclercq, *O cristão e o dinheiro* (São Paulo, 1958), p. 40 and *passim*. The same opinion can be found in other authors such as J. Dupont.
4. Cf J.-M. Castillo, *La alternativa cristiana* (Salamanca, 1978), p. 42 and note 43.
5. Cf R. Sider, *Cristãos ricos em tempos de fome* (São Leopoldo, 1982), ch. 7.
6. Cited by W. Bühlmann, *The Coming of the Third Church* (Maryknoll, N.Y., 1977), p. 122. Cf also V. Codina and N. Zevallos, *Vida Religiosa: História e Teologia* (Petrópolis, 1987, to be translated in this series).
7. Bühlmann, *The Coming of the Third Church*, p. 121.
8. A. Tévoédjrè, *Pobreza: riqueza dos povos* (Petrópolis, 1981).

## CHAPTER VIII: THE OPTION FOR THE POOR DURING A THOUSAND YEARS OF CHURCH HISTORY

1. *Les pauvres au Moyen Age. Etude sociale* (Paris, 1978). The summary given here was made by C. Boff and first published in *Puebla* 7 (1980), pp. 385–402. Mollat has no rival on this subject. His work was based on fourteen years of work, collaborating with his students and others. He gave more than a hundred courses in seminaries and directed more than two hundred theses. Finally, he organized research missions to study the question in cities all over the world: Rome, Moscow, Cambridge, Mass., Beirut, Assisi, Lisbon. . . . He collected all the results in this book, which is consequently unique in its genre.
2. For the history of these periods, we refer to the following classic studies: L. Lallemand, *Histoire de la charité*, 5 vols. (Paris, 1902); L. Prunel, "Les pauvres et l'église," in A. D'Alès, *Dictionnaire Apologétique de la Foi Catholique* (Paris, 1911), vol. 2, col. 1655–1735. Specifically for the early centuries see: J. de Santa Ana, *A Igreja e a desafio dos pobres* (Petrópolis, 1980); U. Benigni, *Storia sociale della Chiesa* (Milan, 1906); M. Giordani, *Ação social da Igreja no Mundo Antigo* (Petrópolis, 1959); I. Giordani, *Il messaggio sociale*

*del'Cristianesimo* (Rome, 1960); A. Hamman, *Riches et pauvres dans l'Eglise ancienne* (Paris, 1962); M. Mara, *Richezza e povertà nel cristianesimo primitivo* (Rome, 1980). Specifically for the later centuries: J. de Santa Ana, ed., *Separation without Hope? Essays on the Relation between the Church and the Poor during the Industrial Revolution and the Western Colonial Expansion* (Geneva, and Maryknoll, N.Y., 1978); D. Menozzi, *Chiesa, Poveri, Società nell'età moderna e contemporanea* (Brescia, 1980), with bibliography, pp. 253–60.
3. Y.-M. Congar, "Les biens temporels de l'Eglise d'après sa tradition théologique et canonique," "Une réalité traditionnelle: l'Eglise recours des faibles et des pauvres," in var., *Eglise et pauvreté*, Unam Sanctam, 57 (Paris, 1965), pp. 233–58 and 259–66.

## CHAPTER IX: THE CHURCHES AND THE POOR TODAY

1. L. Boff, *Church: Charism and Power* (New York and London, 1985), ch. 6: "Roman Catholicism: Structure, Health, Pathologies."
2. Puebla 1134–65.
3. Medellín, Doc. "Peace," 16.
4. "Mensaje del Consejo Latinoamericano de Iglesias (CLAI) a las Iglesias y pueblos del continente americano," in C. Valle, ed., *Semilla de comunión* (Buenos Aires, 1983), pp. 109–12.
5. E. Dussel, "Sobre la historia de la teología en América Latina," *Liberación y cautiverio: Encuentro latinoamericano de teología* (Mexico City, 1976), pp. 19–68, esp. 21–5.
6. P. Richard, *Death of Christendoms, Birth of the Church* (Maryknoll, N.Y., 1987).
7. Var., *La lucha de los dioses* (San José, 1980).

# Select Bibliography

Alfaro, Juan. *Teologia da justiça*. São Paulo: Paulinas, 1978.

Almeida Cunha, R. J. de. *A opção pelos pobres*. Rio de Janeiro: CRB, 1980.

Arns, Card. Paulo Evaristo, D. L. M. de Almeida, D. C. Hummes and Dom Helder Câmara, *Opção pelos pobres: educação e nova sociedade*. XIth National Congress of the AEC, vol. 1 (Col. AEC of Brazil, 8). São Paulo: Loyola, 1983.

Araya, Victorio. *El Dios de los pobres*. San José, Costa Rica: DEI, 1984. Eng. trans.: *God of the Poor*. Maryknoll, N.Y.: Orbis, 1987.

Balera, W. *O direito dos pobres*. São Paulo: Paulinas, 1982.

Barreiro, A. *Os pobres e o Reino: do evangelho a João Paulo II*. São Paulo: Loyola, 1983.

Bastos de Avila, F., F. Taborda and D. Gandin, *Dimensão social, teológica e pedagógica da opção pelos pobres*. XIth National Congress of the AEC, vol. 2 (Col. AEC of Brazil, 9). São Paulo: Loyola, 1983.

Boff, Leonardo. *Church: Charism and Power*. New York and London: Crossroad and S. C. M. Press, 1985.

Bonaventure, St. *Apologia pauperum contra calumniatorem*. In *Obras de San Buenaventura*, vol. 6. Madrid: BAC, pp. 328–707.

Bossuet, C. J. B. "Eminente dignité des pauvres dans l'Eglise." In *Oeuvres de Bossuet*, vol. 7. Paris, 1845, pp. 442–56.

CELAM. *Conclusions*, vol. 2 of the papers from the Medellín Conference. Eng. trans.: *The Church in the Present-day Transformation of Latin America in the Light of the Council*.

Washington, D.C.: USCC, 1970. See esp. the section entitled "Poverty of the Church."

———. *The Final Document* of the Puebla Conference. In John Eagleson and Philip Scharper, eds., *Puebla and Beyond*. Maryknoll, N.Y.: Orbis, 1979. See esp. nos. 1134–65, "The Preferential Option for the Poor."

Comblin, José. *O clamor dos oprimidos, o clamor de Jesus*. Petrópolis: Vozes, 1984. Eng. trans.: *Cry of the Oppressed, Cry of Jesus*. Maryknoll, N.Y.: Orbis, 1988.

*Concilium* (Review). No. 104, *The Poor and the Church*. 1977. No. 130, *The Dignity of the Despised of the Earth*. 1979. No. 176, *La Iglesia Popular: Between Fear and Hope*. 1984.

Cone, James H. *A Black Theology of Liberation*. Maryknoll, N.Y.: Orbis, 1986.

Congar, Yves-Marie. "Les biens temporels de l'Eglise d'après sa tradition théologique et canonique." *Eglise et pauvreté* (Unam Sanctam, 57). Paris: Cerf, 1965, pp. 233–58.

———. *Pour une Eglise servante et pauvre*. Paris.

———. "Une réalité traditionnelle: L'Eglise recours des faibles èt des pauvres." *Eglise et pauvreté*, pp. 259–66.

Cussiánovich, A. *Desde los pobres de la tierra*. Lima: CEP, 1975.

Dupont, J. *Les Béatitudes*, 3 vols. Louvain: Abbaye de Saint-André, 1958.

———. "The Church and Poverty." *The Church of Vatican II*, ed. L. Baraúna. London & New York: Burns & Oates and Herder & Herder, 1968.

———. A. G. Hamman and G. Miccoli. *Seguire Jesù povero*. Magnano: Quiqajon, 1984.

Dussel, Enrique. *El episcopado latinoamericano y la liberación de los pobres, 1504–1602*. Mexico: CRT, 1979.

*Estudios Ecuménicos* (Review). No. 39, *Ecumenismo desde los pobres*. 1980.

Galilea, Segundo. *Evangelizar a los pobres*. Buenos Aires: Paulinas, 1977.

Gauthier, P. *"Consolez mon peuple": Le Concile et "l'Eglise des pauvres."* Paris: Cerf, 1965.

———. *L'évangile de justice*. Paris: Cerf, 1967.

Gelin, Albert. *Les pauvres que Dieu aime.* Paris: Cerf, 1973.

Giordani, I. *Il messaggio sociale del'Cristianesimo.* Rome: Paoline, 1960.

Giordani, M. C. *Ação social da Igreja no mundo antigo.* Petrópolis: Vozes, 1959.

Gómez de Souza, L. A. *Classes populares e Igreja nos caminhos da história.* Petrópolis: Vozes, 1982, esp. Part 3.

González Ruiz, José-María. *Pobreza evangélica y promoción humana.* Barcelona, 1966.

Gottwald, Norman K. *The Tribes of Yahweh: A Sociology of the Religion of Liberated Israel, 1250–1050 BC.* Maryknoll, N.Y.: Orbis, 1979.

Gutiérrez, Gustavo. *The Power of the Poor in History.* Maryknoll, N.Y.: Orbis, 1983.

Hanson, P. D. *The Dawn of Apocalyptic.* 2nd ed. Philadelphia: Fortress, 1979.

Hock, R. F. *The Social Context of Paul's Ministry: Tentmaking and Apostleship.* Philadelphia: Fortress, 1980.

*I-DOC International* (Review). Nos. 1–2, *Bibliografía comentada sobre la Iglesia y la pobreza,* 1980, pp. 65–95.

IECLB. *Responsibilidades sócio-políticas da Igreja Evangélica de Confissão Luterana no Brasil.* CEI 146, 1976.

Julio Maria, P. *A Igreja e o Povo.* São Paulo: Loyola/CEPEHIB, 1983.

Lallemand, L. *Histoire de la charité,* 5 vols. Paris: A. Picard, 1902.

Leclercq, J. *Le chrétien devant l'argent.* Paris: A. Fayard, 1957.

Leclerq, H. "Charité." *Dictionnaire d'archéologie chrétienne et liturgie,* vol. 3. Paris, 1913.

Leuridan, J., and G. Múgica. *Por que a Igreja critica os ricos?* São Paulo: Paulinas, 1983 (anthology of Patristic texts).

Limón, J. J., and others. *Opción por los oprimidos y evangelización.* Mexico: Aportes CRT, 1978.

Lindblom, J. *Prophecy in Ancient Israel.* Oxford: Blackwell, 1962.

Mendenhall, G. E. *The Tenth Generation: The Origins of the Biblical Tradition.* Baltimore: John Hopkins University Press, 1973.

256        Bibliography

Menozzi, D. *Chiesa, Poveri, Società nell'età moderna e contem-poranea*. Brescia: Queriniana, 1980 (anthology of classical texts on poverty with ample bibliography).

Miranda, José P. *Marx y la Biblia. Crítica a la filosofía de la opresión*. Salamanca, 1972. Eng. trans.: *Marx and the Bible: A Critique of the Philosophy of Oppression*. Maryknoll, N.Y.: Orbis, 1973.

Mohana, J. *Pobres e ricos perante Cristo no Brasil*. São Paulo: Loyola, 1982.

Mollat, Michel. *Les pauvres au Moyen Age. Etude sociale*. Paris: Hachette, 1978.

Mowinckel, S. *The Psalms in Israel's Worship*, 2 vols. Oxford: Blackwell, 1962.

Pires, D. J. M. *Do centro para a margem*. João Pessoa: Acaūa, 1978.

Pixley, Jorge V. *God's Kingdom: A Guide for Biblical Study*. Maryknoll, N.Y.: Orbis, 1981.

————. "Jesús y el siervo de Yavé en el Déutero-Isaías." *Servir* 85 (1/1980), pp. 9–47.

————. *On Exodus: A Liberation Perspective*. Maryknoll N.Y.: Orbis, 1987.

Prunel, L. "Les pauvres et l'église." *Dictionnaire apologétique de la foi catholique*, ed. A. D'Alès, vol. 2. Paris, 1911, col. 1655–1735.

*Puebla* (Review). No. 123, *Contribuçoes dos teólogos*. 1979.

Rad, Gerhard von. *Theologie des Alten Testaments*. 9th ed. Munich, 1987.

Rebré, A. *La libertação dos oprimidos no Antigo Testamento*. São Paulo: Paulinas, 1982.

————.*Que tipo de libertador foi Jesus?* São Paulo: Paulinas, 1982.

Richard, Pablo. *Death of Christendoms, Birth of the Church*. Maryknoll, N.Y.: Orbis, 1987.

————, and G. Meléndez, eds. *La Iglesia de los pobres en América Central*. San José, Costa Rica: DEI, 1982.

Rizzi, A. *Escándalo y bienaventuranza de la pobreza*. Madrid: Paulinas, 1978.

Rolim, F. C. *Religião e classes populares*. Petrópolis: Vozes, 1980.

Salem, H., ed. *A Igreja dos oprimidos*. São Paulo: Brasil Debates, 1981.

Santa, Ana, Julio de, ed. *Hacia una Iglesia de los pobres*. Buenos Aires: Aurora, 1983.

——. *A Igreja e o desafio dos pobres*. Petrópolis: Tempo e Presença/Vozes, 1980.

——. ed. *Separation without Hope? Essays on the Relations between the Church and the Poor during the Industrial Revolution and the Western Colonial Expansion*. Maryknoll, N.Y.: Orbis, 1978.

Sider, R. J. *Cristãos ricos em tempos de fome*. São Leopoldo: Sinodal, 1982.

Sierra Bravo, R. *Doctrina social y económica de los Padres de la Iglesia*. Madrid: COMPI, 1967.

Sobrino, Jon. "Archbishop Romero, Martyr for Liberation." *Romero, Martyr for Liberation*. London: CIIR, 1982.

——. *Jesús en América Latina*. San Salvador: UCA, 1982. Eng. trans.: *Jesus in Latin America*. Maryknoll, N.Y.: Orbis, 1987.

Támez, Elsa. *The Bible of the Oppressed*. Maryknoll, N.Y.: Orbis, 1982.

Various. *El credo de los pobres*. Lima: CEP, 1978.

——. "El Dios de los Pobres." *Christus* 519 (Mexico, 1979).

——. *Hacia una teología de los pobres*. Lima: CEP, 1980.

——. *La Iglesia de los pobres en América Latina. Antología*. Santiago, Chile: ECO/SPADE, 1983.

——. *A mensagem das bem-aventuranças*. São Paulo: Paulinas, 1982.

——. *Los pobres. Encuentro y compromiso*. Buenos Aires: Aurora, 1978.

——. *A pobreza evangélica*. São Paulo: Paulinas, 1976.

World Council of Churches. "Por uma Igreja solidária com os pobres." *Cadernos do CEDI*, 4, 1980.

Zanini, O. *O último exame. Reflexões e propostas sobre a opção pelos pobres*. Curitiba, 1984.

Zorrilla, H. *La fiesta de la liberción de los oprimidos. Relectura de Juan 7:1–10, 21*. San José, Costa Rica: DEI, 1981.

# Index

*Already published in this series*

# TRINITY AND SOCIETY
# Leonardo Boff

*Trinity and Society* was written during Leonardo Boff's Vatican-imposed year of silence. He says of it "This book is dangerous for authoritarian mentalities, for the system of centralized power that always sees the (Christian) community as a body that needs to be guided, taught, and strengthened by the sacraments, and not as the great revelation contained in the mytery of Jesus Christ."

The well-known Brazilian theologian guides the reader through the historical controversies and heresies about the Trinity, highlighting those trinitarian interpretations most significant in the context of oppression. Boff illumines the Trinity as the fruitful communion of the three divine Persons – source and model for a human society based on universal collaboration and equality. The Trinity is thus shown to be intimately linked to political, economic, and social justice.

This is Boff at his very best. His meticulous scholarship and thorough historical analysis lead to ground-breaking conclusions, sure to stir heated debate among academics and non-academics alike.

"The communion of the three divine Persons is communion in diversity and therefore is a model to society. Here is a thought which has recently been expounded by, for example, Jürgen Moltmann; but the Latin American context gives it a vividness and an urgency not found in any First World theologians of our time. No one reading this passionate book is likely to echo Kant's dictum that 'the doctrine of the Trinity provides nothing, absolutely nothing of practical value, even if one claims to understand it.'" **David L. Edwards** in the *Church Times*

*Already published in this series*

# ETHICS AND COMMUNITY
## Enrique Dussel

A comprehensive, introductory approach to what liberation
theology has to say about ethics and morals. Dussel begins by
making a fundamental distinction between two types of ethical
systems: community ethics and social morality. The first grows
out of a central concern with community; the second out of
isolated individualism.

In Part 1, Dussel poses ten questions basic to a discussion of
ethics (on good and evil; personal and social sin; relative morals
and absolute ethics, and others). In Part 2, he examines ten
contemporary issues requiring an ethical stance: among them,
labour and the work ethic; capitalism and socialism; the arms
race; the Third World debt and dependency.

Rigorous in structure and scholarship, yet clear and accessibly
written, *Ethics and Community* offers the first single,
systematic, treatment of an ethics rooted, as liberation theology
is rooted, in the concerns of the poor of Latin America – and
the world.

"As an historian he glances back into Latin America's past,
where already the Aztec or Inca warriors were maintained by
a half-starved peasantry and blessed by a subservient
priesthood. But mainly his gaze is fixed on the present, when
'other Christian-murdering empires carry on the Roman
Empire's tradition of sin.' And he is specific in his
denunciations of the transnational corporations which suck the
wealth out of the Third World – and of the US Government
which intervenes disastrously in poor countries' politics . . . .
Obviously Christians who stand outside the problems of Latin
America ought to listen carefully to any voice from where it
hurts."

**David L. Edwards** in the *Church Times*

*Already published in this series*

# THE HOLY SPIRIT AND LIBERATION
## José Comblin

The Holy Spirit is the "great unknown" of Western Theology and one of the great rediscoveries of liberation theology. Few books, however, have yet given it the attention and analysis it deserves. This volume remedies this defect, and in a fresh and challenging way.

Speaking from his own experiences living among the very poor in North-eastern Brazil, Comblin examines the effects of the presence of the Spirit in the world and the church. In the world it is present whenever the poor act on their own initiative, the weak organise, the unlettered speak out, the down-trodden discover new ways of living in community: all characteristics of the new base communities of Latin America. In the liberation struggle, experience of God is experience of the Spirit; the Spirit lies at the root of the cry of the poor.

Christianity, Comblin argues, has two sources: the "Jesus event" and the coming of the Spirit: Easter and Pentecost. Yet Western tradition has consistently undervalued the place of the Holy Spirit, substituting the chain "Father-Son-Church" for the Trinitarian order, and invoking the Spirit only as a prop for decisions already taken by a hierarchical church.

Finally, he puts forward a new model of spirituality, a spirituality of austerity, commitment and action, finding God in service to the poor, but shot through with "joy in the Spirit".

"This is one of the most remarkable books to come from Latin America; a serious yet accessible theological study." – *Renew*

*Already published in this series*

# THE MEMORY OF THE CHRISTIAN PEOPLE

## Eduardo Hoornaert

For nine years Eduardo Hoornaert lived and worked in a poor quarter of the megalopolis of Recife, Brazil, among the people of the basic Christian communities. With insights gained through this experience, he here examines the early church from the perspective of the living, practising communities of the poor. He focuses on the basic communities that comprised the church at its beginnings, and on the role of the poor and marginalized.

The early church, then, is understood as articulated in communities rather than in a hierarchical institution. Those communities themselves, Hoornaert says, lived "at the margin of society, in *paroikia*, between strangers and marginalized people." Christian mission was, then, not only the work of the great apostles: it was a large, popular, anonymous movement, manifested in cycles, during Christianity's first three centuries.

*The Memory of the Christian People* reveals striking similarities between the church's first communities and the grassroots communities transforming the church today. "The oppressed persons of the base communities today can enthusiastically exclaim, 'the first Christian‿ iived as we do'". *The Memory of the Christian People* should be read and re-read by pastoral workers, students, scholars, and all those involved with local church communities.

---

Books of general Christian interest as well as books on theology, scripture, spirituality and mysticism are published by Burns and Oates and Search Press Limited. A free catalogue will be sent on request:
**BURNS AND OATES Dept A,**
Wellwood, North Farm Road, Tunbridge Wells, Kent TN2 3DR
Tel. (0892) 510850